ENHANCING GLOBAL COMPARABILITY

ASIA AND THE PACIFIC IN THE INTERNATIONAL COMPARISON PROGRAM

A Special Supplement of *Key Indicators for Asia and the Pacific 2025*

DECEMBER 2025

ASIAN DEVELOPMENT BANK

ADB

6 ADB Avenue, Mandaluyong City, 1550 Metro Manila, Philippines
Tel +63 2 8632 4444; Fax +63 2 8636 2444
www.adb.org

ISBN 978-92-9277-600-8 (print); 978-92-9277-601-5 (electronic); 978-92-9277-602-2 (ebook)
Publication Stock No. FLS250527-3
DOI: http://dx.doi.org/10.22617/FLS250527-3

Notes:
In this publication, "$" refers to United States dollars.
ADB recognizes "China" as the People's Republic of China.

Cover design by Mike Cortes.

Contents

Tables, Figures, and Boxes

Tables

Figures

Boxes

Foreword

The International Comparison Program (ICP) stands as a cornerstone of the global statistical system, delivering essential data on purchasing power parities (PPPs) that enable meaningful economic comparisons across more than 175 economies. By moving beyond the limitations of exchange-rate-based metrics, PPPs offer a more accurate representation of relative price levels, real economic output, and standards of living worldwide. These insights are invaluable for policymakers, researchers, and international organizations tracking economic performance and progress toward development goals.

Globally coordinated by the World Bank under the United Nations Statistical Commission, the ICP operates through a unique partnership of regional and national agencies. In Asia and the Pacific, the Asian Development Bank (ADB) has served as the regional implementing agency since 2005, successfully leading the 2005, 2011, 2017, and 2021 ICP cycles, and currently spearheading the 2024 cycle.

This special supplement to *Key Indicators for Asia and the Pacific 2025* marks 2 decades of ADB's leadership and innovation in the ICP. It highlights the critical role of PPP-based economic comparisons in shaping policy and analysis, and underscores the region's growing significance in the global economy. According to the latest ICP results for 2021, Asia and the Pacific, with nearly 55% of the world's population, accounts for almost 45% of global gross domestic product in PPP terms. The region is home to the world's largest economy, the People's Republic of China (PRC), and four of the top 10 economies globally—the PRC, India, Japan, and Indonesia—collectively contributing about one-third of global output in 2021.

Analysis of PPPs and related macroeconomic indicators reveals that Asia and the Pacific has become the principal engine of global economic growth. From 2011 to 2021, around two-thirds of global growth originated from this region. The data also point to narrowing disparities in real incomes among the region's economies over this period. With comparatively low price levels as seen from the program's results and comparative lower domestic production costs, Asia and the Pacific exports competitively priced goods and therefore play an important role in driving down inflationary pressures in advanced economies around the world.

ADB and the participating economies from the Asia and Pacific region have made substantial contributions to the evolution of global ICP methods and standards. Innovations include new methodologies for complex cross-economy comparisons of government expenditure and housing services, research on poverty-specific PPPs, and the development of robust approaches for producing more reliable PPPs. ADB's technological advancements have streamlined price data management by adopting user-friendly software tools and improved data validation and comparability using innovative data visualization tools. ADB has further enhanced dissemination of ICP data and methods through a centralized portal (icp.adb.org).

Since 2005, ADB has fostered strong cooperation among participating economies in Asia and the Pacific. This collaboration has been vital in overcoming operational challenges and ensuring the production of high-quality, representative data. The bank has supported knowledge sharing through extensive training and capacity building in price and national accounts statistics, complemented by regional workshops that facilitate the exchange of experiences, solutions, and best practices.

The achievements of the ICP in Asia and the Pacific are a testament to the dedication of the region's participating economies. Their commitment to data collection and validation and integration of the ICP into their statistical programs—often amid competing priorities—deserve special recognition. The resilience of the region's national implementing agencies was particularly evident during the 2021 ICP cycle, when innovative approaches to price surveys ensured continuity, despite the disruptions caused by the coronavirus disease (COVID-19) pandemic.

Special thanks are extended to the specialist groups whose expertise has been instrumental to the ICP's success in our region. These include the ICP Regional Advisory Board for Asia and the Pacific for their guidance, the ICP's group of experts for their technical advice, and the World Bank ICP Global Office for their ongoing support.

Kaushal Joshi led this report's preparation under the guidance of Elaine S. Tan, with technical and coordination support from Criselda de Dios. The main authors were Kaushal Joshi and Prasada Rao, with contributions from Criselda de Dios, Paolo Kris Adriano, and Kristine Faith Maningding as the core team. Additional inputs were provided by Rhea-Ann Bautista, Juan Miguel dela Cruz, and Mario Ilagan II. Paul Dent provided manuscript support, Mike Cortes handled the cover design and select infographics with team support, and Joe Mark Ganaban managed typesetting.

Over the past 20 years, the partnership between ADB and more than 20 regional economies has exemplified effective regional cooperation, producing comparable economic statistics that are of significant regional and global public value. Looking ahead, the ICP will continue to play a pivotal role in economic measurement and comparison, both regionally and globally.

Albert F. Park
Chief Economist and Director General,
Economic Research and Development Impact Department
Asian Development Bank

Abbreviations

ADB	Asian Development Bank
AICH	actual individual consumption by households
CCEG	collective consumption expenditure by government
CIS-STAT	Interstate Statistical Committee of the Commonwealth of Independent States
CPD	country-product-dummy
CPI	consumer price index
ECOSOC	United Nations Economic and Social Council
Eurostat	Statistical Office of the European Communities
GDP	gross domestic product
GEKS	Gini–Èltetö–Köves–Szulc
GFCE	government final consumption expenditure
GFCF	gross fixed capital formation
HDI	human development index
ICEG	individual consumption expenditure by government
ICEH	individual consumption expenditure by households
ICP	International Comparison Program
ICP APSS	International Comparison Program Asia and the Pacific Software Suite
IMF	International Monetary Fund
LCU	local currency unit
MDG	Millennium Development Goals
NIA	national implementing agency
NPISH	nonprofit institutions serving households
OECD	Organisation for Economic Co-operation and Development
PLI	price level index
PPP	purchasing power parity
RAB	Regional Advisory Board
RIA	regional implementing agency
SDG	Sustainable Development Goal
SNA	System of National Accounts
SPD	structured product description
SUT	supply and use table
UNSC	United Nations Statistical Commission

Executive Summary

Challenges in comparing gross domestic product and living standards. Comparing gross domestic product (GDP) and living standards across economies is inherently complex. Differences in local currencies and price levels mean that market exchange rates—often used as currency converters—do not accurately reflect domestic purchasing power. These rates are also subject to volatility, making them unreliable for cross-economy comparisons. As a result, alternative approaches are needed to ensure meaningful and consistent international economic analysis.

The role of purchasing power parities. Purchasing power parities (PPPs) are essential for overcoming the limitations of market exchange rates. PPPs adjust for differences in currency values and price levels, providing a more reliable basis for comparing economic output and living standards across economies. This adjustment makes PPPs indispensable for global economic analysis and policymaking, as they enable direct comparisons of well-being indicators such as per capita GDP, health and education expenditures, and capital formation. PPPs are also critical for tracking progress on many Sustainable Development Goals (SDGs), by ensuring cross-economy comparability.

The influence of the International Comparison Program. The International Comparison Program (ICP) is a global initiative under the United Nations Statistical Commission, tasked with producing PPPs for international economic comparisons. Since its inception in 1968 as a small research project involving just 10 economies, the ICP has evolved into a permanent fixture of the global statistical system and now encompasses more than 175 economies worldwide. This expansion reflects the growing recognition of the ICP's importance in generating harmonized economic data for global development, research, and policy coordination.

Ensuring methodological rigor and accurate data collection. A hallmark of the ICP is its methodological rigor. The program adheres to the System of National Accounts, focusing on the expenditure approach to GDP measurement, which is appropriate for collecting price data on final expenditures. The ICP's commitment to methodological soundness has built trust among users. It involves comprehensive price data collection across more than 175 economies, with rigorous validation processes to ensure accurate price comparisons. This collaborative effort enhances data quality and fosters transparency and mutual learning among national statistical agencies.

Uses and applications of purchasing power parities. PPPs produced by ICP serve a wide range of research and policy analysis beyond comparing well-being indicators, such as per capita GDP, health and education expenditures, and gross fixed capital formation across economies. PPPs are essential for estimating global and regional poverty, monitoring SDGs such as eradicating extreme poverty, and tracking SDG targets on inequality, health, energy, productivity, and emissions. They inform cost-of-living adjustments for expatriates and competitiveness assessments, and ICP price data now help develop nutrition-based poverty measures. International organizations use PPPs for policy, development indexes, fund allocation, and tracking progress, highlighting their global significance.

Asia and the Pacific's economic weight in the global economy. The latest ICP results (from the 2021 cycle) highlight the significant influence of Asia and the Pacific on the global economy. The region accounts for nearly 45% of global GDP in PPP terms. The People's Republic of China (PRC) was the world's largest economy in real (PPP) terms in 2021, with a GDP of $28.82 trillion, followed by the United States ($23.59 trillion) and India ($10.96 trillion). The PRC (18.9%), India (7.2%), Japan (3.7%), and Indonesia (2.3%) were among the world's top 10 economies for 2021, collectively contributing close to one-third (32.1%) of global economic output. This underscores the region's growing importance in the global economic landscape.

Disparities in per capita real gross domestic product. Despite large size of GDP, the PRC and India ranked much lower globally in per capita real (PPP) GDP for 2021. There were also wide disparities in per capita incomes across Asia and the Pacific. For example, Tajikistan (a lower-middle-income economy) contrasted sharply with Singapore (a high-income economy), with a per capita income ratio of nearly 1:33. Singapore (ranked second in 2021); Brunei Darussalam (eighth); Hong Kong, China (14th); and Taipei,China (15th) were among the top 15 economies globally in per capita real GDP.

Assessing trends in income inequality. The Asia and Pacific region has experienced a consistent reduction in intereconomy income inequality as revealed by the results of the recent ICP cycles. The Gini coefficient decreased from 0.3635 in 2011 to 0.3273 in 2021, indicating narrowing disparities. In comparison, the global intereconomy Gini coefficient was 0.4610 in 2021, highlighting Asia and the Pacific's relative progress in reducing inequality.

Price level indexes and comparable price levels. Most Asia and the Pacific economies had price level indexes (PLIs) significantly below those of advanced economies in 2021, indicating lower price levels and making many of the region's economies among the least-expensive globally. In terms of GDP, PLIs for 2021 were below 30.0 in several economies, compared to the US benchmark (PLI = 100.0). Lower price levels and domestic production costs enable Asia and the Pacific to export competitively priced goods, helping to drive down inflationary pressures in advanced economies.

Rapid economic growth across Asia and the Pacific. From 2011 to 2021, Asia and the Pacific experienced rapidly accelerating economic growth, with real GDP (in current PPPs) expanding by over 83%. This growth was driven by a 62% expansion in output and a price effect of 13%. By comparison, global real (in current PPPs) GDP increased by 63%, with a growth component of 36% and a price effect of 20%. The region contributed nearly two-thirds of the global growth in economic output for 2011–2021, underscoring its central role in driving economic expansion worldwide. Asia and the Pacific also accounted for over half of global gross fixed capital formation, attracting investment through sustained growth and competitive production costs. This investment supports ongoing economic expansion and development across the region.

Asian Development Bank leadership in Asia and the Pacific. Since the 2005 ICP cycle, the Asian Development Bank (ADB) has played a pivotal role as the regional implementing agency for the ICP in Asia and the Pacific. Under ADB's leadership, four ICP cycles of 2005, 2011, 2017, and 2021 in the region have been successfully accomplished, while the 2024 cycle is progressing. ADB has expanded participation, improved methodologies, and built statistical capacity in the region. Its leadership has strengthened the ICP both regionally and globally, contributing to the development and refinement of the program's methodologies and practices.

Vital refinements to price comparison methodologies. ADB, with the help of the region's participating economies, has contributed to refinements in the global ICP methodology for comparing government services. It did so by introducing productivity adjustments to the relevant PPPs in order to account for differences in labor productivity across economies. The methodology, with further refinements by the ICP Global Office, is now uniformly applied in all regions needing such adjustments. A new methodology for housing comparisons in Asia and the Pacific was also developed by ADB. This methodology suitably accounts for the quality differences in housing services in the widely diverse economies of Asia and the Pacific, enhancing the accuracy of PPPs. The new housing methodology was endorsed by the ICP Technical Advisory Group and recommended for testing in other regions.

Pioneering research on poverty-specific purchasing power parities. ADB implemented a research study for compiling PPPs specific for use in calculating poverty by tailoring price data collection to the consumption patterns of poor households. With poverty reduction central to international development and policymaking worldwide, the ADB study showed that identifying consumption items of particular relevance to the poor and conducting targeted surveys to capture prices paid by the poor for those items, would yield PPPs more relevant to poverty measurement.

Bolstering statistical capacity in Asia and the Pacific. Through various regional initiatives, ADB has played a central role in enhancing price and national accounts statistics for economies of Asia and the Pacific, with positive outcomes achieved via technical assistance and regular training workshops. The bank has supported economies in harmonizing data collection for consumer price index and ICP surveys, using existing common infrastructure for both processes, and thereby enhancing operational and resource efficiencies. ADB regional technical assistance has also helped economies develop "supply and use" tables aligned with System of National Accounts standards, improving the accuracy and consistency of the GDP expenditure estimates essential for PPP calculations. These efforts have established uniform data collection protocols, improved the accuracy of GDP and price statistics, and built a foundation for sustained progress in economic measurement.

The crucial role of statistical agencies. The commitment of the statistical agencies in participating economies is the key driver of success for the ICP in Asia and the Pacific. With the successful completion of four ICP benchmarks for 2005, 2011, 2017, and 2021—and the fifth for 2024 ongoing—the dedication and adaptability of these agencies in challenging times, most especially during the coronavirus disease (COVID-19) pandemic, have ensured the continuity and integrity of the program, even in the face of unprecedented disruptions. This commitment to the ICP's success provides the foundation for region's future agenda of continued innovations in statistical methodologies and advancements in digital applications to further strengthen the ICP surveys, data collection, dissemination, and policy applications.

CHAPTER 1

Introduction

The Asia and Pacific region serves as a vital engine for global economic growth. Home to more than half the world's population, it accounts for nearly 45% of global gross domestic product (GDP) when measured using purchasing power parities (PPPs). The economic landscape of the region is marked by a diverse set of economies, ranging from small, high-income economies such as Singapore and Hong Kong, China to large and rapidly growing economies such as the People's Republic of China, India, and Indonesia. Asia and the Pacific continues to be the most dynamic region in the global economy.

Comparing the size of economies in such a diverse region (as well as comparing these economies to others across the world) poses significant challenges, particularly due to differences in currencies and price levels. GDP, which represents the total value of final expenditures in an economy, continues to be the key indicator of economic capacity and, when expressed as a per capita measure, suggests comparative levels of material well-being across economies.

To facilitate comparisons between economies, market exchange rates are often used to convert macroeconomic aggregates published by the economies in their local currency units into a common currency. However, exchange rates—being volatile and often misaligned with domestic purchasing power—are not suitable currency converters for meaningful economic comparisons. The International Comparison Program (ICP), established in 1968 and implemented across all regions of the world under the auspices of the United Nations Statistical Commission, aims to fill this gap by estimating PPPs of individual currencies. These PPPs also adjust for differences in price levels across economies, providing stable and uniform economic comparisons. The PPPs from the ICP are used to convert GDP and its expenditure components from local currency units into a common currency to compile internationally comparable macroeconomic aggregates of economies.

Since the 2005 ICP cycle,[1] the Asian Development Bank (ADB) has served as the regional implementing agency for the Asia and Pacific region of the ICP. ADB successfully implemented the 2005, 2011, 2017, and 2021 ICP cycles and is currently leading the 2024 ICP cycle. Over these 2 decades of regional leadership, the bank has played a pivotal role in expanding program participation by the region's economies, standardizing methodologies, improving data quality, and building capacity among statistical agencies in the participating economies. Its contributions range from innovative region-specific methods to developing tools and technologies for efficient data handling and quality assurance. ADB's involvement has also ensured the full participation of the People's Republic of China and India—two of the world's most populous and influential economies. The collaborative partnership between ADB and more than 20 regional economies over two decades has exemplified effective regional cooperation, producing comparable economic statistics of significant public value at both the regional and global levels.

1 Comparisons under the ICP have been conducted for reference years 1970, 1973, 1975, 1980, 1985, 1993, 2005, 2011, 2017, and 2021, with 2024 comparisons in progress at the time of this report. Each benchmark exercise was referred to as a "round" until the 2011 ICP. Starting with the 2017 ICP, it is now termed as a "cycle", with the intention to implement the program in a cycle of every 3 years.

Objectives of this Special Supplement

This special supplement to *Key Indicators for Asia and the Pacific 2025* has three interrelated objectives.

The supplement aims to **demonstrate the value of PPPs and their use in comparing real incomes across economies.** This includes highlighting the significance of PPPs (compared with the use of market exchange rates) in measuring real income, comparing economic output, and assessing standards of living. This report also exhibits how ICP data support evidence-based policymaking, poverty assessments, and tracking of the Sustainable Development Goals.

The supplement seeks to use ICP results to **analyze economic performance of the Asia and Pacific region** in a global context. It includes a comprehensive analysis of the region's economic size, structure, and price levels using PPPs and real GDP in relation to the world economy, based on the results of the 2021 ICP cycle (the most recent global comparisons). The publication examines household consumption, government expenditure, investment, and regional growth trends, highlighting the diversity of the economies in Asia and the Pacific and the region's growing role in global output.

The supplement also **showcases the region's contributions to the ICP.** The report demonstrates how economies of Asia and the Pacific have contributed to the ICP through collaboration and technical innovation, and underscores how ADB's leadership has helped advance the ICP both regionally and globally. This includes the bank's role as the regional implementing agency in mobilizing economy participation and resources, improving methodologies, developing data management tools, enhancing data quality, and strengthening the statistical capacities of participating economies for successful implementation of this complex program.

Scope and Structure of the Report

The early chapters of this special supplement provide vital background to understanding the importance of the ICP to Asia and the Pacific. Chapter 2 explains key concepts of international economic comparisons: PPPs, exchange rates, price level indexes, and nominal and real expenditures. It also illustrates the value of PPPs in providing real comparisons of economic output and measures of living standards across economies. Chapter 3 provides a brief evolution of the ICP since 1968 and its establishment as a permanent element of the global statistical program. The chapter also explains the governance structure for the ICP and its conceptual framework, which draws from the System of National Accounts, and the uses of PPPs in areas such as monitoring the Sustainable Development Goals, poverty analysis, inequality, and productivity comparisons. Chapter 4 profiles the Asia and Pacific region in a global context, including economic size in terms of GDP and other macroeconomic measures such as household consumption, government expenditure, and investment based on ICP results. It examines standards of living, regional inequality, diversity, and contributions to global growth.

The latter chapters of the report delve more deeply into the functioning of the ICP and detail ADB's contribution to the global program and in fostering regional cooperation in Asia and the Pacific. Chapter 5 provides insights into the role played by ADB as the regional implementing agency since the 2005 ICP cycle. It details regional governance arrangements and the partnerships needed with the region's economies for successful implementation of the regional program. Chapter 6 outlines the bank's important contributions to ICP methodology, particularly in developing tailored approaches to solve region-specific implementation challenges. Chapter 7 describes the statistical capacity building that has taken place within the participating economies of Asia and the Pacific. This includes efforts to integrate ICP and consumer price index processes, along with emerging work on subnational PPPs for improved policy targeting. Chapter 8 wraps up the report with a range of summary conclusions.

CHAPTER 2

Fundamentals of International Economic Comparisons

Demand for standardized and globally comparable data for public policymaking and research has surged with increasing globalization and interconnectedness across economies. By conducting extensive price surveys across hundreds of goods and services, the International Comparison Program (ICP) calculates purchasing power parities (PPPs)—currency conversion factors that reflect the real cost of living in each economy. Unlike market exchange rates, which can fluctuate due to speculation, capital flows, or monetary policy, PPPs offer a more stable and accurate basis for meaningful international comparisons of gross domestic product (GDP), consumption, and investment. These statistics support evidence-based policymaking, strengthen academic research, and inform decision-making in both the public and private sectors. The ICP's global reach (covering nearly all the world's economies) and periodical updating make it central to global economic comparisons and research.

For international development organizations, comparable measures of economic activity are indispensable as they are used to assess progress, allocate funds, and conduct economic analysis. As a central example, the Sustainable Development Goals (SDGs) rely on harmonized economic indicators to measure global poverty levels, health outcomes, and environmental sustainability. Without consistency and uniformity in measurement, tracking global progress toward these goals would be almost impossible. Internationally comparable measures of economic activity are therefore not merely indicators to be applied in bureaucracy or academia: they enable meaningful comparisons across economies of the world, foster economic cooperation, and ensure that policymaking is based on sound, objective evidence.

Measuring Economic Activity: Gross Domestic Product

GDP is the most widely accepted measure of the size of an economy. It is produced by national statistics offices in accordance with the System of National Accounts (SNA) of the United Nations.

The SNA is the internationally agreed framework used to compile various measures of economic activity by all economies.[1] This macroeconomic framework is based on the premise that all goods and services produced in the domestic economy are used in some form or other. It also accounts for the circular flows of income and expenditure of all residents and nonresidents participating in the transactions of the domestic economy. The framework ensures balance of the supply and use of goods and services produced; the market value of producing goods and services within the economy's geographic boundaries; the income generated in production; and the expenditures on goods and services.

In theory, there are three ways to measure GDP in an economy, with all three methods leading to the same monetary value.

Expenditure Approach: whereby GDP is calculated as the aggregate of final consumption expenditures by households and government, gross capital formation, and net exports (exports *less* imports).

1 The System of National Accounts 2008 (2008 SNA) is currently the most widely used standard for compiling national accounts statistics by the national statistics offices. In March 2025, the United Nations Statistical Commission endorsed a revised System of National Accounts 2025 (2025 SNA). More information can be found at https://unstats.un.org/unsd/nationalaccount/default.asp.

Production Approach: also known as output approach whereby GDP is calculated as the value of gross output, *less* intermediate consumption, *plus* taxes on products not already included in output values, *less* subsidies on products.

Income Approach: whereby GDP is calculated as the sum of compensation of employees, gross operating surplus (including mixed income), and taxes, *less* subsidies on production and imports.

Table 2.1 illustrates these three approaches to calculating GDP, using data for India over 2 consecutive financial years expressed in Indian rupee.

Of the three approaches for measuring GDP, the ICP focuses on the expenditure method. This choice is primarily due to the practicality and feasibility of collecting data on purchaser prices for the items of final expenditure. Such data are essential for compiling PPPs, real GDP, and GDP components of final consumption and investment. By contrast, the output approach requires detailed data on both gross output and intermediate consumption.

Table 2.1: Gross Domestic Product of India by the Expenditure, Production, and Income Approaches

Aggregates	at current prices (₹ billion)	
	FY 2022-23	FY 2023-24
GDP - Expenditure Approach		
Final consumption expenditure	**192,854.90**	**212,347.29**
Household Nonprofit institutions serving households	165,278.62	181,304.31
Government	27,576.28	31,042.98
Gross capital formation	**87,715.73**	**94,681.15**
Gross fixed capital formation	83,960.38	91,652.24
Changes in inventories	2,998.51	4,595.71
Acquisition less disposal of valuables	3,444.89	4,249.19
External balance of goods and services	**-9,605.78**	**-6,312.10**
Exports	62,524.49	64,609.82
Imports	72,130.27	70,921.92
Statistical discrepancies	-4,748.17	-5,302.77
GDP	**268,904.73**	**301,229.56**
GDP - Production Approach		
Total Gross Value Added at basic prices	246,466.98	274,128.88
Taxes less subsidies on products[a]	22,437.75	27,100.68
GDP at market prices	**268,904.73**	**301,229.56**
GDP - Income Approach		
Compensation of employees	89,101.18	99,064.70
Gross operating surplus and mixed income	158,055.09	175,741.84
Taxes less subsidies on production[b]	21,748.46	26,423.02
GDP	**268,904.73**	**301,229.56**

₹ = Indian rupees, FY = financial year, GDP = gross domestic product.

Notes:

[a] Refers to taxes on products including import duties *less* subsidies on products.

[b] Refers to sum of taxes on products including import duties, *less* subsidies on products and production taxes, *less* production subsidies.

Source: Government of India, Ministry of Statistics and Programme Implementation. National Accounts Statistics 2025, "Statement 1.1: Key aggregates of National Accounts" and "Statement 7.1: Output, Value Added, CE, OS/MI by industry." https://www.mospi.gov.in/publication/national-accounts-statistics-2025 (accessed 11 June 2025).

The expenditure approach is less data-intensive and more manageable for implementing across all regions of the world. Additionally, expenditure-based comparisons for per capita GDP and its components (e.g., food, health, and education) provide valuable insights into living standards across the globe. In contrast, the income approach does not allow for separating values into price and volume components, rendering it unsuitable for producing comparable international measures.

Issues in Comparing Gross Domestic Product Across Economies

National statistics offices compile and publish estimates of GDP and its components, in the local currency units, on a quarterly and annual basis, following the SNA.

GDP expressed in value terms is a function of prevailing prices and quantities or volumes of all goods and services consumed or acquired by households, government, and firms along with net exports during the reference year. As these macroeconomic aggregates are expressed in local currency units and in the prices prevailing in each economy during the reference period, they are not especially useful for the direct comparison of volumes of goods and services across economies.

To facilitate international comparisons of economic activity, macroeconomic aggregates must be converted into a common currency using currency conversion factors that also adjusts for differences in the prices prevailing in the economies during the reference period. The two main instruments available for converting the aggregates into a common currency are **market exchange rates** and **PPPs** of currencies.

Exchange Rates as Conversion Factors

An exchange rate between two currencies is the rate at which one currency can be exchanged for the other. The International Monetary Fund describes exchange rates thus:

> The price of one currency in terms of another. Most commonly, exchange rates are expressed as the number of units of domestic currency that will purchase one unit of foreign currency (e.g., units of currency per United States [US] dollar). An exchange rate may also be defined as the inverse: the number of units of foreign currency that one unit of domestic currency will purchase.[2]

Exchange rates, while useful for converting currencies in trade and finance, are not ideal for comparing the size of economies and standards of living of their populations. Exchange rates are determined by the demand and supply of currencies and fluctuate daily due to market speculation, interest rate changes, and geopolitical events. The exchange rates are also not aligned with relative price levels between economies and this often results in misrepresentation of the real economic capacity.

The effect of fluctuating exchange rates on the measurement of Japan's GDP from 2020 to 2024 can be seen in Table 2.2.

Table 2.2: Effect of Exchange Rates on the Gross Domestic Product of Japan, 2020–2024

Year	GDP of Japan (¥ trillion)	Exchange Rate (¥/$)	Nominal GDP of Japan ($ trillion) = Col2/Col3	GDP of US ($ trillion)	Comparative Size of Japan's Economy in Nominal GDP (% of US GDP)
(1)	(2)	(3)	(4)	(5)	(6)
2020	539.646	106.775	5.054	21.354	23.7
2021	553.068	109.754	5.039	23.681	21.3
2022	560.464	131.498	4.262	26.007	16.4
2023	591.913	140.491	4.213	27.721	15.2
2024	609.433	151.366	4.026	29.185	13.8

$ = United States dollars, ¥ = yen, GDP = gross domestic product, US = United States.

Sources: For 2020–2024 GDP and Exchange Rates of Japan: Asian Development Bank. Key Indicators Database. https://kidb.adb.org/ (accessed 18 November 2025). For 2020–2024 GDP of US: U.S. Bureau of Economic Analysis, "Table 1.1.5. Gross Domestic Product." https://www.bea.gov/ (accessed 26 June 2025); Asian Development Bank estimates.

From 2020 to 2024, Japan's GDP (when measured in yen) grew by about 13.0% at current prices and by about 5.3% at constant prices. During the same period, the GDP of the US grew by about 36.7% at current prices and by 15.0% at constant prices. From Table 2.2 (col 4) it can be seen that, when Japan's GDP is converted using exchange rates for yen to US dollar (often referred as XR-based or Nominal expenditure for the purpose of ICP), the economy's GDP is seen to have fallen from $5.054 trillion in 2020 to $4.026 trillion in 2024 (a contraction of around 20%). Comparing the size of Japan's economy to that of the US (col 6), the contraction is proportionately greater, i.e., from about 23.7% in 2020 to only 13.8% in 2024. Much of this contraction is attributed to the weakening of Japanese yen from ¥106.8 per $1 to ¥151.4 per $1 from 2020 to 2024 (a depreciation of about 42%) as shown in Figure 2.1.

The distortion in comparative economic size, as seen in the above example for Japan, highlights that relying solely on exchange rates can give misleading conclusions about the real size of an economy, per capita real incomes, and living standards. It also shows that the movements in exchange rates are not aligned with relative prices or with price levels across economies. Thus, for these reasons, exchange rates are not considered appropriate conversion factors for comparing the volumes of goods and services of economies.

2 The International Monetary Fund's glossary of terms can be found at https://www.imf.org/en/About/glossary (accessed 4 August 2025).

Figure 2.1: Exchange Rates and Purchasing Power Parities Between Japan and the United States, 2020–2024

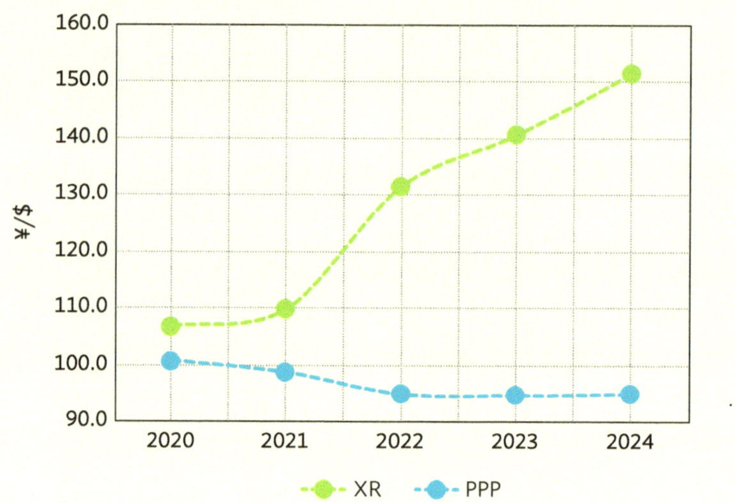

$ = United States dollars, ¥ = yen, GDP = gross domestic product, ICP = International Comparison Program, PPP = purchasing power parity, XR = exchange rate.

Sources: For 2020–2024 Exchange Rates: Asian Development Bank. Key Indicators Database. https://kidb.adb.org/ (accessed 18 November 2025). For 2020–2023 PPPs: World Bank. DataBank: ICP 2021. https://databank.worldbank.org/source/icp-2021# (accessed 4 June 2024). For 2024 PPP: Asian Development Bank estimates.

Purchasing Power Parities as Conversion Factors

PPPs are currency conversion factors that address the shortcomings of exchange rates by adjusting for differences in currency denominations and relative price levels. The PPPs produced by the ICP are specifically designed to facilitate international comparisons of real volumes or GDP and its several expenditure components. PPPs are measured relative to the currency of a reference economy. The Hong Kong dollar is used as the reference currency for comparisons within the Asia and Pacific region. In the case of global comparisons, the US dollar is the reference currency.

Under the 2025 SNA, a PPP is defined as:

> ... the number of units of country B's currency that are needed in country B to purchase the same quantity of an individual good or service as one unit of country A's currency will purchase in country A.
>
> (United Nations 2025, para. 18.267).

Continuing with the example of Japan, Table 2.3 shows the PPP conversion factors (in reference to the US dollar) applied for 2020–2024 and provides Japan's corresponding GDP in PPP terms.

Table 2.3: Effect of Purchasing Power Parities on the Gross Domestic Product of Japan, 2020–2024

Year	GDP of Japan (¥ trillion)	PPP (¥/$)	Real (PPP) GDP of Japan ($ trillion) = Col2/Col3	GDP of US ($ trillion)	Comparative Size of Japan's Economy in Real (PPP) GDP (% of US GDP)
(1)	(2)	(3)	(4)	(5)	(6)
2020	539.646	100.742	5.357	21.354	25.1
2021	553.068	98.691	5.604	23.681	23.7
2022	560.464	94.936	5.904	26.007	22.7
2023	591.913	94.677	6.252	27.721	22.6
2024	609.433	94.942	6.419	29.185	22.0

$ = United States dollars, ¥ = yen, GDP = gross domestic product, ICP = International Comparison Program, PPP = purchasing power parity, US = United States.

Sources: For 2020–2024 GDP of Japan: Asian Development Bank. Key Indicators Database. https://kidb.adb.org/ (accessed 18 November 2025). For 2020–2024 GDP of US: U.S. Bureau of Economic Analysis, "Table 1.1.5. Gross Domestic Product." https://www.bea.gov/ (accessed 26 June 2025). For 2020–2023 PPPs: World Bank. DataBank: ICP 2021. https://databank.worldbank.org/source/icp-2021# (accessed 4 June 2024); For 2024 PPP: Asian Development Bank estimates.

As inflation for 2020–2024 was much lower in Japan (at 7.3%) than in the US (at 18.9%), the PPP of the yen with reference to the US dollar strengthened from ¥100.742 per $1 to ¥94.942 per $1 over the period (Figure 2.1).

When using PPPs as the conversion factor (often referred as PPP-based or real expenditures for the purpose of ICP), the GDP of Japan increased from $5.357 trillion in 2020 to $6.419 trillion in 2024, compared to $4.026 trillion if measured using exchange rates (Figure 2.2). This PPP-based figure equates to about 22.0% of the US GDP in 2024, as opposed to only 13.8% under exchange rates. This demonstrates that the 41% depreciation in the yen–US dollar exchange rate does not reflect the changes in the relative prices between the two economies from 2020 to 2024.

Purchasing Power Parities for Single Items and Groups of Items

PPPs can be calculated for a single item—such as a Big Mac—or based on a grouping of items, such as food, clothing, transport, or medical services. Within the ICP, PPPs are published from a national expenditure perspective for baskets of items or expenditure aggregates. These cover 45 expenditure aggregates, including broader categories such as household consumption, government consumption, gross capital formation, and GDP as a whole.

Figure 2.2: Japan's Gross Domestic Product Converted Using Exchange Rates and Purchasing Power Parities, 2020–2024

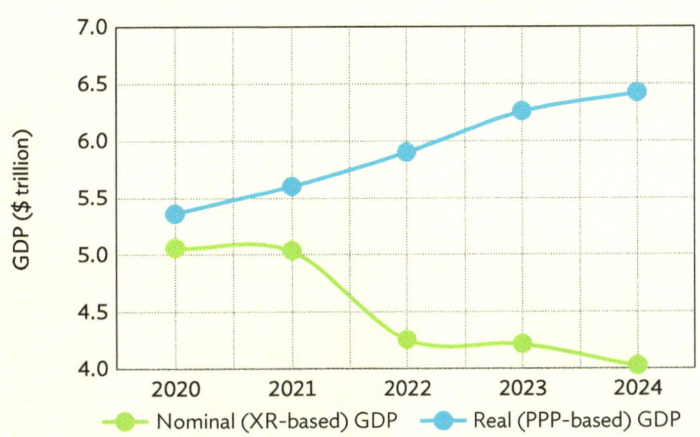

$ = United States dollars, ¥ = yen, GDP = gross domestic product, ICP = International Comparison Program, PPP = purchasing power parity, XR = exchange rate.

Sources: For 2020–2024 GDP and Exchange Rates of Japan: Asian Development Bank. Key Indicators Database. https://kidb.adb.org/ (accessed 18 November 2025). For 2020–2023 PPPs: World Bank. DataBank: ICP 2021. https://databank.worldbank.org/source/icp-2021# (accessed 4 June 2024); For 2024 PPP: Asian Development Bank estimates.

Due to its wide availability around the world, the Big Mac provides a convenient example of a comparable product for price comparison (Figure 2.3). If a Big Mac costs $4.93 in the US and RM9.99 in Malaysia, the Big Mac PPP for Malaysia is RM2.03 per $1. The Big Mac PPP is based on the prices of one single item in Malaysia in Malaysian ringgit and that of the US—the reference economy in US dollar. However, comparison of broader household consumption in the national accounting context requires comparing prices of a basket of goods and services consumed by households in each economy and then constructing PPPs for higher level aggregates such as food or clothing and footwear. As shown in Figure 2.3, if a weekly food basket costs an average of $225.00 in the US and RM659.25 in Malaysia, the food basket PPP is RM2.93 per $1. Meanwhile, the ringgit–US dollar exchange rate is higher at RM4.14 per $1.

It should be noted from this example that PPPs for the Big Mac are not a substitute for PPPs for a broader basket of items. The Big Mac Index[3] is often cited in the media as a shorthand measure of price levels. However, Big Mac PPPs can diverge considerably from PPPs for general food consumption. This highlights the limitation of using a single product, like the Big Mac, to represent broader consumption categories.

Using results from the 2021 ICP cycle for five specific economies, Box 2.1 presents PPPs for select broad expenditure aggregates of commodity groups and compares these PPPs to exchange rates, PPPs for overall GDP, and PPPs for the Big Mac for selected economies.

Figure 2.3: Purchasing Power Parities and Exchange Rate Between Malaysia and the United States, 2021

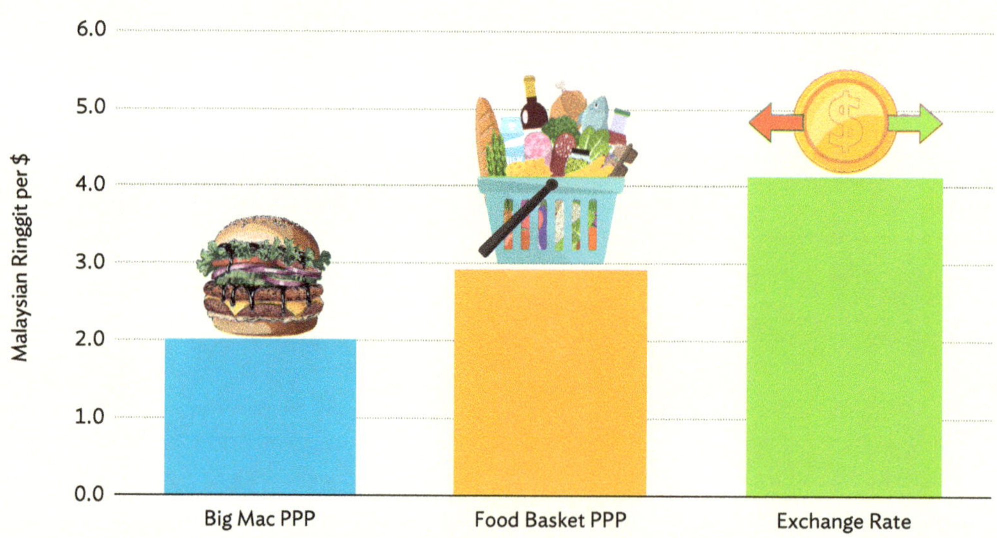

$ = United States dollars, ICP = International Comparison Program, PPP = purchasing power parity.

Sources: For Big Mac PPP: Asian Development Bank estimates based on price data in local currency units as of July 2021 from The Big Mac Index. https://www.economist.com/big-mac-index (accessed 7 May 2025). For Food Basket: World Bank DataBank. https://databank.worldbank.org/embed/ICP-2021-Cycle/id/3a11040d?inf=n (accessed 26 June 2025). For Exchange Rate: World Bank. Databank: ICP 2021. https://databank.worldbank.org/source/icp-2021# (accessed 13 May 2025).

3 The Big Mac Index published by *The Economist* can be accessed at https://www.economist.com/big-mac-index.

Box 2.1: Purchasing Power Parities in Five Economies for Different Commodity Groups: An Illustration

The table below compares exchange rates with purchasing power parities (PPPs) for total gross domestic product (GDP), select GDP expenditure aggregates from the 2021 International Comparison Program (ICP), and the Big Mac, for five economies of varying income levels: the People's Republic of China, India, Japan, Singapore, and Viet Nam. One important difference to be noted is that exchange rates for an economy remain the same for all aggregates, whereas PPPs are different for each aggregate. This is because the PPPs reflect relative prices of the basket of goods and services corresponding to that aggregate.

Exchange Rates Versus Purchasing Power Parities for Selected Expenditure Aggregates, 2021
(number of currency units per United States dollar)

Economy	Exchange Rate	Purchasing Power Parity							
		Gross Domestic Product	Food	Transportation	Recreation and Culture	Restaurants and Hotel	Machinery and Equipment	Construction	Big Mac
People's Republic of China	6.45	3.99	7.16	4.57	4.33	3.85	9.92	1.93	4.54
India	73.92	20.73	36.59	39.29	27.15	20.37	84.13	9.05	38.54
Japan	109.75	98.69	186.32	142.33	135.55	114.28	131.32	89.47	79.11
Singapore	1.34	0.81	1.50	2.00	0.88	0.66	1.89	0.43	1.20
Viet Nam	23,159.89	7,120.01	15,663.69	13,955.33	8,508.66	5,867.14	27,800.92	3,220.80	13,995.94

ICP = International Comparison Program.

Sources: For Exchange Rate and Purchasing Power Parity: World Bank data. DataBank: ICP 2021. https://databank.worldbank.org/source/icp-2021# (accessed 4 June 2024). For Big Mac: Asian Development Bank estimates based on data in local currency units as of July 2021 from The Big Mac Index. https://www.economist.com/big-mac-index (accessed 7 May 2025).

Key insights of the assessment include:

- Across all five economies and all categories of expenditure assessed, there was a wide divergence between market exchange rates and PPPs. This reinforces the importance of using PPPs rather than exchange rates when comparing living standards and economic output.
- In all the economies assessed (including high-income economies such as Japan and Singapore), PPPs for GDP were lower than the corresponding exchange rates. This implies that the general price level in these economies was lower than in the United States. As a result, when GDP was converted using PPPs rather than exchange rates, the implied size of these economies in real terms was larger.
- The differences between exchange rates and PPPs for GDP were especially pronounced, most notably in Viet Nam, India, and the People's Republic of China. This means that when comparing income or per capita GDP, these economies appear substantially wealthier when using PPPs instead of exchange rates as conversion factors. Conversely, for high-income economies such as Japan and Singapore, these differences were narrower.
- PPPs differed across specific expenditure aggregates. This reflects variation in relative prices of different categories of goods and services. For instance, traded goods such as machinery and equipment tend to have PPPs closer to exchange rates, while nontraded goods such as food or services can show wider disparities. The data show that the PPPs for machinery and equipment were significantly higher than the PPPs for all other aggregates in each economy and were somewhat closer to exchange rates. Thus, unlike exchange rates, each PPP is specific to a basket of final goods and services, and it is important for users to choose the relevant PPPs for converting expenditures in local currency units.
- Except in India, Big Mac PPPs were lower than food PPPs, suggesting that Big Macs were relatively cheaper than broader food baskets in most economies. This highlights the limitation of using a single product to represent complex consumption categories.

Source: Asian Development Bank compilation and analysis.

Comparing Price Levels Across Economies: The Price Level Index

Purchasing power parity reflects the amount of an economy's currency needed to buy the same basket of goods and services domestically that one unit of a reference currency (the US dollar in global comparisons) will buy in a reference economy (the US in global comparisons). The price level index (PLI), on the other hand, compares "price levels" between economies in international comparisons. The PLI is defined as the ratio of an economy's PPP to its exchange rate, multiplied by 100.

Use of the PLI helps quickly answer the following question: Is the price level of an economy higher or lower than that of another economy (or higher or lower than a global average price level) with a given value of 100? A PLI equal to 100 implies the same price level as the reference economy (or global average); below 100 means prices are lower than in the reference economy (or global average); above 100 means they are higher. By extension, an economy with a lower PLI generally has, on average, a lower price level than an economy with a higher PLI.

Table 2.4 presents PLIs for GDP, select expenditure aggregates, and the Big Mac in six economies. These PLIs are drawn from the 2021 ICP cycle, with the US = 100 (reference economy).

In 2021, India and Viet Nam typically had PLIs well below 100, except for highly tradable machinery and equipment, indicating relatively low prices for nontradable goods, especially under the aggregates for restaurants and hotels and construction. Meanwhile, Japan had PLIs close to or above 100, with a particularly high PLI for food.

Table 2.4 also shows that, like PPPs, PLIs vary depending upon the goods and services under consideration—because the indexes reflect a ratio of the PPP to the market exchange rate. The PLIs for machinery and equipment for all economies other than the US in Table 2.4 are above 100, reflecting the internationally traded nature of these goods.

PPPs and PLIs offer a clearer lens into comparative price levels and measures of real income, consumption, and investments. They are essential tools in global comparisons, policy planning, and equitable development.

Table 2.4: Price Level Indexes for Selected Aggregates and Economies, 2021

Economy	Gross Domestic Product	Food	Transportation	Recreation and Culture	Restaurants and Hotel	Machinery and Equipment	Construction	Big Mac
People's Republic of China	61.81	110.97	70.83	67.12	59.65	153.77	29.97	70.43
India	28.04	49.50	53.16	36.73	27.56	113.81	12.24	52.14
Japan	89.92	169.77	129.68	123.50	104.13	119.65	81.52	72.08
Singapore	60.34	111.25	149.08	65.32	49.05	140.60	31.72	89.04
Viet Nam	30.74	67.63	60.26	36.74	25.33	120.04	13.91	60.43
United States	100.00	100.00	100.00	100.00	100.00	100.00	100.00	100.00

ICP = International Comparison Program.

Source: World Bank data. DataBank: ICP 2021. https://databank.worldbank.org/source/icp-2021# (accessed 4 June 2024).

CHAPTER 3

International Comparison Program: Governance and Conceptual Framework

The International Comparison Program (ICP) represents one of the most ambitious and technically demanding statistical initiatives ever undertaken, aimed at measuring the size and structure of economies in real terms by generating purchasing power parities (PPPs). The ICP has evolved from a small project to become a truly global program covering 176 economies in its recent cycles. This chapter provides a brief evolution of the ICP, its governance structure, its conceptual framework, and the uses of PPPs in global policy, monitoring of global development goals, and poverty and inequality analysis and research.

Background and Evolution

The limitations of using foreign exchange rates to convert economic aggregates for international comparisons—especially of measures of per capita real gross domestic product (GDP) and measures of material well-being—led to recommendations by the United Nations Statistical Commission (UNSC) in its 15th session in 1968 to develop methods for PPP-based comparisons of GDP (ECOSOC 1968). These recommendations led to the beginnings of the ICP as a modest research project in 1968, with collaborative work between the then United Nations Statistical Office[1] and the University of Pennsylvania, under the leadership of Irving Kravis, Alan Heston, and Robert Summers.

Expansion Phases (1970–1993)

The first cycle of the ICP was conducted in 1970, delivering comparisons for just 10 economies globally. The program steadily increased to 16 economies for the 1973 ICP round and to 34 economies for the 1975 comparisons. These phases were crucial in establishing a technical framework linked to the System of National Accounts, developing appropriate survey frameworks, and implementing an aggregation methodology for the compilation of PPPs.

By the 1980s, the ICP had transformed from a research project to a formal program within the United Nations Statistical Office, covering 60 economies globally in the 1980 round, then increasing to 64 economies for the 1985 round. The 1985 round also influenced the development of the "dollar-a-day" poverty line, which is now a recognized metric for measuring the incidence of extreme poverty at the regional and global levels.

The 1993 ICP round saw participation almost double to 115 economies, but the program's administrators faced difficulties in creating consistent global comparisons due to regional disparities in product lists, classification structures, and data collection processes. In addition, funding issues were limiting the ability of the ICP to produce robust, reliable, and globally comparable results. These difficulties, along with the significant expansion in the number of participating economies, highlighted the need for more coherent governance, improved technical standards, and sustainable support to ensure the comparability and credibility of the ICP.

1 Currently the United Nations Statistics Division.

Restructuring and Consolidation Phases (2005–2021)

Due to the problems encountered during the expansion phases of the program, the ICP went into hiatus after the completion of the 1993 cycle. In 1999, an evaluation of the program was conducted by Jacob Ryten, concluding that the ICP was vital to global economic comparisons and should be continued (ECOSOC 1999). The evaluation also recommended that, with the rapid expansion of economies participating from all the regions of the world, the ICP needed better funding and governance arrangements.

Meanwhile, in 2000, the UNSC appointed a specialist group to report on issues concerning comparisons of per capita incomes across economies as a component of the Human Development Index (HDI) published in the *Human Development Report* by the United Nations Development Programme. These issues included the choice between PPPs and market exchange rates to convert economic aggregates. The specialist group recommended the use of PPPs because of their inherent appropriateness in intereconomy economic comparisons (UNSC 2001). These recommendations led to the revival of the ICP, with the World Bank demonstrating strong interest because the PPPs from the ICP were also used in the calibration of the dollar-a-day poverty line, which aligned with the bank's mandate to reducing absolute poverty around the world.

The 2005 cycle of the ICP marked a new phase in the program's evolution, both in terms of scope and institutional structure. A major transformation occurred when the ICP adopted a new global governance framework[2] with a decentralized regional coordination structure involving national statistics offices and regional coordinating agencies. The World Bank assumed overall responsibility for global coordination and established the ICP Global Office, while regional coordinating agencies (now known as regional implementing agencies) took responsibility for managing the program within their respective regions.

The 2005 ICP cycle therefore marked the beginning of a regionally coordinated ICP outside the European Union and Organisation for Economic Co-operation and Development (OECD) members. The regional agencies that now serve as implementing agencies in their respective regions are: the African Development Bank, the Asian Development Bank (ADB), the Interstate Statistical Committee of the Commonwealth of Independent States, Eurostat, the OECD, the United Nations Economic Commission for Latin America and the Caribbean, and the United Nations Economic and Social Commission for Western Asia.

The 2005 ICP cycle covered 146 economies globally. Significantly, this included India rejoining the program while the People's Republic of China (PRC) joined for the first time, although the PRC's survey coverage was limited to 11 capital cities. The inclusion of both India and the PRC helped boost ICP coverage of the world population to 95%.

The 2011 ICP round marked a high point for the program, with 199 economies participating. This included 178 economies participating in the comparison of all components of GDP, and partial participation, i.e., for comparisons covering household consumption only, of 20 Pacific island economies and one economy from the Latin America and Caribbean regional program.

In 2016, the UNSC endorsed the ICP as a permanent element of its global statistical work program and recommended to conduct the program at more frequent intervals, in a 3-year cycle, with 2017 as the next benchmark year (ECOSOC 2016).

Subsequent ICP cycles in 2017 and 2021 each attracted 176 economies, covering over 99% of the global population and total GDP generated. This confirmed the ICP's status as a truly global statistical endeavor. In the 2024 ICP cycle (under implementation at the time of this report), a similar level of participation is expected globally.

2 The new global governance framework was adopted by the UNSC based on the evaluation of the ICP prepared by Jacob Ryten, which strongly recommend that the "ICP should not be ended nor should it be allowed to languish." (ECOSOC 1999)

Figure 3.1 shows the evolution of ICP and economies' participation in ICP cycles from the 1970 benchmark to the 2021 benchmark, delineating global participation and economies in Asia and the Pacific.

Table 3.1 outlines the number of economies that participated under each regional agency in the 2021 ICP cycle. It may be noted that these regions are defined for ICP purposes largely based on homogeneity of each grouping and practical considerations of program implementation.

Figure 3.1: Economy Participation and History of International Comparison Program Benchmarks, 1970–2021

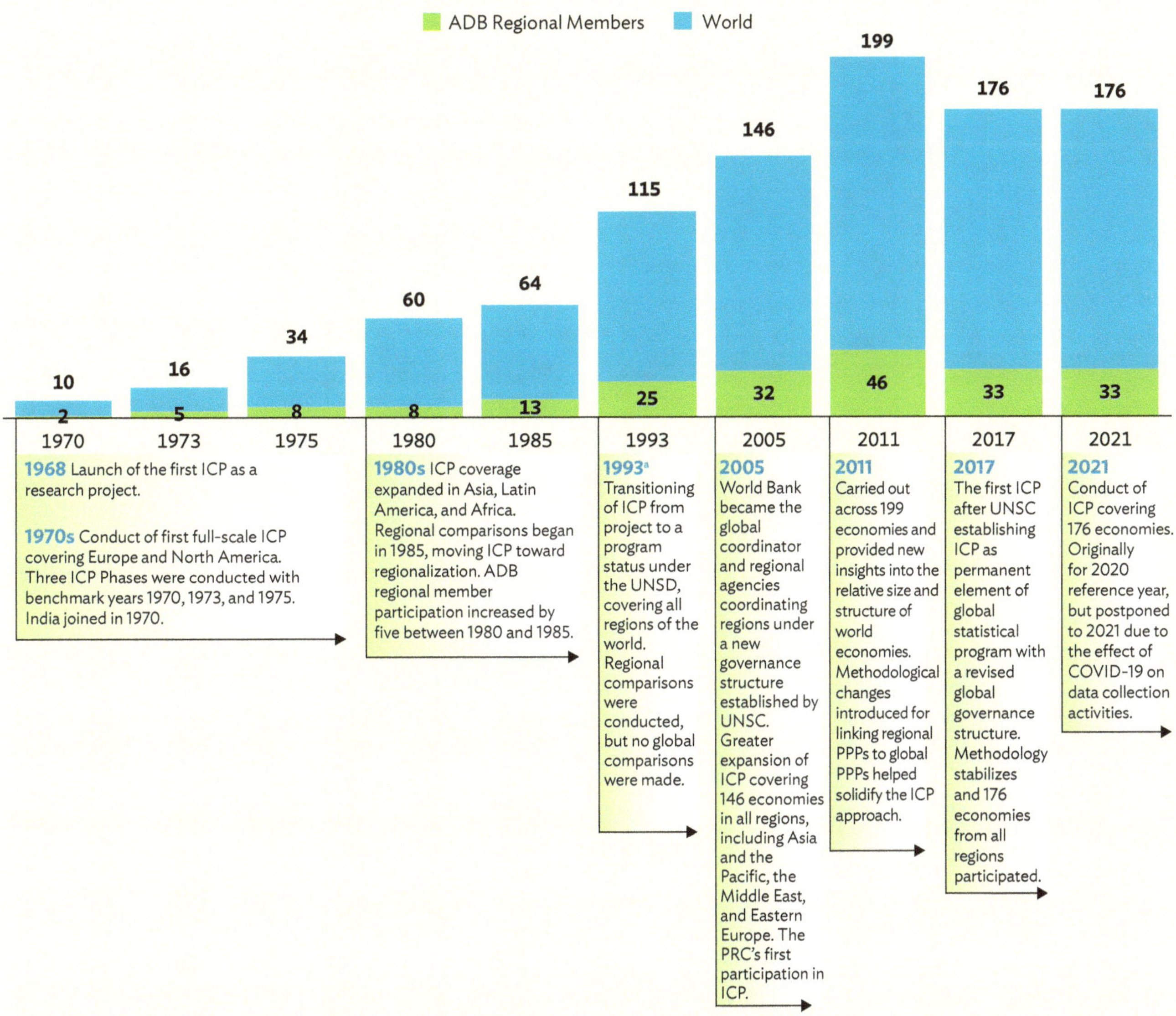

ADB = Asian Development Bank, COVID-19 = coronavirus disease, ICP = International Comparison Program, PPP = purchasing power parity, PRC = People's Republic of China, UNSC = United Nations Statistical Commission, UNSD = United Nations Statistics Division.

Notes: In the 2011 ICP benchmark cycle, a total of 199 economies participated globally. These included 178 economies that participated for the full coverage of gross domestic product and 21 economies (including 20 Pacific island economies) that participated partially, covering only household consumption. Of the 20 Pacific economies, 13 are ADB regional members. Other than Fiji, which has participated regularly in the ADB ICP Asia and Pacific region, other Pacific island economies have participated only in 2011 benchmark.

[a] In 1990, the International Comparison Project was renamed the International Comparison Program.

Sources: United Nations Statistics Division. Handbook of the International Comparison Programme. https://unstats.un.org/unsd/methods/icp/ipc6_htm.htm; World Bank. International Comparison Program: Participation of Economies in ICP cycles. https://www.worldbank.org/en/programs/icp/history; and ADB. 2023. Part IV: Stories Behind Data—Using Price Data and Statistics to Track Socioeconomic Development. Key Indicators for Asia and the Pacific 2023. https://www.adb.org/sites/default/files/publication/900716/part4-sbd.pdf.

Table 3.1: Distribution of Economies in the 2021 Cycle of the International Comparison Program, by Region

ICP Regions	Regional Implementing Agency	Number of Economies
Africa	African Development Bank	52
Asia and the Pacific	Asian Development Bank	21
Commonwealth of Independent States	Interstate Statistical Committee of the Commonwealth of Independent States	9
Europe and OECD	Eurostat and OECD	51
Latin America and the Caribbean	United Nations Economic Commission for Latin America and the Caribbean	32
Western Asia	United Nations Economic and Social Commission for Western Asia	16

OECD = Organisation for Economic Co-operation and Development.

Note: A total of 176 economies participated, which included a few dual participating economies or economies which participated simultaneously in two regional comparisons.

Source: ICP Global Office of the World Bank: History of International Comparison Program. https://www.worldbank.org/en/programs/icp/history, accessed 18 June 2025.

Global Governance Structure

A complex statistical program on the global scale of the ICP requires highly effective coordination across all stakeholders for its successful implementation.

With the program maintaining a regionalized approach since the 2005 cycle, in the first stage, comparisons are organized in each of the ICP regions to compile regional PPPs and PPP-based real expenditures. These comparisons use the currency of one of the regional economies as the reference currency, e.g., the Hong Kong dollar is used in Asia and the Pacific. In the next stage, the World Bank calculates global PPPs and corresponding real expenditures, with the United States dollar as the reference currency, by linking together regional results using established methods. This involves complex processes and methods that need to be effectively coordinated and for which a global governance framework has been established to support the active participation of all stakeholders.

The global governance structure of the ICP since the 2017 ICP cycle is depicted in Figure 3.2. It shows how the program brings together national, regional, and global agencies in a coherent and systematic approach. The structure is designed to ensure that all implementation activities at the economy, regional, and global levels—i.e., every activity needed to produce reliable measures of PPPs and real GDP

Figure 3.2: Global Governance Structure for the International Comparison Program

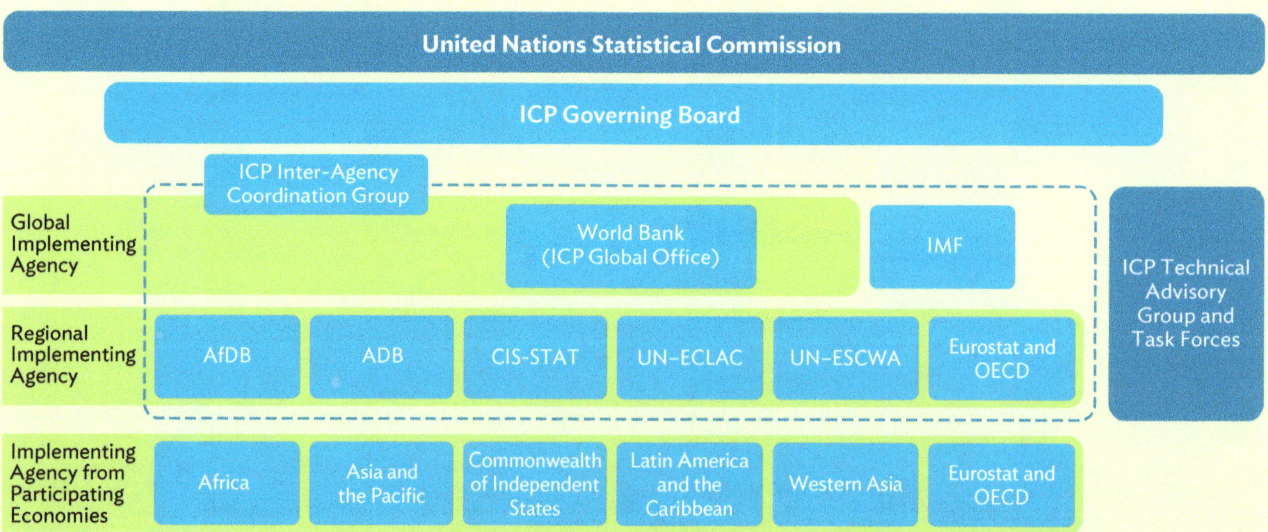

ADB = Asian Development Bank, AfDB = African Development Bank, CIS-STAT = Interstate Statistical Committee of the Commonwealth of Independent States, Eurostat = Statistical Office of the European Union, ICP = International Comparison Program, IMF = International Monetary Fund, OECD = Organisation for Economic Co-operation and Development, UN-ECLAC = United Nations Economic Commission for Latin America and the Caribbean, UN-ESCWA = United Nations Economic and Social Commission for Western Asia.

Source: World Bank. 2020. *Purchasing Power Parities and the Size of the World Economies: Results from the 2017 International Comparison Program*. https://openknowledge.worldbank.org/handle/10986/33623.

and its expenditure components—are based on robust protocols, methods, and quality assurance standards.

The UNSC is the ultimate statistical stakeholder, providing full program oversight. The **Governing Board**, with representation from 11 economies across ICP regions and international and regional partners, sets the ICP's strategic directions and priorities. The **Inter-Agency Coordination Group** (comprising the World Bank, the International Monetary Fund, and regional implementing agencies) is responsible for harmonizing ICP procedures and operations across the regions. **Regional implementing agencies** steer specific ICP regional programs in collaboration with national implementing agencies, with this collaboration focusing on the collection of data, quality assurance, and calculating regional PPPs and real expenditures. The **ICP Global Office** at the World Bank coordinates the program worldwide and produces global PPPs by linking the regional results. The Global Office works in collaboration with the Inter-Agency Coordination Group. Technical guidance on standardized methodology, technical oversight of quality of results, and transparency of PPP estimation processes comes from the **Technical Advisory Group**, a panel of prominent experts in the fields of index numbers, PPPs, price statistics, and national accounts.

Program Framework, Methodology, and Operations

Framework and Methodology for the Global Program

The ICP framework is defined by the System of National Accounts, with pricing concepts, definitions, and classifications used in the ICP being consistent with the compilation of GDP under the expenditure approach as defined in the 2008 System of National Accounts. The six main aggregates forming GDP from the expenditure side, along with two analytically important derived expenditure aggregates, are outlined in Figure 3.3. ICP results are currently published for 45 selected aggregates on the expenditure side of GDP.

The classification used by the ICP for price collection and GDP expenditure-side disaggregation is based on five standard statistical classifications followed under the System of National Accounts. These classifications correspond to the main six aggregates of GDP from the expenditure side. As shown in Figure 3.3, GDP is comprised of six main aggregates and the five standard statistical classifications corresponding to these main expenditure aggregates are: (i) classification of individual consumption according to purpose (COICOP) for individual consumption expenditure by households (ICEH); (ii) classification of the purposes of nonprofit institutions serving households (COPNI) for individual consumption expenditure by nonprofit institutions serving households (NPISHs); (iii) classification of the functions of government (COFOG) for individual consumption expenditure by government (ICEG) and collective consumption expenditure by government (CCEG); (iv) central product classification (CPC) for gross capital formation (GCF), i.e., gross fixed capital formation plus changes in inventories and net acquisition of valuables; and (v) harmonized system (HS) classification for exports and imports.

The ICP classification of GDP at the detailed levels comprises the six main aggregates broken down into 28 categories, 63 groups, 126 classes, and 155 basic headings. While the main aggregates and expenditure categories are outlined in Figure 3.3, Table 3.2 shows the number of ICP expenditure categories, groups, classes, and basic headings under each main aggregate of the ICP classification (World Bank 2016).

Calculations of PPPs are first made at the "basic heading" level, which is the lowest level in the classification hierarchy, and PPPs for aggregates above the "basic heading" level are calculated using the PPPs of underlying basic headings and corresponding GDP expenditures, which serve as weights in the aggregation process.

Figure 3.3: Expenditure Side of Gross Domestic Product

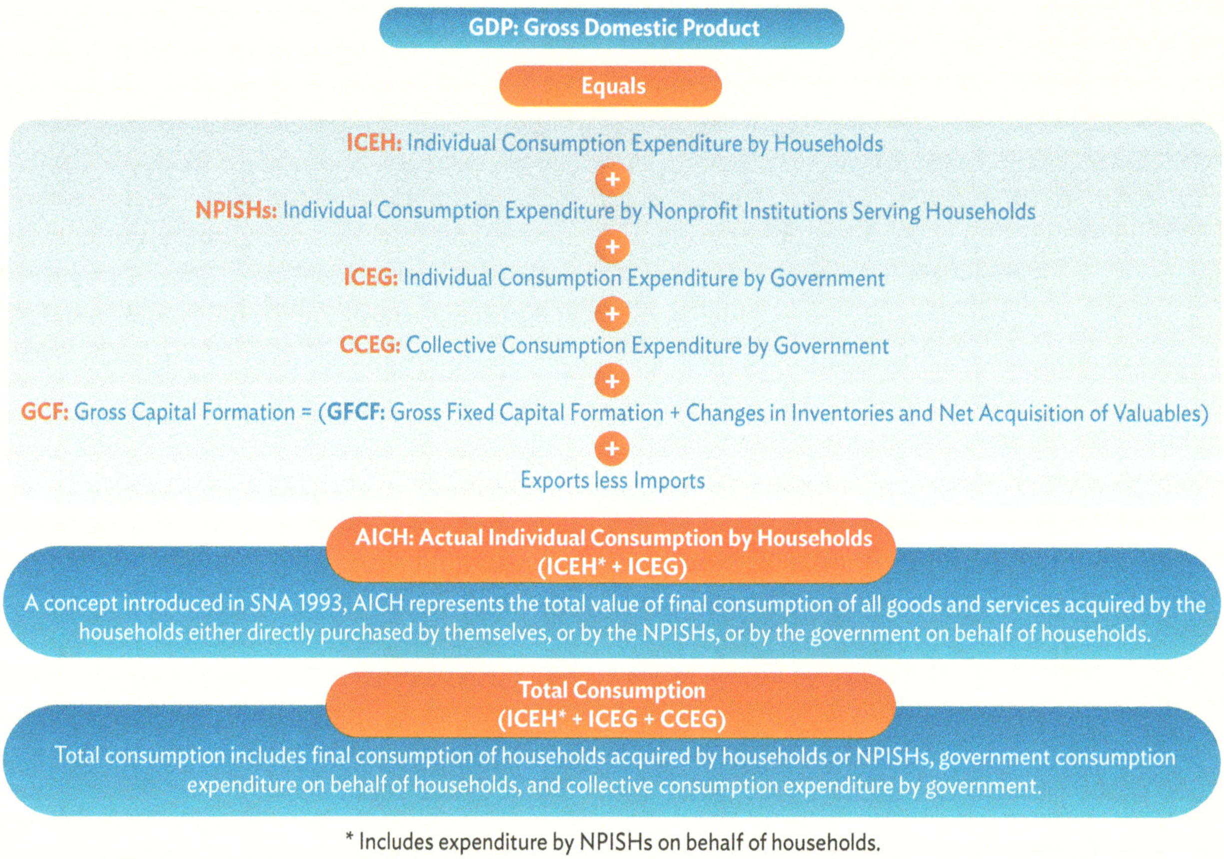

SNA = System of National Accounts.
Source: Asian Development Bank.

Table 3.2: Number of Categories, Groups, Classes, and Basic Headings by Aggregate

Gross Domestic Product and Main Aggregates	Category	Group	Class	Basic Heading
Gross Domestic Product	28	63	126	155
Individual Consumption Expenditure by Households	13	44	91	110
Individual Consumption Expenditure by NPISH	5	5	5	5
Individual Consumption Expenditure by Government	5	7	16	21
Collective Consumption Expenditure by Government	1	1	5	5
Gross Capital Formation	3	5	8	12
Balance of Exports and Imports	1	1	1	2

NPISH = nonprofit institutions serving households.

Source: Asian Development Bank based on World Bank. 2016. *International Comparison Program: Classification of Final Expenditure on GDP*. Washington, DC. http://pubdocs.worldbank.org/en/708531575560035925/pdf/ICP-Classification-description-2019-1205.pdf.

The PPP for total GDP is based on the aggregation of PPPs of the 155 basic headings, with corresponding GDP expenditures for those 155 headings serving as weights.

Data Collection Requirements

The calculation of PPPs for economies across the world, following standardized procedures, must be backed by an intensive data collection exercise that is possible only with collaborative partnerships with the national statistics offices in participating economies. While exchange rates are readily available through open financial markets, estimation of PPPs requires dedicated price collection surveys for a well-defined basket of items of goods and services in all participating economies. These surveys conducted by the national statistics offices, collect prices for goods and services for the reference year and are currently undertaken every 3 years.

These surveys must gather several price quotations from representative outlets in selected markets during the reference year to estimate national **annual average prices** for items representative of the consumption and investment expenditures of the economies. The item lists are developed for collection of prices of well specified items of expenditures on household consumption, housing rental, compensation paid to government employees, construction inputs, and machinery and equipment. These annual average prices of items from each survey facilitate price comparisons between economies for the calculation of PPPs at the basic heading level. Other essential inputs in PPP calculations are the GDP expenditures broken down by 155 basic headings for the benchmark ICP year, which serve as weights for the compilation of PPPs for components of GDP above the basic headings.

Workflow of the Global Program

The ICP follows a structured process for preparing product lists; selecting representative products; conducting price surveys at the economy level; validating data at the national, regional, and global levels; and calculating regional and global comparisons using index number methods endorsed by the ICP Technical Advisory Group. This ensures comparability and transparency in published PPPs and related real expenditures. Figure 3.4 outlines the workflow between national implementing agencies, regional implementing agencies, and the ICP Global Office.

Product List Development

Standardized product lists are prepared in consultation with all the stakeholders prior to ICP price surveys. They cover household consumption, housing rental, government compensation, construction, and machinery and equipment. Product lists provide a "structured product description" for each item. These descriptions contain price-determining characteristics to ensure that the items priced by all economies are "like with like" comparisons. Items to be priced are grouped by basic heading comprising a homogeneous set of two or more items. Thus on the price collection side, a basic heading is a homogeneous set of items for price collection, for which corresponding expenditure is compiled from the GDP expenditure side. As mentioned before, a basic heading is the lowest level in the ICP classification hierarchy for which PPPs are calculated.

Price Surveys by Participating Economies

National implementing agencies, typically national statistics offices in each economy, undertake ICP price surveys from a nationally representative sample of outlets for a representative and comparable set of items from the predefined product lists. Prices are collected on a monthly, quarterly, six-monthly, or annual basis, depending on the product characteristics and price variability to estimate the national annual average price for each item priced. The national implementing agencies also prepare GDP expenditures disaggregated by 155 basic headings and provide national annual average prices and GDP expenditures to the regional implementing agency.

Figure 3.4: Workflow of the International Comparison Program

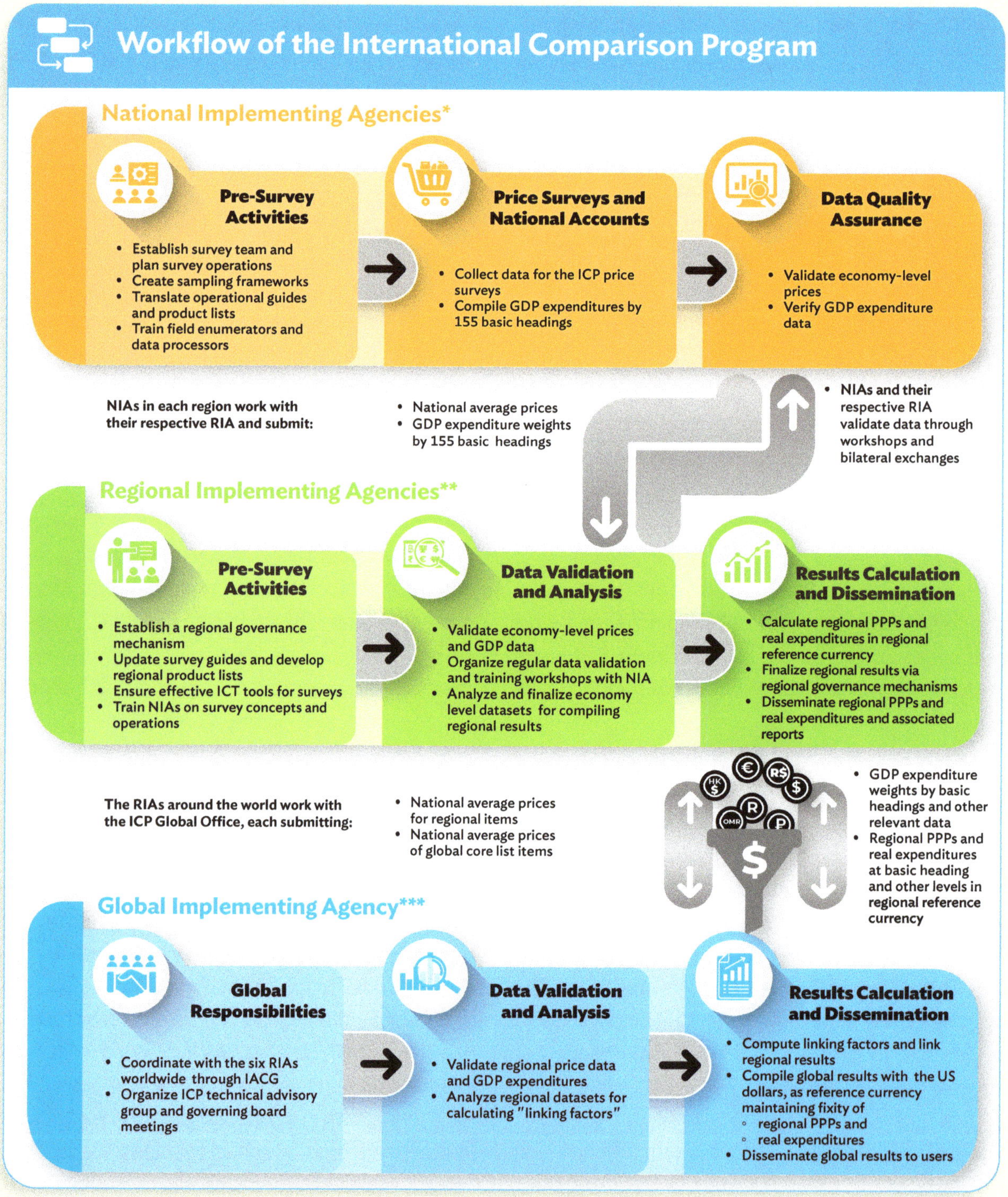

GDP = gross domestic product, IACG = Interagency Coordination Group, ICP = International Comparison Program, ICT = information and communication technology, NIA = national implementing agency, PPP = purchasing power parity, RIA = regional implementing agency, US = United States.

* Globally, 176 economies participated in the 2017 and 2021 ICP cycles, with a similar number involved in the 2024 ICP cycle.

** The seven regional implementing agencies are: ADB = Asian Development Bank, AfDB = African Development Bank, CIS-STAT = Interstate Statistical Committee of the Commonwealth of Independent States, Eurostat = Statistical Office of the European Union, OECD = Organisation for Economic Co-operation and Development, UN-ECLAC = United Nations Economic Commission for Latin America and the Caribbean, UN-ESCWA = United Nations Economic and Social Commission for Western Asia.

*** The World Bank serves as the ICP Global Implementing Agency.

Source: Asian Development Bank compilation.

Table 3.3: Price Surveys and Number of Items in the 2021 International Comparison Program Cycle for Asia and the Pacific

Price Survey	Survey Description	Number of Items in Product List
Household Consumption	Captures the prices paid by the household for the goods and services typically consumed by the households in an economy from the regional product list.	990 items, including 857 items for regional comparisons and 563 items for global linking.
Housing	Captures annual average rents paid for a representative sample of dwelling types prevalent in the economy. Additionally, housing stock (number of dwellings, rooms, floor area), and data on housing quality indicators such as facilities of inside water, private toilet, and electricity in the economy are collected.	20 dwelling types representing apartments and houses of different sizes.
Government Compensation	Captures annual average compensation paid to government employees engaged in selected occupations in the production of health, education, and collective services provided by the government.	34 government occupations.
Construction	Captures prices of construction material inputs, rental paid for construction equipment, and labor inputs commonly used in the construction of residential buildings, nonresidential buildings, and civil engineering works.	51 construction inputs comprising materials (33), equipment rental (10), and labor (8).
Machinery and Equipment	Captures prices for representative items of fixed assets of machinery and equipment used by the firms in the production of goods and services.	179 items of machinery and equipment.

Source: Asian Development Bank.

Table 3.3 lists the price surveys and the number of items in product lists for the 2021 ICP cycle implemented in Asia and the Pacific.

Data Quality Assurance

Since high data quality is integral to ICP implementation, sophisticated statistical tools are used to validate data quality and comparability. The price data validation process is carried out in three stages: economy-level validation by the national implementing agencies, intereconomy data validation by the regional implementing agencies, and interregional or global data validation by the World Bank. These validations ensure high data quality and comparability across all participating economies.

Aggregation of Price Data

Items for which price data have been collected are grouped into the 155 basic headings in the GDP breakdown. These basic headings are aggregated into 126 classes, such as "bread and cereals" (which may include rice, other cereals, flour, bread, and pasta). These classes are then clustered into 63 groups—e.g., the "food" group includes meat, fish, dairy, oils, fruits, and vegetables—and these groups are further combined into 28 categories, such as "food and nonalcoholic beverages." At the top of the hierarchy, the categories are grouped to form the six main aggregates that make up GDP: (i) individual consumption expenditure by households, (ii) individual consumption expenditure by nonprofit institutions serving households, (iii) individual consumption expenditure by government, (iv) collective consumption expenditure by government, (v) gross capital formation, and (vi) net exports.

Compilation of PPPs

The PPPs are first compiled by each region with a regional economy's currency as the reference currency for comparisons. In Asia and the Pacific, Hong Kong dollar serves as the regional reference currency. Each region compiles regional level PPPs at the basic heading and higher levels aggregates and real expenditures.

Within a region, PPPs are compiled for higher levels of aggregation by progressively combining the PPPs derived at the "basic heading" level, similar to how national statistics offices calculate indexes such as the consumer price index. At the basic heading level, the country-product-dummy (CPD) method is used to estimate PPPs , while higher-level aggregates use the Gini-Eltetö-Köves-Szulc (GEKS) method (ADB 2020). This hierarchical process of compiling PPPs is depicted in Figure 3.5.

Relevant regional results are provided by each region to the World Bank, the global implementing agency, for calculating linking factors and the global ICP results.

Figure 3.5: Hierarchical Structure for Compiling Purchasing Power Parities in the International Comparison Program

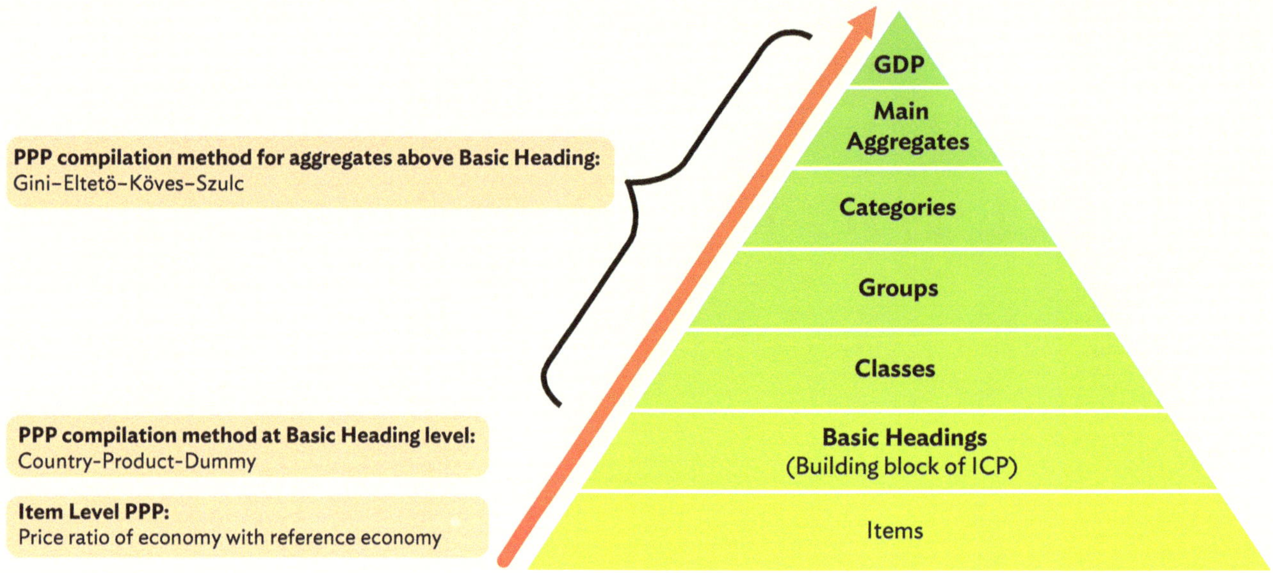

GDP = gross domestic product, ICP = International Comparison Program, PPP = purchasing power parity.

Source: D. S. Prasada Rao. 2013. The Framework of the International Comparison Program. In World Bank, ed. *Measuring the Real Size of the World Economy*. World Bank. pp 13–45.

Note that a key principle in the compilation of global PPPs is "fixity", which ensures that the relative positions of economies within regional comparisons are preserved in the global results, which are calculated by linking regional results. (For more details on compilation methodology, refer to ADB 2020).

Uses and Applications of Purchasing Power Parities and Real Expenditures

The increased coverage of the ICP (which now covers almost 180 economies around the world) and improvements in the program's methodology have led to the increasing adoption of PPP-based measures in empirical research and policy analysis. Comparisons of real incomes based on PPPs are now frequently used in the study of poverty and inequality, economic convergence, international development, and structural transformation. Some of the most popular applications of PPPs and real expenditures are briefly presented in the next subsections.

Applications for the Sustainable Development Goals Monitoring

By expressing outcomes in common purchasing power terms, PPPs from the ICP contribute to the monitoring of development progress against agreed global benchmarks. PPPs play a vital role in both the formulation and the ongoing evaluation of the Sustainable Development Goal (SDG) agenda. The SDGs, which were established by the United Nations General Assembly, include several indicators that depend on PPP-based expenditure measures to ensure comparability across economies. One of the most critical global goals under the SDG agenda is the elimination of extreme poverty, and PPPs are a critical input in the consistent monitoring of extreme poverty (SDG 1) across economies as well as providing the basis for the estimation of the international poverty line (Ravallion et al. 1991). The extreme poverty line has been recently updated from $2.15 per person per day at 2017 PPP to $3.00 per person per day in 2021 PPP terms (Alfani et al. 2025), based on prices collected in the 2021 ICP cycle.

In addition to tracking the progress of SDG 1 on extreme poverty, PPPs and real expenditures provide a basis for measuring indicators used to track other goals of the SDG agenda. Some examples of these applications where PPPs are used to estimate comparable expenditures/income include: agricultural incomes and productivity for indicators 2.3.1 and 2.3.2 under the goal on achieving zero hunger (SDG 2); providing measures for maternal mortality rate for indicator 3.1.1 and household expenditures on health for indicator 3.8.2 under the goal on good health and well-being (SDG 3); measuring energy intensity, indicator 7.3.1, under the goal on affordable and clean energy (SDG 7); comparing labor productivity, indicator 8.2.1, under the goal on decent work and economic growth (SDG 8); analyzing greenhouse gas emissions per unit of economic output (in PPPs), indicators 9.4.1 and 9.5.1, under the goal on industry, innovation, and infrastructure (SDG 9); and per capita consumption of households in PPP terms for indicator 10.1.1 under the goal on reducing income inequality (SDG 10). Changes in the PPP-based measures over time help in analyzing the policy drivers aimed at achieving these important global objectives. Figure 3.6 lists the SDGs and indicators that depend on the PPP-based expenditure aggregates.

Figure 3.6: Uses of Purchasing Power Parities in Tracking Sustainable Development Goals

CO_2 = carbon dioxide, GDP = gross domestic product, PPP = purchasing power parity.

Source: United Nations. Sustainable Development Goals Metadata repository. https://unstats.un.org/sdgs/metadata. World Bank. 2021. *Purchasing Power Parities for Policy Making: A Visual Guide to Using Data from the International Comparison Program*. https://openknowledge.worldbank.org/entities/publication/dc4deba0-339b-5dca-af4c-4881445d1dce.

Use by International Organizations

PPPs and PPP-based expenditures are increasingly being used by international organizations for administrative purposes, research and policy analysis, and economic comparisons as well as for the tracking of development progress on various global goals and targets.

Administrative Uses

Several international organizations have incorporated PPP-based measures into their operational and administrative frameworks (Figure 3.7). The International Monetary Fund (IMF) includes PPP-based GDP in the formula used for the calculation of member quota subscriptions; a formula that also determines the IMF's financial assistance and economies' voting power in decisions relevant to the IMF. The World Bank uses PPP-based GDP for calculating the shareholding rights of the International Bank for Reconstruction and Development members. The European Commission employs regional per capita GDP in PPP terms to allocate structural funds designed to reduce disparities between and within member economies. These metrics are also used for budgetary contributions by European Union members (World Bank 2021).

Uses in Compiling Development and Growth Indicators

PPP-based GDP and per capita incomes are important components in several international development indicators and feature prominently in the construction of such indicators (Figure 3.7). Some examples include the Human Development Index (HDI), the Inequality-Adjusted HDI, and the Gender Development Index. All these indicators incorporate per capita gross national income

Figure 3.7: Administrative and Other Policy Applications of Purchasing Power Parities

GDP = gross domestic product, PPP = purchasing power parity, OECD = Organisation for Economic Co-operation and Development.

Sources: Asian Development Bank. Asian Development Outlook. International Monetary Fund (IMF). World Economic Outlook. OECD. Better Life Index. OECD. Economic Outlook. United Nations Development Programme. Human Development Report. World Bank. Poverty and Inequality Platform Publications. World Bank. 2021. *Purchasing Power Parities for Policy Making: A Visual Guide to Using Data from the International Comparison Program*. https://openknowledge.worldbank.org/entities/publication/dc4deba0-339b-5dca-af4c-4881445d1dce. World Economic Forum. 2020. *The Global Competitiveness Report Special Edition 2020: How Countries Are Performing on the Road to Recovery*. https://www3.weforum.org/docs/WEF_TheGlobalCompetitivenessReport2020.pdf.

expressed in PPP terms as one of the components. These are published annually in the United Nations Development Programme's Human Development Reports.[3]

PPP-based economic measures also allow for the calculation of averages for a group of economies or a particular region. This is done by aggregating individual economy values weighted by their share in the PPP-based GDP of the group in order to reflect the contribution of each economy in the region's average or regional growth rate. Organizations such as ADB, the IMF, and the OECD rely on the PPP-based GDP of individual economies to estimate regional and global GDP growth and inflation in their respective macroeconomic reports: *Asian Development Outlook*, *World Economic Outlook*, and *Economic Outlook*. ADB's Corporate Results Framework, 2025–2030 is aligned with regional development priorities under the 2030 Agenda for Sustainable Development and includes the indicator "people in poverty and vulnerable situations," which relies on the PPP-based international poverty line (ADB 2024b).

Other Common Applications

In addition to their core uses, PPPs from the ICP support a wide range of analyses, including productivity comparisons, assessments of economic catch-up and convergence of incomes across economies, and the measurement of regional and global inequality trends. They are also used for calculating cost-of-living adjustments for expatriates and in evaluating national competitiveness.[4] The annual average prices collected for PPP estimation have been applied to nutrition-based measures and costs of healthy diets (FAO et al. 2025).

Domestic Economic Analysis and Policy

The use of PPPs and real expenditure data within economies is a relatively unexplored area. PPPs from the ICP, while primarily used for intereconomy comparisons, also have important applications for domestic economic analysis and policymaking. By adjusting for differences in price levels, PPPs can enable more accurate assessments of real income, living standards, and poverty across geographic areas within an economy. In Asia and the Pacific, for instance, the National Statistics Office of Viet Nam annually produces a subnational Spatial Cost of Living Index.[5] This index compares prices collected in six economic zones of Viet Nam and includes data for 2010 onwards. Such applications make PPPs a useful instrument for tailored policy formulation within economies.

Domestic social policies can also benefit from PPP data by benchmarking national poverty lines against international standards, improving the design and targeting of welfare programs. Similarly, PPPs allow for meaningful comparisons of per capita spending relative to economies at similar levels of development. For example, national policymakers can evaluate whether domestic food prices are higher than in comparable economies within the region, whether government expenditure for households aligns with international norms, or whether prices of tradeable goods are competitive from a trade perspective. Such comparisons can help identify inefficiencies in domestic budgeting, set more realistic and attainable economic benchmarks, and guide evidence-based policy decisions by national and subnational governments.

3 Human Development Reports are available at https://hdr.undp.org/.
4 For more applications of PPPs as outlined by the World Bank, go to http://hdl.handle.net/10986/35736.
5 The online portal for the Spatial Cost of Living Index can be found at https://www.nso.gov.vn/en/px-web/?pxid=E1121&theme=Trade%2C%20Price%20and%20Tourist.

Limitations and Caution

While PPPs are valuable for international comparisons and policy analysis, their use requires some caution and important considerations.

PPPs generated by the ICP are estimated using prices collected in a given reference year and are designed for spatial comparisons across participating economies for that year. This means they are not suitable for temporal comparisons or analyzing trends over time, such as economic growth or inflation.

PPPs rely on complex methodologies and use economy-specific data, which can vary in quality and consistency, potentially affecting comparability. Additionally, PPPs reflect relative price levels, not market exchange rates, and therefore are not appropriate for financial forecasting or exchange rate analysis.

It is important to consider the appropriate PPP needed to study a given problem, because PPPs refer to specific baskets of goods and services. Users are often not aware that PPPs are specific to a basket of final goods and services defined in the ICP classification, and it is important to familiarize these users with the scope and coverage of each PPP available from the ICP. Moreover, as PPPs under the ICP are currently updated only once every 3 years, their relevance may become limited when applied toward the end of the ICP cycle, especially for rapidly changing economies.

Finally, because they are national averages, PPPs do not provide information on regional price variations within economies, making them unsuitable for subnational analysis without further adjustments. These limitations highlight the need for the careful, context-aware application of PPPs in domestic and international policy settings.

Nevertheless, the PPPs generated under the ICP remain central to evidence-based policymaking at the economy, regional, and global levels. The global governance framework and the conceptual framework established for the ICP since 1970 have provided the program with strong organizational and technical foundations to produce reliable PPPs and real income comparisons through transparent processes and methods. These PPPs and measures of real income, standard of living, and material well-being have myriad policy applications from national and international perspectives.

CHAPTER 4

Asia and the Pacific in the Global Context

Background

The Asia and Pacific region occupies a position of central importance in the contemporary global economy. Since the 1970s, Asia in particular has transformed from a region of mostly developing economies into a major engine of economic growth. This metamorphosis began with Japan, which rose rapidly after World War II to become the world's second-largest economy by the 1980s, thanks to its strong industrial base, export-led growth, and innovations in technology and manufacturing.

Following Japan's lead, the so-called "Asian Tigers"—Hong Kong, China; the Republic of Korea; Singapore; and Taipei,China—emerged in the 1970s and 1980s as dynamic, high-growth economies. With heavy investments in education, infrastructure, and export-driven industries, these economies achieved rapid modernization and became key players in global trade and finance.

The spotlight has since shifted to the People's Republic of China (PRC) and India. The PRC's economic reforms, starting in the late 1970s, have unleashed unprecedented growth, lifting hundreds of millions out of poverty and turning the economy into the largest exporter globally and, in real terms, the world's largest economy. India, has also made significant strides since liberalizing its economy in the early 1990s, becoming a global hub for services, technology, and pharmaceuticals. Indonesia, Malaysia, the Philippines, Thailand, and Viet Nam have also experienced rapid growth, often inspired by the performance of the Asian Tiger economies.

As a significant outcome of their flourishing growth over 5 decades, Singapore and Hong Kong, China have become major international financial hubs, attracting foreign investment and fostering even greater economic expansion.

More broadly, trends in demography further highlight the economic potential of the Asia and Pacific region, with many of its economies possessing large, young, and increasingly urbanized populations. This demographic dividend is contributing to rising domestic consumption and expanding middle classes, creating new opportunities for investment and economic diversification. While aging populations in economies such as Japan and the Republic of Korea present long-term challenges, the region continues to benefit from strong labor market growth and human capital development.

Drawing exclusively on results from the latest 2021 cycle of the International Comparison Program (ICP), and its precursor benchmarks of 2011 and 2017, this chapter highlights the extent to which Asia and the Pacific contributes to the global economy when economic comparisons are made using purchasing power parities (PPPs). The 2011, 2017, and 2021 ICP cycles have maintained the same methodology for the calculation of PPPs, which allows comparing the results over the three ICP benchmarks.

Coverage

For the purposes of this chapter, the Asia and Pacific region comprises the following 33 members of the Asian Development Bank (ADB) who have participated in the most recent 2021 ICP cycle.

Armenia; Australia; Azerbaijan; Bangladesh; Bhutan; Brunei Darussalam; Cambodia; the PRC; Fiji;

Georgia; Hong Kong, China; India; Indonesia; Japan; Kazakhstan; the Republic of Korea; the Kyrgyz Republic; the Lao People's Democratic Republic; Malaysia; Maldives; Mongolia; Nepal; New Zealand; Pakistan; the Philippines; Singapore; Sri Lanka; Taipei,China; Tajikistan; Thailand; Türkiye; Uzbekistan; and Viet Nam.[1]

The United States (US) is included in some of the tables and graphs as it is the reference economy for global comparisons, with the US dollar as the reference currency for global PPPs and real expenditures (Chapter 2 includes details of these concepts). In addition, Africa, Europe, and the Rest of the World are included in relevant tables and figures to provide a more comprehensive global perspective on international comparisons.

Purchasing Power Parities Versus Exchange Rates

When comparing the size of economies, or measuring the total size of the global economy, a conversion method is required to express data in a common currency. The options available for this purpose are market exchange rates or PPPs. As discussed in Chapter 2, PPPs from ICP reflect differences in price levels across economies by comparing the cost of a standard basket of goods and services, and are used as conversion factors to express macroeconomic aggregates in a common currency. By contrast, exchange rates are determined by currency markets and can fluctuate due to financial flows and/or investor sentiment, thereby failing to reflect the relative purchasing power of the currencies.

Figure 4.1 presents the ratios of PPPs for gross domestic product (GDP) to exchange rates across economies of Asia and the Pacific in 2021 (shown on the vertical axis) against the per capita real GDP of those economies (shown on the horizontal axis). It reveals that, except for the developed economies of Australia and New Zealand, the PPPs for 2021 were consistently lower than market exchange rates (ratio of PPP to exchange rate is less than 1).

Key Findings:

- Among lower-middle-income and upper-middle-income economies, the PPP-to-exchange-rate ratio was often below 0.50. This means real economic output was significantly understated when measured using exchange rates instead of using PPPs as currency converters.
- For Tajikistan, the ratio was just 0.22. This indicates that the economy's nominal GDP was less than one-fourth of its real GDP. Similarly, India's ratio of 0.28 suggests its real GDP was over three and half times larger than its nominal figure. For the PRC, the ratio was 0.62, implying a real GDP nearly 62% greater than its nominal value.
- Among the high-income economies, Australia and New Zealand, the PPP-to-exchange-rate ratios were greater than 1.00, with real GDP lower than nominal GDP, implying GDP is overstated when market exchange rates are used instead of PPPs as currency converters. For other high-income economies, the ratios were below 1.00 implying relatively lower prices than in the US.

The differences between PPPs and market exchange rates highlight a key issue: Using exchange rates tends to exaggerate income disparities between economies. In particular, it understates the economic size of lower-income economies and overstates the income gap in comparison with developed economies.

For these reasons—and considering that PPPs not only convert different currencies into a common currency but also adjust for the difference in the price levels between economies—PPPs produced by the ICP are better measures than market exchange rates in providing real comparisons of the economic size and per capita incomes of economies around the world. This chapter primarily uses real (PPP-adjusted) GDP and other aggregates from the results of the 2021

1 ADB member Myanmar participated in the 2011 and 2017 ICP cycles while Uzbekistan has participated only in the 2021 cycle.

Figure 4.1: Ratio of Purchasing Power Parity for Gross Domestic Product to Market Exchange Rate, 2021

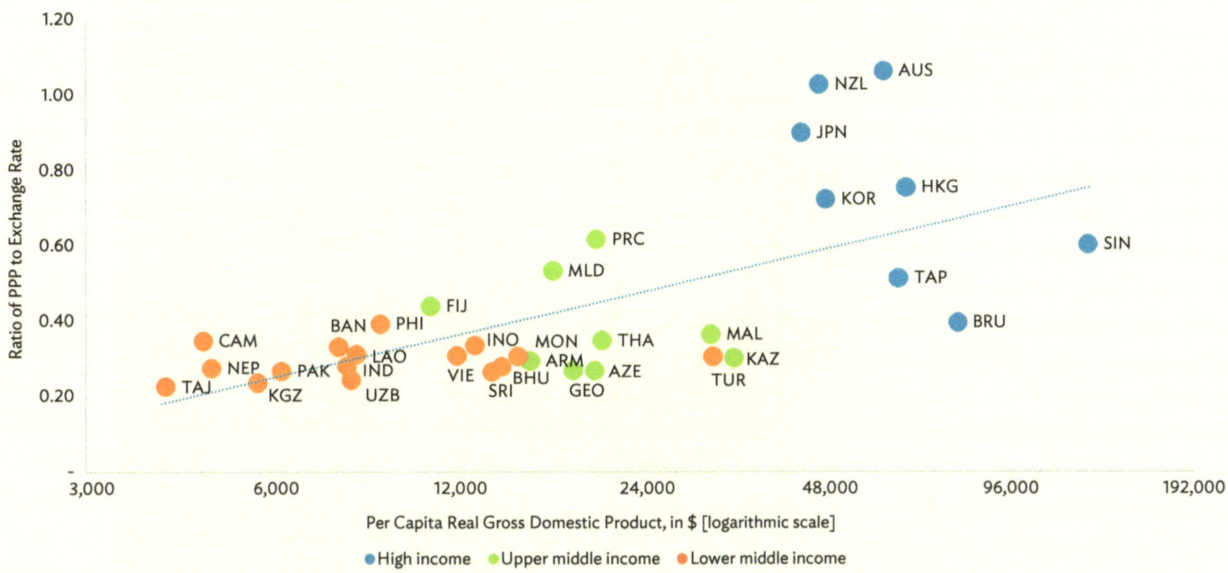

$ = United States dollars; ARM = Armenia; AUS = Australia; AZE = Azerbaijan; BAN = Bangladesh; BHU = Bhutan; BRU = Brunei Darussalam; CAM = Cambodia; FIJ = Fiji; GEO = Georgia; HKG = Hong Kong, China; ICP = International Comparison Program; IND = India; INO = Indonesia; JPN = Japan; KAZ = Kazakhstan; KOR = Republic of Korea; KGZ = Kyrgyz Republic; LAO = Lao People's Democratic Republic; MAL = Malaysia; MLD = Maldives; MON = Mongolia; NEP = Nepal; NZL = New Zealand; PAK = Pakistan; PHI = Philippines; PPP = purchasing power parity; PRC = People's Republic of China; SIN = Singapore; SRI = Sri Lanka; TAJ = Tajikistan; TAP = Taipei,China; THA = Thailand; TUR = Türkiye; UZB = Uzbekistan; VIE = Viet Nam.

Note: Data presented are for 33 economies that participated in the 2021 ICP globally.

Source: Asian Development Bank estimates using World Bank data. DataBank: ICP 2021. https://databank.worldbank.org/source/icp-2021# (accessed 4 June 2024).

ICP cycle, as they provide more accurate measures of the volumes of goods and services produced and consumed across economies.

Asia and the Pacific in the Global Economy

Regional Contribution to Global Gross Domestic Product

Figure 4.2 shows that the Asia and Pacific region (designated by segments in shades of blue) is the single-greatest contributor to the world economy. The outer circle of the figure presents GDP in nominal (exchange-rate based) terms while the inner circle denotes GDP in real (PPP-adjusted) terms. As a reference point for the key findings below, the total size of the world economy in 2021 was $152.413 trillion in real or PPP-adjusted terms and $96.187 trillion in nominal or exchange-rate terms, based on the 2021 ICP results.

Key Findings:

- When measured in real terms, i.e., adjusted for purchasing power, the Asia and Pacific region accounted for 44.6% of global GDP in 2021. When using exchange rates, its share was about 7 percentage points lower at 37.7%.

- The US contributed 15.5% of the global economy in real terms, but a much higher 24.5% when measured in exchange-rate or nominal terms. This reflects the strength of the US dollar in international markets.

Figure 4.2: Nominal and Real Shares of Global Gross Domestic Product, 2021
(%)

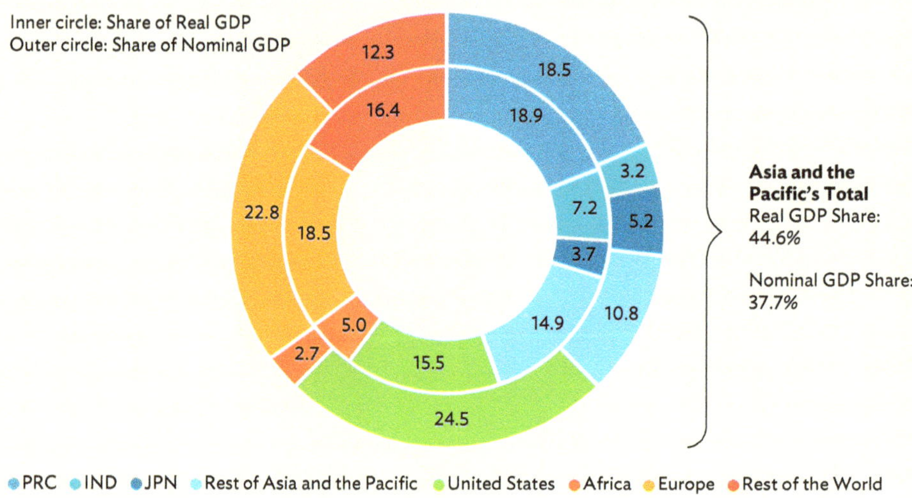

GDP = gross domestic product, ICP = International Comparison Program, IND = India, JPN = Japan, PPP = purchasing power parity, PRC = People's Republic of China.
Note: The outer circle shows each share of nominal (exchange-rate-based) global GDP. The inner circle shows each share of real (PPP-adjusted) global GDP.
Source: Asian Development Bank estimates using World Bank data. DataBank: ICP 2021. https://databank.worldbank.org/source/icp-2021# (accessed 4 June 2024).

- The PRC, with a contribution of 18.9% to global real GDP was the biggest economy in the world in 2021. However, in exchange-rate terms, its share of 18.5% made it much smaller than the US economy at 24.5% (Box 4.1 discusses this for the year 2024).
- The share of Europe in global GDP was 18.5% when measured in PPP terms, smaller than its 22.8% share measured via exchange rates.
- Africa and "the rest of the world" (which excludes all of Asia and the Pacific, the US, and Europe) made up 21.4% of global GDP in real terms and 15.0% in nominal terms.

It is clear from the above income shares from the 2021 ICP cycle that exchange-rate-based measures of GDP tend to overestimate the size of developed economies while understating the size of developing economies.

Analysis of Gross Domestic Product for Individual Economies

Table 4.1 summarizes real (PPP-adjusted) and nominal (exchange-rate-based) GDP results from the 2021 ICP cycle for 33 economies of the Asia and Pacific region. The table also provides GDP comparisons with the US and other regions of the world.

Figure 4.3a presents GDP results (in billions of US dollars) in both real and nominal terms for the top 10 economies of Asia and the Pacific in the 2021 ICP cycle. Figure 4.3b presents these data (in millions of US dollars) for the remaining 23 economies of the region who participated in the 2021 ICP cycle. These charts illustrate the relative size of each economy in the region.

Box 4.1: Which is the World's Biggest Economy?

Being the world's largest economy depends on whether a nominal or real measure of gross domestic product (GDP) is used. When measuring GDP in current United States (US) dollars, the US was still leading in 2024. According to the International Monetary Fund's World Economic Outlook Database (updated in April 2025), the US economy was valued at $29.185 trillion in 2024—about 56% larger than the $18.748 trillion for the People's Republic of China (PRC)—and this nominal measure based on market exchange rates, is commonly reported in the media. However, the corresponding GDP figures based on purchasing power parity (PPP) show the US economy was about 24% smaller than the PRC in 2024.

Gross Domestic Product by Market Exchange Rates and Purchasing Power Parity, 2024
($ billion)

GDP (market exchange rates)			GDP (purchasing power parity)		
PRC	US	US-PRC (%)	PRC	US	US-PRC (%)
18,748.0	29,184.9	155.7	38,154.2	29,184.9	76.5

$ = United States dollars, GDP = gross domestic product, PRC= People's Republic of China, US = United States.
Source: International Monetary Fund. World Economic Outlook Database: April 2025. https://www.imf.org/en/Publications/WEO/weo-database/2025/april (accessed 31 July 2025).

This comparison of the real size of the US and the PRC economies is an example of why market exchange rates fall short in measuring GDP, i.e., by not accounting for price differences across economies. This is why economists often rely on PPPs, which adjust for price-level differences and give a more accurate analysis of goods and services produced in any given economy.

Eminent economic historian, the late Angus Maddison, predicted that the PRC would become the world's largest economy by 2030 (Maddison 2006). He was nearly right—it happened much earlier as revealed by the 2017 ICP results.

The results from the 2017 ICP cycle showed that the PRC slightly edged out the US in real (PPP-adjusted) GDP terms and, since then, it has widened the gap. According to the 2021 ICP results, the PRC's real GDP reached $28.822 trillion, ahead of the US at $23.594 trillion. By these measures, the PRC has been the world's largest economy for some years.

Reference: Maddison, A.. 2006. China in the World Economy: 1300–2030. *International Journal of Business*. 11 (3).
Source: Asian Development Bank compilation and analysis.

Key Findings:

- The PRC was the largest economy in the Asia and Pacific region (and globally) in real terms, with a GDP of $28.822 trillion for 2021. India ranked second in the region (and third globally), with a real GDP of $10.963 trillion.

- Japan was the third-largest economy in the region (and fifth globally), with a real GDP of $5.567 trillion, while Indonesia was the fourth-largest in the region (and 10th globally), with a real GDP of $3.531 trillion.

- Together, the PRC, India, Japan, and Indonesia accounted for $48.882 trillion in real GDP in 2021, or close to a third (32.1%) of global output, reflecting the influence of the Asia and Pacific region on the world economy.

- Other major economies of the region in 2021 included Türkiye (13th globally); the Republic of Korea (14th globally); Australia (19th); Taipei,China (21st); Thailand (22nd); Pakistan (23rd); and Bangladesh (24th).

- By comparison, the US remained the second-largest economy in real terms globally in 2021, with a GDP of $23.594 trillion—or roughly 82% of the PRC's output.

Table 4.1: Summary Results for Gross Domestic Product, 2021

Economy	Purchasing Power Parity ($ = 1.00)	Exchange Rate ($ = 1.00)	Expenditure ($ billion)		Shares (World = 100.00)		Per Capita Expenditure, in $		Per Capita Expenditure Indexes (US = 100)		Price Level Indexes		Reference Data	
			Real	Nominal	Real	Nominal	Real	Nominal	Real	Nominal	US = 100	World = 100	Expenditure, in LCU billion	Population, in million
Developing ADB Member Economies	...	...	**60,652.6**	**29,329.2**	**39.79**	**30.49**	**14,798**	**7,156**	**21**	**10**	**48**	**77**	...	**4,098.8**
Armenia	148.24	503.77	47.2	13.9	0.03	0.01	15,922	4,685	22	7	29	47	6,992	3.0
Azerbaijan	0.46	1.70	203.9	54.8	0.13	0.06	20,298	5,458	29	8	27	43	93	10.0
Bangladesh	28.30	85.10	1,325.6	440.8	0.87	0.46	7,786	2,589	11	4	33	53	37,510	170.3
Bhutan	19.61	73.94	10.4	2.8	0.01	0.00	13,803	3,661	19	5	27	42	205	0.8
Brunei Darussalam	0.53	1.34	35.3	14.0	0.02	0.01	80,203	31,786	113	45	40	63	19	0.4
Cambodia	1,426.96	4,098.72	77.4	27.0	0.05	0.03	4,667	1,625	7	2	35	55	110,506	16.6
China, People's Republic of	3.99	6.45	28,821.6	17,813.5	18.91	18.52	20,407	12,613	29	18	62	98	114,924	1,412.4
Fiji	0.91	2.07	9.8	4.3	0.01	0.00	10,963	4,818	15	7	44	70	9	0.9
Georgia	0.87	3.23	69.3	18.6	0.05	0.02	18,691	5,016	26	7	27	43	60	3.7
Hong Kong, China	5.87	7.77	488.4	368.9	0.32	0.38	65,877	49,760	93	70	76	120	2,868	7.4
India	20.73	73.92	10,963.1	3,074.3	7.19	3.20	8,019	2,249	11	3	28	44	227,243	1,367.2
Indonesia	4,808.43	14,308.14	3,530.6	1,186.5	2.32	1.23	12,948	4,351	18	6	34	53	16,976,751	272.7
Kazakhstan	129.06	426.03	650.5	197.1	0.43	0.20	34,231	10,370	48	15	30	48	83,952	19.0
Korea, Republic of	827.27	1,143.95	2,514.5	1,818.4	1.65	1.89	48,594	35,142	68	50	72	115	2,080,198	51.7
Kyrgyz Republic	19.92	84.64	39.3	9.2	0.03	0.01	5,736	1,350	8	2	24	37	783	6.9
Lao People's Democratic Republic	3,031.70	9,697.92	61.0	19.1	0.04	0.02	8,315	2,599	12	4	31	50	184,982	7.3
Malaysia	1.51	4.14	1,022.5	373.8	0.67	0.39	31,389	11,476	44	16	37	58	1,549	32.6
Maldives	8.21	15.38	9.8	5.3	0.01	0.01	17,309	9,243	24	13	53	85	81	0.6
Mongolia	870.18	2,849.29	50.1	15.3	0.03	0.02	15,247	4,657	21	7	31	48	43,555	3.3
Nepal	32.48	118.13	139.9	38.5	0.09	0.04	4,813	1,323	7	2	27	44	4,543	29.1
Pakistan	43.44	162.63	1,409.5	376.5	0.92	0.39	6,271	1,675	9	2	27	42	61,230	224.8
Philippines	19.38	49.25	1,001.8	394.1	0.66	0.41	9,091	3,576	13	5	39	62	19,411	110.2
Singapore	0.81	1.34	719.1	433.9	0.47	0.45	131,864	79,571	186	112	60	96	583	5.5
Sri Lanka	55.53	198.88	317.0	88.5	0.21	0.09	14,306	3,994	20	6	28	44	17,600	22.2
Taipei,China	14.40	28.02	1,504.8	773.1	0.99	0.80	64,120	32,941	90	46	51	81	21,663	23.5
Tajikistan	2.54	11.31	39.7	8.9	0.03	0.01	4,053	912	6	1	22	36	101	9.8
Thailand	11.15	31.98	1,452.1	506.2	0.95	0.53	20,838	7,264	29	10	35	55	16,189	69.7
Türkiye	2.73	8.89	2,662.2	816.4	1.75	0.85	31,638	9,702	45	14	31	49	7,256	84.1
Uzbekistan	2,591.11	10,609.98	285.0	69.6	0.19	0.07	8,162	1,993	11	3	24	39	738,425	34.9
Viet Nam	7,120.01	23,159.89	1,191.0	366.1	0.78	0.38	12,090	3,717	17	5	31	49	8,479,667	98.5
Developed ADB Member Economies	...	...	**7,366.7**	**6,912.8**	**4.83**	**7.19**	**47,132**	**44,227**	**66**	**62**	**94**	**149**	...	**156.3**
Australia	1.42	1.33	1,557.5	1,657.5	1.02	1.72	60,639	64,532	85	91	106	169	2,207	25.7
Japan	98.69	109.75	5,566.7	5,005.5	3.65	5.20	44,355	39,884	62	56	90	142	549,379	125.5
New Zealand	1.46	1.41	242.5	249.7	0.16	0.26	47,426	48,834	67	69	103	163	353	5.1
Asia and the Pacific (33)	...	...	**68,019.3**	**36,242.0**	**44.63**	**37.68**	**15,985**	**8,517**	**23**	**12**	**53**	**84**	...	**4,255.1**
Africa	...	...	**7,605.3**	**2,631.7**	**4.99**	**2.74**	**5,655**	**1,957**	**8**	**3**	**35**	**55**	...	**1,344.8**
Europe	...	...	**28,249.5**	**21,891.6**	**18.53**	**22.76**	**51,876**	**40,200**	**73**	**57**	**77**	**123**	...	**544.6**
United States	**1.00**	**1.00**	**23,594.0**	**23,594.0**	**15.48**	**24.53**	**70,988**	**70,988**	**100**	**100**	**100**	**158**	**23,594**	**332.4**
Rest of the World	...	...	**24,944.5**	**11,827.4**	**16.37**	**12.30**	**23,939**	**11,351**	**34**	**16**	**47**	**75**	...	**1,042.0**
World	...	...	**152,412.5**	**96,186.7**	**100.00**	**100.00**	**20,271**	**12,793**	**29**	**18**	**63**	**100**	...	**7,518.8**

... = not available/applicable, $ = United States dollars, ADB = Asian Development Bank, ICP = International Comparison Program, LCU = local currency unit, US = United States.

Source: World Bank. DataBank: ICP 2021. https://databank.worldbank.org/source/icp-2021# (accessed 4 June 2024).

Figure 4.3: Gross Domestic Product in Real and Nominal Terms, 2021

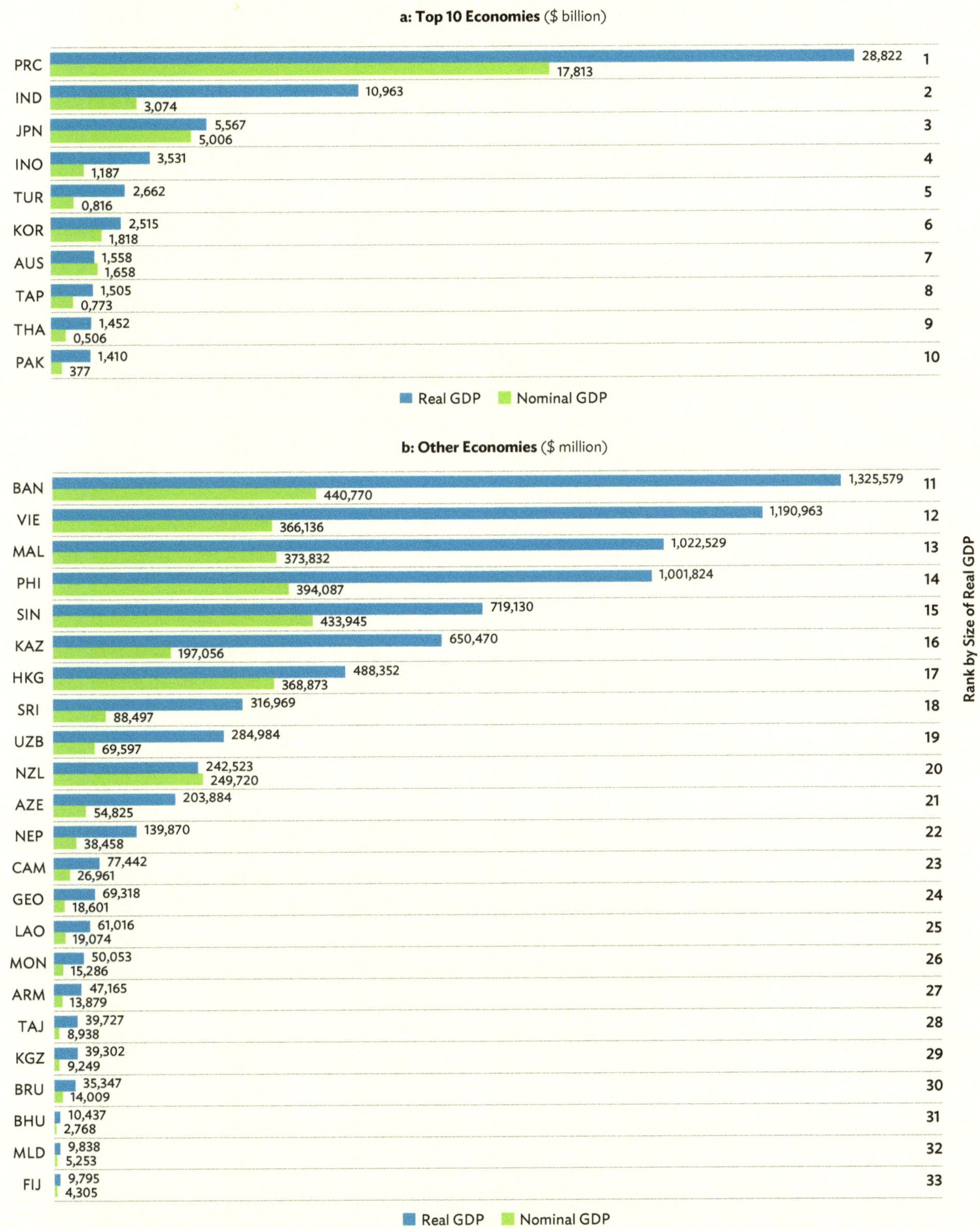

$ = United States dollars; ARM = Armenia; AUS = Australia; AZE = Azerbaijan; BAN = Bangladesh; BHU = Bhutan; BRU = Brunei Darussalam; CAM = Cambodia; FIJ = Fiji; GEO = Georgia; GDP = gross domestic product; HKG = Hong Kong, China; ICP = International Comparison Program; IND = India; INO = Indonesia; JPN = Japan; KAZ = Kazakhstan; KGZ = Kyrgyz Republic; KOR = Republic of Korea; LAO = Lao People's Democratic Republic; MAL = Malaysia; MLD = Maldives; MON = Mongolia; NEP = Nepal; NZL = New Zealand; PAK = Pakistan; PHI = Philippines PRC = People's Republic of China; SIN = Singapore; SRI = Sri Lanka; TAJ = Tajikistan; TAP = Taipei,China; THA = Thailand; TUR = Türkiye; UZB = Uzbekistan; VIE = Viet Nam.

Note: Data presented are for 33 economies that participated in the 2021 ICP globally.

Source: World Bank. DataBank: ICP 2021. https://databank.worldbank.org/source/icp-2021# (accessed 4 June 2024).

Table 4.1 and Figure 4.3 show that the nominal GDP figures for most economies of Asia and the Pacific were significantly lower than their real GDP results for 2021. This is due to PPPs being lower than market exchange rates relative to the US dollar. This gap highlights how conversions based on exchange rates can understate economic size, especially for developing economies.

Contributions to the World Economy and Population Shares

One way to understand global economic dynamics is to ask: do individual economies contribute in proportion to their population size? If share of global economic output were to match share of global population, it would suggest a degree of global income equality. In simple terms, if economies with more people are also producing more, it is a sign of a convergence of average incomes across economies.

Figure 4.4 helps explore this notion by comparing shares of real GDP globally (as shown in the outer circle of the figure) with corresponding global population shares (as shown in the inner circle) for selected economies and regions in 2021.

Key Findings:

- Europe, with a population share of only 7.3%, accounted for 18.5% of real (PPP-adjusted) global GDP in 2021, exhibiting a starkly higher measure of per capita well-being than Asia and the Pacific (represented in shades of blue), which had a population share of 56.6% and a real GDP share of about 44.6%.
- Africa had the lowest share of real global GDP at only 5.0%, despite its population share of 17.9%.
- The average share of "the rest of the world" in real GDP at 16.4% is higher than its global share population share of 13.9%.
- These findings reflect wide disparities in average per capita incomes between developed and developing regions.
- High-income economies such as the US, Japan, and Australia (the latter not shown in Figure 4.4) posted real GDP shares much higher than their population shares, reflecting advanced economy status.
- The PRC exhibited near equality between its global GDP and population shares for 2021, with both at around 19%, reflecting a per capita real GDP close to the global average.
- India's population share was about two and a half times larger than its share of global real GDP. This suggests lower income per person compared to the global average.

Table A1.1 in Appendix 1 offers full GDP results for the 33 economies of Asia and the Pacific that participated in the 2021 ICP cycle, including comparisons with other major regions of the world.

Figure 4.4: Shares in Global Real Gross Domestic Product and Global Population, 2021

(%)

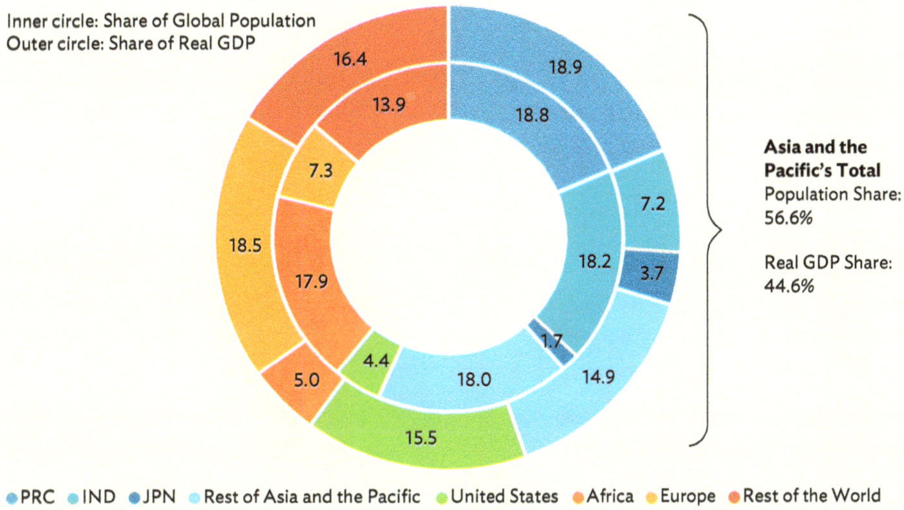

GDP = gross domestic product, ICP = International Comparison Program, IND = India, JPN = Japan, PPP = purchasing power parity, PRC = People's Republic of China.

Note: The outer circle represents share of real (PPP-adjusted) global GDP. The inner circle refers to share of global population.

Source: World Bank. DataBank: ICP 2021. https://databank.worldbank.org/source/icp-2021# (accessed 4 June 2024).

Measuring Living Standards and Material Well-Being

Per capita real (PPP-adjusted) GDP is widely used as a measure of a population's standard of living. It reflects the total economic output or expenditure of an economy, adjusted for population size. This provides a broad reflection of the affluence of the economy's residents.

However, GDP is comprised of various expenditure components. Some of these components—such as individual consumption expenditure by households (ICEH), expenditures by nonprofit institutions serving households (NPISHs), and government spending on behalf of households—relate to material well-being, but others—such as investment, changes in inventories, and trade balances—are not so directly relevant. Therefore, while GDP as a holistic indicator may be useful for comparing overall economic activity, it may not accurately capture the material well-being experienced by individuals.

For this reason, economists often turn to ICEH as a more direct indicator of living standards. This refers to the goods and services consumed by households. Additionally, households benefit from expenditures by NPISHs, such as charities or religious organizations. In many economies, data limitations make it difficult to separate NPISH spending from household spending and, in ICP results, these two expenditures are grouped together under the term ICEH. Data from the ICP on ICEH are especially valuable for analyzing poverty and inequality, as they more closely reflect consumption patterns of households.

Governments also spend directly on behalf of individuals, covering services such as housing, health care, education, and social protection. This spending is categorized as individual consumption expenditure by government (ICEG) and, in many economies, such public services play a crucial role in improving quality of life.

Introduced by the System of National Accounts 1993, a broader measure of the goods and services consumed by households is termed "actual individual consumption by households" (AICH), which is obtained by adding ICEG to ICEH. This cumulative figure presents a better measure of material well-being, since AICH includes goods and services consumed by households from all three sources: consumption expenditure by households; expenditures by NPISHs on behalf of households; and expenditures by government on behalf of households.

Measuring Material Well-Being Under the International Comparison Program

To capture a nuanced analysis of the material well-being of populations across economies, the ICP provides three key analytical measures:

(i) Per capita real GDP, the broadest measure of economic output or income per person;
(ii) Per capita real ICEH, individual consumption expenditure by households and nonprofit institutions serving households; and
(iii) Per capita real AICH, adding government-provided services for individuals (ICEG) to ICEH.

Together, these indicators help move beyond headline GDP figures and toward a deeper understanding of the material well-being of any given population.

Table 4.2 presents three key indicators of living standards—per capita GDP, per capita ICEH, and per capita AICH for 33 economies in the Asia and Pacific region as well as the US, based on 2021 ICP data with an index (World = 100). The table also includes the global ranking of each economy for each measure.

Key Findings:

- As expected, both per capita ICEH and per capita AICH were consistently lower than per capita GDP for 2021. This reflects the basic point that per capita GDP can overstate material well-being by including nonconsumption components of economic output.

- All three per capita measures of economic well-being indicate that the average for the Asia and Pacific region was below the global average for 2021.

- Within Asia and the Pacific, there were wide disparities in global rankings for per capita real GDP. While Singapore and Brunei Darussalam ranked second and eighth in the world, respectively, the region also includes some economies with very low per capita real GDP, such as Cambodia (ranked 143rd globally in 2021) and Tajikistan (ranked 146th globally).

- There were big gaps in the per capita measures of GDP, ICEH, and AICH between the developing and developed economies of Asia and the Pacific in 2021, with each of these measures at least three times higher for the developed economies.

- Importantly, the ratio of per capita ICEH or AICH to per capita GDP varied across economies. In economies such as Brunei Darussalam and Kazakhstan (which are resource-rich), Singapore (with strong trade surpluses), and the PRC (with high investment levels), per capita ICEH was significantly lower than per capita GDP. This suggests that a large portion of GDP in these economies stems from components other than consumption expenditure by or for households.

Table 4.2: Measures of Living Standards and Associated Global Rankings, 2021

ADB Economy Name	Gross Domestic Product			Individual Consumption Expenditure by Households and NPISH			Actual Individual Consumption by Households		
	Per Capita, in $	Per Capita Index (WLD = 100)	Global rank	Per Capita, in $	Per Capita Index (WLD = 100)	Global rank	Per Capita, in $	Per Capita Index (WLD = 100)	Global rank
Developing ADB Member Economies	**14,798**	**73**	...	**7,098**	**67**	...	**8,406**	**65**	...
Armenia	15,922	79	92	10,239	96	87	12,842	99	86
Azerbaijan	20,298	100	77	10,065	94	88	12,800	99	87
Bangladesh	7,786	38	124	5,198	49	125	5,707	44	127
Bhutan	13,803	68	102	6,605	62	113	8,852	68	107
Brunei Darussalam	80,203	396	8	17,504	164	53	23,492	181	49
Cambodia	4,667	23	143	2,781	26	146	3,284	25	144
China, People's Republic of	20,407	101	76	7,755	73	104	9,286	72	102
Fiji	10,963	54	111	8,646	81	98	10,212	79	97
Georgia	18,691	92	80	12,582	118	76	15,769	122	75
Hong Kong, China	65,877	325	14	39,345	369	2	44,577	344	4
India	8,019	40	123	5,213	49	123	5,745	44	126
Indonesia	12,948	64	104	6,469	61	115	7,642	59	113
Kazakhstan	34,231	169	51	16,026	150	58	20,469	158	59
Republic of Korea	48,594	240	31	19,584	184	41	25,885	200	41
Kyrgyz Republic	5,736	28	135	4,019	38	135	5,270	41	129
Lao People's Democratic Republic	8,315	41	121	3,634	34	140	4,296	33	137
Malaysia	31,389	155	54	17,720	166	51	21,122	163	54
Maldives	17,309	85	87	6,544	61	114	8,907	69	106
Mongolia	15,247	75	96	7,342	69	108	9,455	73	101
Nepal	4,813	24	140	3,844	36	138	4,338	34	136
Pakistan	6,271	31	131	5,425	51	121	6,022	47	123
Philippines	9,091	45	117	6,390	60	116	7,381	57	117
Singapore	131,864	651	2	29,336	275	9	35,066	271	20
Sri Lanka	14,306	71	100	8,339	78	101	10,146	78	98
Taipei,China	64,120	316	15	26,340	247	18	33,061	255	22
Tajikistan	4,053	20	146	2,575	24	151	3,421	26	142
Thailand	20,838	103	75	10,459	98	84	13,429	104	83
Türkiye	31,638	156	53	15,757	148	62	22,121	171	53
Uzbekistan	8,162	40	122	4,350	41	131	5,956	46	124
Viet Nam	12,090	60	108	6,292	59	118	7,624	59	114
Developed ADB Member Economies	**47,132**	**233**	...	**22,672**	**213**	...	**31,018**	**240**	...
Australia	60,639	299	21	28,023	263	14	37,030	286	17
Japan	44,355	219	39	21,448	201	32	29,637	229	29
New Zealand	47,426	234	34	25,831	242	19	34,710	268	21
United States	70,988	350	10	48,269	452	1	52,654	407	1
Asia and the Pacific (33)	**15,985**	**79**	...	**7,670**	**72**	...	**9,237**	**71**	...
World	**20,271**	**100**	...	**10,668**	**100**	...	**12,948**	**100**	...

... = not available/applicable, $ = United States dollars, ADB = Asian Development Bank, ICP = International Comparison Program, NPISHs = nonprofit institutions serving households, WLD = World.

Source: Asian Development Bank estimates using World Bank data. DataBank: ICP 2021. https://databank.worldbank.org/source/icp-2021# (accessed 4 June 2024).

- Comparing per capita ICEH with per capita AICH provides additional insights. The difference between the two reveals the extent to which governments support household consumption by providing public services such as health care, education, and housing (refer to section on "Measuring the Role of Government on Material Well-Being" for more discussion). Notably, per capita ICEH in developing economies of Asia and the Pacific averaged around 84% of per capita AICH in 2021, while this proportion was only about 73% for the region's developed economies. This shows that the governments in developed economies generally had the resources to play a greater role in delivering essential services to their households.

Using the United States as a Well-Being Benchmark

Another useful perspective on living standards comes from comparing each economy's per capita real GDP and per capita real ICEH with those two measures for the US. Figure 4.5 plots the relative income gaps (based on per capita real GDP) and the relative household consumption gaps (based on per capita real ICEH) between the US and the 33 economies of Asia and the Pacific that participated in the 2021 ICP cycle.

Key Findings:

- Most economies fell well below the US benchmark on both per capita real GDP and per capita real ICEH for 2021. In general, the gaps were much larger for per capita real ICEH for 28 economies.
- Two-third out of 33 economies had an income gap of at least 70% compared to the US for both per capita real GDP and per capita real ICEH, including four economies—Cambodia, the Kyrgyz Republic, Nepal, and Tajikistan—with gaps for both exceeding 90%, implying level of material well-being was below 10% of that in the US.
- The only two economies with *negative gap ratios* for per capita real GDP, meaning they exceeded the US on this measure were Brunei Darussalam (-13%) and Singapore (-86%). However, when per capita real ICEH is considered, all economies of the region including Brunei Darussalam (64%) and Singapore (39%) fell below the US. This reveals that their apparent affluence reflected in per capita real GDP was contributed in large measures by components other than household consumption.

Figure 4.5: Gross Domestic Product and Household Consumption Relative to the United States, 2021
(%)

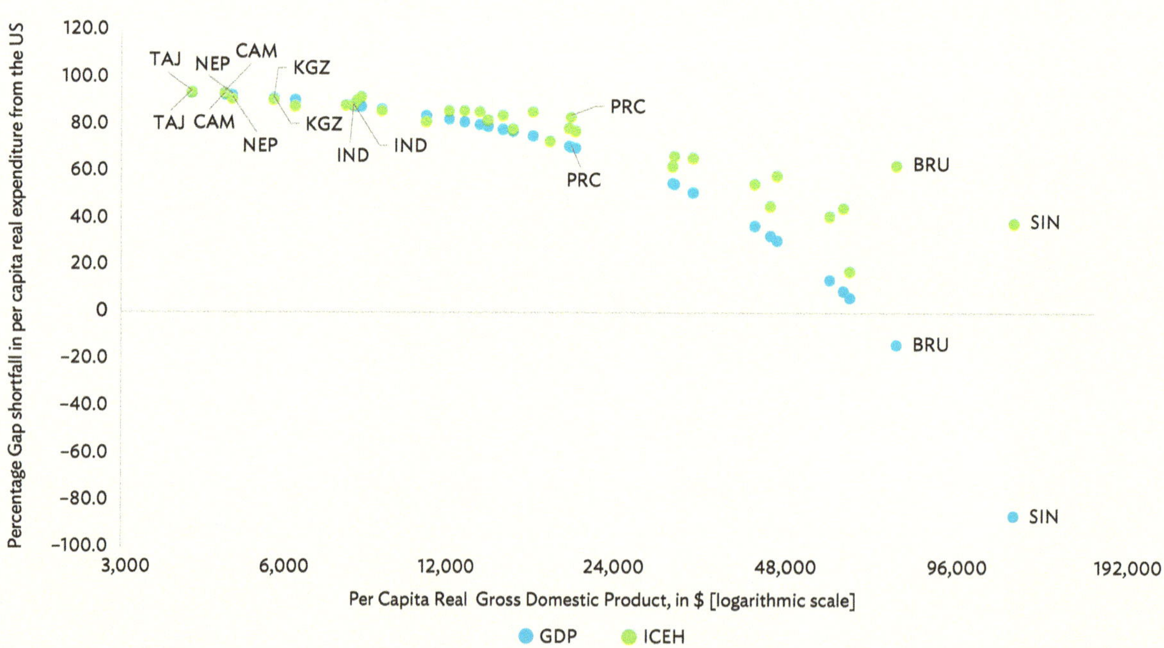

$ = United States dollars, ADB = Asian Development Bank, BRU = Brunei Darussalam, CAM = Cambodia, GDP = gross domestic product, ICEH = individual consumption expenditure by households, ICP = International Comparison Program, IND = India, KGZ = Kyrgyz Republic, NEP = Nepal, PRC = People's Republic of China, SIN = Singapore, TAJ = Tajikistan, US = United States.

Note: Data is for the 33 ADB regional member economies participating in 2021 ICP.

Source: ADB estimates based on data from World Bank. DataBank: ICP 2021. https://databank.worldbank.org/source/icp-2021# (accessed 4 June 2024).

- While the PRC and India have consistently exhibited high growth rates since 2000 and were the world's largest and third-largest economies, respectively, in real GDP terms in 2021, on a per capita basis they were still far from the US living standards. The gaps between per capita real GDP of the PRC and India with respect to the US were 71% and 89%, respectively, and the gaps with respect to per capita real ICEH were 84% and 89%, respectively, implying that the PRC and India would need many more years of sustained growth to reach the current per capita levels of the US.

Table A1.2 and Table A1.3 in Appendix 1 present full results on ICEH and AICH for the 33 economies of Asia and the Pacific that participated in the 2021 ICP cycle, including comparisons with other major regions of the world.

Measuring the Role of Government on Material Well-Being

The role of government in enhancing the material well-being of households can be assessed by each economy's ratio of ICEG to AICH. Figure 4.6 plots these ratios (shown on the vertical axis) for 173 economies of the world, including 33 economies of Asia and the Pacific for 2021, against per capita real GDP in natural logarithms (shown on the horizontal axis).

Note that the ICP uses the Gini-Éltető-Köves-Szulc (GEKS) method for the aggregation of basic heading level PPPs to derive higher-level aggregates of ICEH, ICEG, and AICH. PPP-based aggregates derived using the GEKS method for an individual economy are not additive, implying that ICEH and ICEG do not sum to AICH in real terms. In local currency

Figure 4.6: Ratio of Real Individual Consumption Expenditure by Government to Real Actual Individual Consumption by Households, 2021

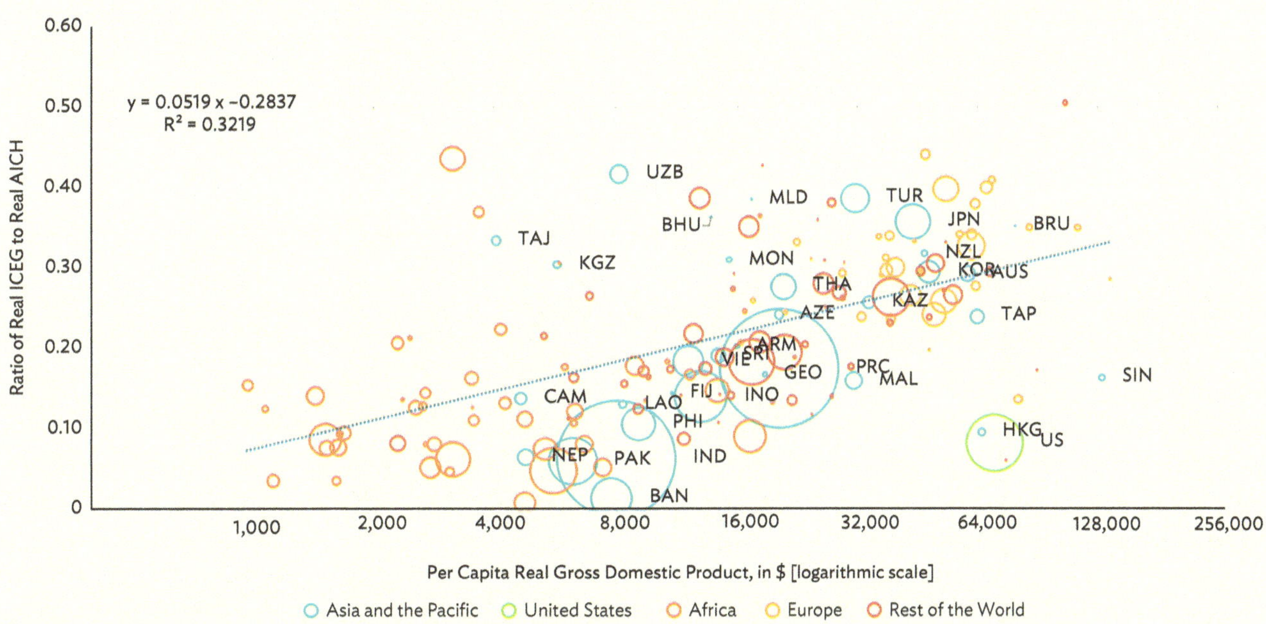

$ = United States dollars; AICH= actual individual consumption by households; ARM = Armenia; AUS =Australia; AZE = Azerbaijan; BAN = Bangladesh; BHU = Bhutan; BRU = Brunei Darussalam; CAM = Cambodia; FIJ = Fiji; GEKS = Gini-Éltető-Köves-Szulc; GEO = Georgia; HKG = Hong Kong, China; ICEG= individual consumption expenditure by government; ICEH = individual consumption expenditure by households; ICP = International Comparison Program; IND = India; INO =Indonesia; JPN = Japan; KAZ = Kazakstan; KGZ = Kyrgyz Republic; KOR = Republic of Korea; LAO = Lao People's Democratic Republic; MAL = Malaysia; MLD = Maldives; MON = Mongolia; NEP = Nepal; NZL = New Zealand; PAK = Pakistan; PPP = purchasing power parity; PHI = Philippines; PRC = People's Republic of China; SIN = Singapore; SRI = Sri Lanka; TAJ = Tajikistan; TAP = Taipei,China; THA = Thailand; TUR = Türkiye; US = United States; UZB = Uzbekistan; VIE = Viet Nam.

Notes: Bubble sizes reflect midyear population from ICP 2021 results. Due to the use of the GEKS aggregation method, PPP-based estimates of ICEH and ICEG are not additive: they do not sum to AICH in real terms. In local currency units, however, the components are additive. Therefore, the ICEG-AICH ratio on the y-axis should be interpreted with caution.

Source: Asian Development Bank estimates using World Bank data. DataBank: ICP 2021. https://databank.worldbank.org/source/icp-2021# (accessed 4 June 2024).

units, however, the components are additive. Therefore, the ratio of real ICEG to real AICH on the vertical axis should be interpreted with caution. Nonetheless, the use of real (PPP-adjusted) aggregates helps account for differences in relative price levels for each component, making it suitable for evaluating a government's role in household welfare.

Key Findings:

- There was a general upward trend between per capita real GDP and the government's contribution to material well-being in 2021, with some notable exceptions: the US had a low ratio of 0.08 despite its high income levels, while Singapore also registered a relatively low ratio of 0.16 despite being a high-income economy.

- Among lower- and upper-middle income economies of Asia and the Pacific, the real ICEG–AICH ratios fell below the fitted trend line. The ratios for India and the PRC were 0.06 and 0.18, respectively.

- Several middle-income economies exhibited notably higher ratios, e.g., the Kyrgyz Republic at 0.30, Mongolia at 0.31, Tajikistan at 0.33, and Uzbekistan at 0.42. Bhutan (0.36) and Maldives (0.39) also exhibited higher ratios among the economies of Asia and the Pacific. This suggests stronger government provisioning of goods and services for households, especially for education and health.

- Among high-income economies—including Australia (0.29), Brunei Darussalam (0.35), Japan (0.36), the Republic of Korea (0.30), and New Zealand (0.32)—government contributions to household consumption were relatively high.

Tables A1.4, A1.5, and A1.6 in Appendix 1 offer full results for ICEG, collective consumption expenditure by government, and general government final consumption expenditure, respectively. These tables cover the 33 economies of Asia and the Pacific that participated in the 2021 ICP cycle, including comparisons with other major regions of the world.

Disparities in Per Capita Real Incomes and Expenditures

Disparities in Per Capita Real Gross Domestic Product

Based on 2021 ICP results, economies of Asia and the Pacific vary widely with respect to per capita real income (GDP). The region has low-middle income economies such as Tajikistan ($4,053 per capita real income in 2021), Cambodia ($4,667), and Nepal ($4,813); upper-middle income economies such as the PRC ($20,407), Malaysia ($31,389), and Kazakhstan ($34,231); and high-income economies such as Hong Kong, China ($65,877); Brunei Darussalam ($80,203); Singapore ($131,864); and Taipei,China ($64,120). In fact, the region's richest economy, Singapore, has per capita real income nearly 33 times that of Tajikistan (the economy with the lowest per capita real income).

Figure 4.7 features a Lorenz curve that graphically represents the distribution of per capita real incomes (GDP) for 33 economies of Asia and the Pacific across three ICP cycles of 2011, 2017, and 2021. The figure measures the cumulative percentage of the population (shown on the horizontal axis) and the income shares of the corresponding population percentage (shown on the vertical axis) by arranging the economies from the lowest per capita income to the highest. The diagonal line represents the line of equal distribution, while the deviation of the Lorenz curve from the diagonal indicates the extent of inequality. The Gini coefficient of inequality is equal to twice the area that lies between the line of equality and the Lorenz curve and lies between 0 (absolute equality) to 1 (absolute inequality).

Figure 4.7: Lorenz Curves for Distribution of Per Capita Real Gross Domestic Product

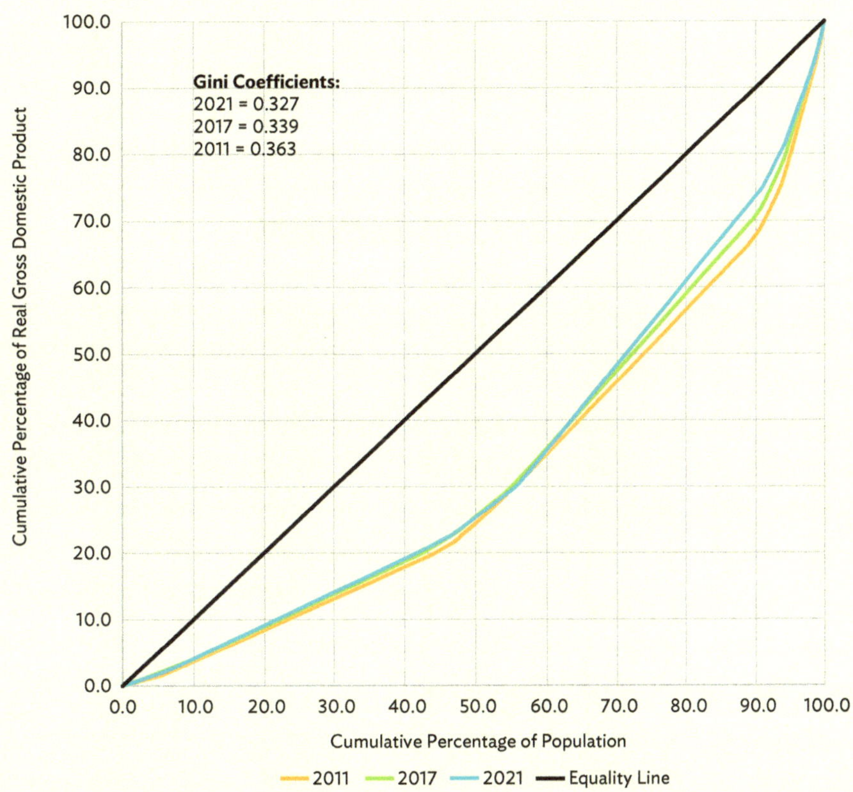

Notes: Gini coefficients are population-weighted and based on data for the 33 Asian Development Bank member economies that participated in the 2021 cycle of the International Comparison Program (ICP). For 2011 and 2017, data for economies that did not participate in the 2011 and 2017 ICP cycles are sourced from the estimates available in the World Bank's World Development Indicators.

Sources: For 2011, Asian Development Bank estimates using World Bank data. DataBank: ICP 2017. https://databank.worldbank.org/source/icp-2017 (accessed 4 June 2024). For 2017 and 2021, Asian Development Bank estimates using World Bank data. DataBank: ICP 2021. https://databank.worldbank.org/source/icp-2021# (accessed 4 June 2024). For economies not participating in 2011 and 2017 ICP cycles World Bank. World Development Indicators Database. https://databank.worldbank.org/source/world-development-indicators# (accessed 15 April 2025).

Key Findings:

- Inequality in per capita real incomes between economies of Asia and the Pacific has reduced over time. Beyond 60% of population, the Lorenz curve for 2021 lies above the curves for 2011 and 2017.
- The Gini measure of inequality reduced from 0.363 in 2011 to 0.339 in 2017 and 0.327 in 2021. This steady, albeit slow, improvement in the distribution of per capita real income is a sign of convergence of average incomes across the economies of the region over this 10-year period.
- However, the population-weighted Gini measure for the world was 0.461[2] for 2021, significantly higher than the 0.327 observed for Asia and the Pacific.

Disparities in Per Capita Consumption Measures Versus Per Capita Gross Domestic Product

As the Asia and Pacific region includes economies with high trade balances—namely, Brunei Darussalam; Singapore; and Taipei,China—it is quite likely that per capita real ICEH exhibits lower levels of inequality compared to per capita real income (GDP).

2 Gini coefficient is estimated using data from 176 economies participating in the 2021 ICP cycle.

In terms of per capita real ICEH, a measure of household material well-being, the region's leading economies in 2021 were Hong Kong, China ($39,345); Singapore ($29,336); and Australia ($28,023). The lowest per capita ICEH was recorded for Tajikistan at $2,575. The region's highest per capita real ICEH was 15.28 times the lowest, which is less than half the 33 times multiple for per capita real income.

Similarly, when considering per capita real AICH—the third measure of the well-being of households, which adds ICEG to ICEH—the region's three leading economies in 2021 were again Hong Kong, China ($44,577); Australia ($37,030); and Singapore ($35,066). Cambodia recorded the lowest per capita real AICH at $3,284 followed by Tajikistan at $3,421.

Figure 4.8 features a Lorenz curve that represents the expenditure distribution of the three key measures of material well-being: per capita real GDP, per capita real ICEH, and per capita real AICH. Each curve represents data for the 33 economies of Asia and the Pacific that participated in the 2021 ICP cycle.

Key Findings:

- Among the economies of Asia and the Pacific in 2021, intereconomy inequality as measured by the Gini coefficient was lowest for per capita real ICEH (0.231), i.e., the Lorenz curve for ICEH is closer to the equal distribution line than the curves for per capita real income (GDP), which had a Gini coefficient of 0.327, or per capita real AICH, whose Gini coefficient was 0.268.

Figure 4.8: Lorenz Curves for Distribution of Key Measures of Material Well-Being, 2021

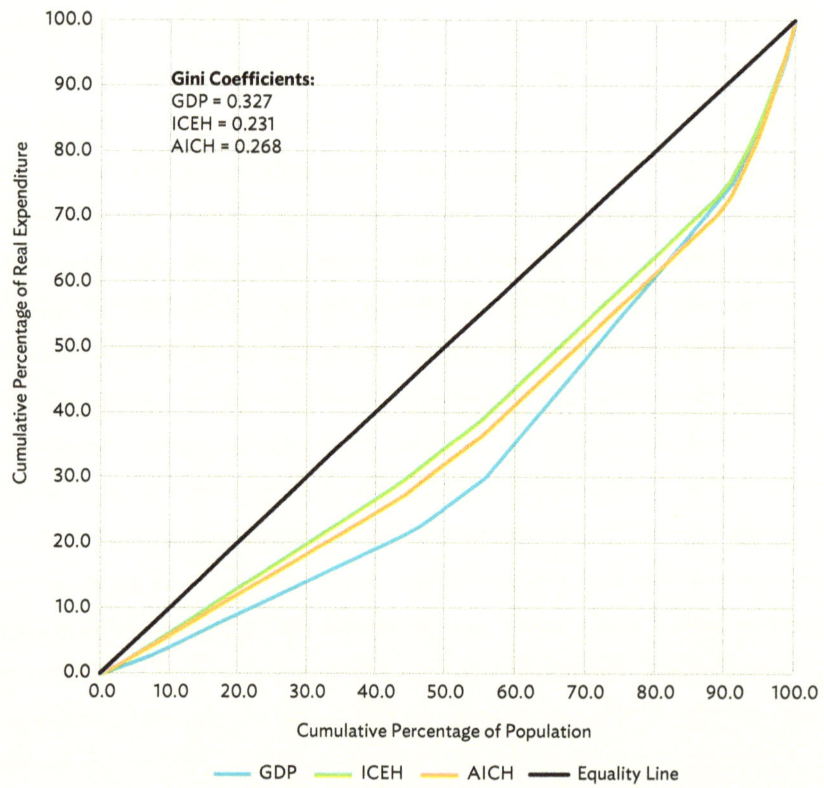

AICH= actual individual consumption by households, GDP = gross domestic product, ICEH= individual consumption expenditure by households, ICP = International Comparison Program.

Note: Gini coefficients are population-weighted and based on data for the 33 Asian Development Bank member economies that participated in the 2021 ICP cycle.

Source: Asian Development Bank estimates using World Bank data. DataBank: ICP 2021. https://databank.worldbank.org/source/icp-2021# (accessed 4 June 2024).

- Up to the 80th population percentile, the shares of AICH are higher than the corresponding income (GDP) shares, but lower than the shares for ICEH. This suggests that government expenditure on households in 2021 was relatively higher in economies with higher per capita incomes.

Labor Productivity and Per Capita Income

The relationship between labor productivity and per capita income (GDP) has important ramifications for an economy's general performance and living standards. As discussed, per capita real GDP shows the average income or output per person in the population and is often used as a general proxy for material well-being. Labor productivity, on the other hand, measures the output produced per worker and reflects the efficiency and technological level of an economy.

Figure 4.9 maps per capita real GDP against labor productivity for 160 economies that participated in the 2021 ICP cycle globally.

Figure 4.9 shows that labor productivity, measured as GDP per person employed, is a strong determinant of per capita income. However, observations for the economies are scattered around the fitted line and there are various factors that explain these deviations. For instance,

Figure 4.9: Per Capita Real Gross Domestic Product Versus Labor Productivity, 2021

($)

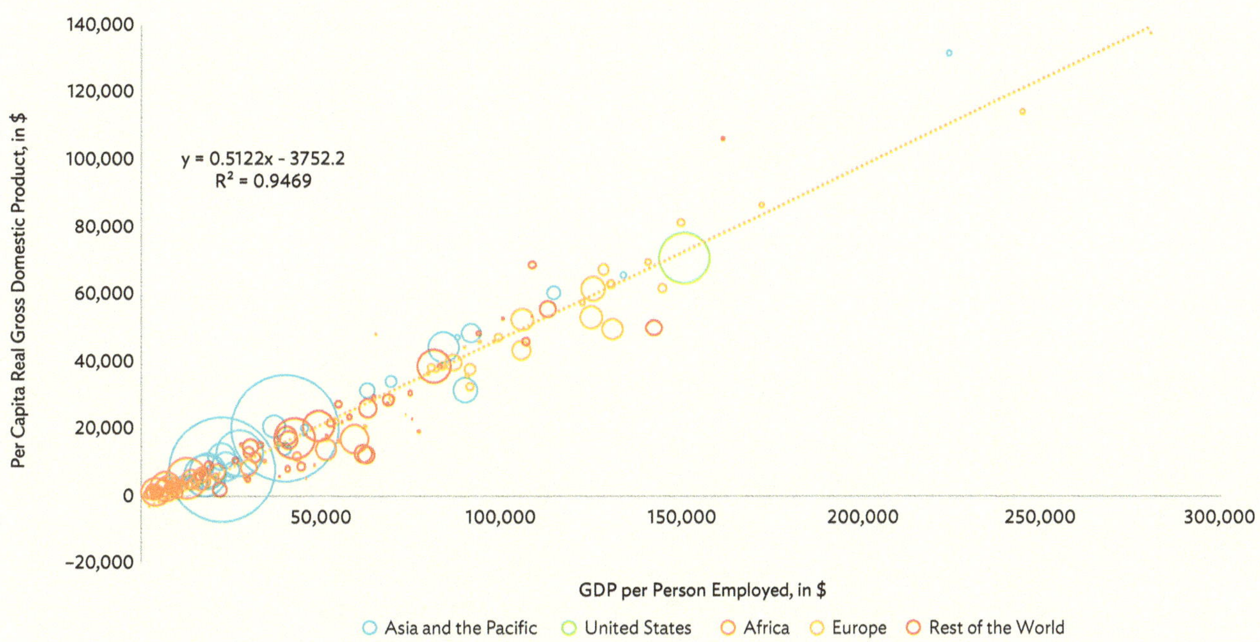

$ = United States dollars, GDP = gross domestic product, ICP = International Comparison Program, PPP = purchasing power parity.

Notes: Bubble sizes reflect midyear population from ICP 2021 results. Data presented are for 160 economies that participated in the 2021 ICP globally.

Sources: For Per Capita Real GDP, Asian Development Bank estimates using World Bank data. DataBank: ICP 2021. https://databank.worldbank.org/source/icp-2021# (accessed 4 June 2024); and for GDP per person employed, World Development Indicators Database. https://databank.worldbank.org/source/world-development-indicators (accessed 28 July 2025).

while higher labor productivity typically contributes to higher per capita income, the relationship is not one-to-one and depends on demographic and labor market conditions. A more precise decomposition of per capita real GDP is given by:

$$\frac{Y}{N} = \frac{Y}{L} \times \frac{L}{LF} \times \frac{LF}{WAP} \times \frac{WAP}{N}$$

where Y = total GDP; N = total population; *L* = number of persons employed; *LF* = labor force (employed plus unemployed seeking work); and *WAP* = working-age population (population aged 15–64 years).

Therefore, per capita income can be expressed using the following components:

Per capita GDP = labor productivity × (1 – unemployment rate) × labor force participation rate x working-age share of the population.

Key Findings:

- The decomposition highlights that raising per capita income requires not just improvements in productivity but also inclusive labor market participation, low unemployment, and a favorable age structure in the labor force.
- When components on the right-hand side of the equation (labor force participation, employment rate, and demographic structure) are relatively stable or slow to change, improvements in labor productivity become the primary engine of sustained growth in per capita income.
- Rapid aging of the population in many economies of Asia and the Pacific—and potentially fewer people in the workforce in the future—underscores the critical importance of investing in education, skills, technology, artificial intelligence, and innovation to boost productivity and, in turn, enhance living standards.

Better Health Outcomes and Life Expectancy

Life expectancy—the average number of years a newborn is expected to live—serves as a powerful indicator of a population's overall health and well-being. It reflects the cumulative impact of various factors, including income levels, education, lifestyle, environmental conditions, and access to health care. Comparing life expectancy across economies not only highlights health disparities but also reveals the broader social and economic determinants of health.

Per Capita Income and Life Expectancy

Based on results from the 2021 ICP cycle, Figure 4.10 presents the relationship between the natural logarithm of per capita real income (GDP) and life expectancy for the US and 170 other economies in different regions of the world.

Key Findings:

- There was a strong positive correlation between per capita real income and life expectancy across the world in 2021. On average, wealthier economies tended to have higher life expectancy, as demonstrated by a high coefficient of determination (R^2 = 0.7134).
- The results are more nuanced for some individual economies: many economies cluster around the expected trend line, but several others performed better or worse than predicted by their per capita income levels.
- Many African economies tended to fall below the trend line, indicating life expectancy outcomes lower than their per capita income would suggest.

Figure 4.10: Life Expectancy Versus Per Capita Real Gross Domestic Product, 2021

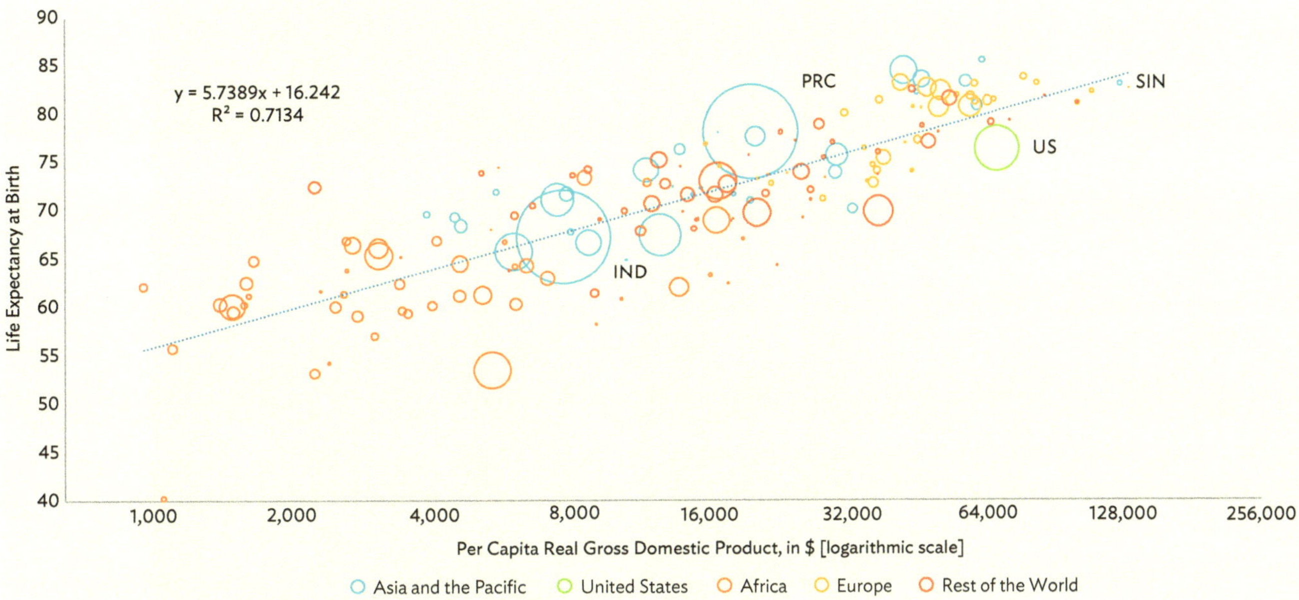

$ = United States dollars, ICP = International Comparison Program, IND = India, PPP= purchasing power parity, PRC = People's Republic of China, SIN = Singapore, US = United States.

Note: Bubble size reflects population size in 2021 for 171 economies that participated in the 2021 ICP cycle.

Sources: For per capita real gross domestic product, World Bank. DataBank: ICP 2021. https://databank.worldbank.org/source/icp-2021# (accessed 4 June 2024). For life expectancy, World Bank. World Development Indicators Database, https://databank.worldbank.org/source/world-development-indicators# (accessed 18 July 2025). For Taipei,China, data for life expectancy and population, Asian Development Bank. Key Indicators Database. https://kidb.adb.org/ (accessed 15 May 2025).

- Most economies of Asia and the Pacific, including the PRC, lie above the trend line, signaling better-than-expected health outcomes in relation to per capita income. India, meanwhile, aligns closely with expectations for its per capita income.

- Strikingly, the US recorded life expectancy noticeably lower than what might be anticipated for its per capita income level.

Asia and the Pacific is Powering Global Growth

The Asia and Pacific region has consistently been recognized as a primary engine of global economic growth. Home to several of the world's most dynamic and rapidly expanding economies—such as the PRC, India, Indonesia, and Viet Nam—the region has made substantial contributions to the expansion of global GDP. These assessments are grounded in the national accounts data of world economies published in the International Monetary Fund's World Economic Outlook and the World Bank's World Development Indicators.

Complementing these sources, the results from various ICP cycles offer a robust set of data for evaluating the contribution of Asia and the Pacific to global growth. Drawing on extensive price and expenditure data, ICP results across multiple cycles enable the estimation of global GDP in PPP terms. When combined with an analytical framework developed by Balk, Rambaldi, and Rao (2022), it becomes possible not only to assess the size of the global economy at different points in time but also to decompose changes in global GDP—expressed in US dollars—into components attributable to real growth and price-related effects as well as by geographic regions and individual economies.

Growth Trends in the Global Economy

A recent study by Hajargasht, Rambaldi, and Rao (2025) utilizes data from the University of Queensland International Comparison Database (UQICD) Version 3.0[3] to examine global economic trends over a 49-year period from 1970 to 2019. The analysis reveals that global GDP, measured in PPP terms and current prices, rose from $3.428 trillion in 1970 to $125.929 trillion in 2019—an approximate 37-fold increase in the size of the world economy. The decomposition of this growth indicates that about 50% of the overall change can be attributed to real economic expansion across economies. Furthermore, the research disaggregates this growth contribution by economy, identifying the major contributors as the PRC (25.36%), the US (18.51%), India (8.37%), Japan (3.9%), and Germany (2.62%).

The expansion of the ICP to encompass most of the world allows analysts to assess regional contributions to global growth between ICP cycles.

Table 4.3 illustrates the components of growth and price effects that underpinned changes in the size of both the global economy and the Asia and Pacific region from 2011 to 2021, based on results from the ICP. For the purposes of this analysis, "the world" is represented by 169 economies covering 95% (7.55 billion people) of the global population (7.94 billion people) in 2021. With a focus on Asia and the Pacific vis-à-vis the rest of the world, the table presents specific results for these two groupings.

Key Findings:

The size of the world economy increased from $93.215 trillion in 2011 in current prices (prices and PPPs in 2011) to $152.359 trillion in 2021 current prices (prices and PPPs in 2021). This represents a 63% increase over the decade. Employing the decomposition methodology developed by Balk, Rambaldi, and Rao (2022), this change can be broken down into three components:

(i) actual growth between 2011 and 2021 in economic activity in constant price terms,
(ii) inflation between 2011 and 2021 within economies as measured by the changes in the GDP deflator, and
(iii) changes in PPPs between 2011 and 2021 used to convert national GDP into comparable units.

Table 4.3: Real Growth and Price Effects in Asia and the Pacific and Globally, Between 2011 and 2021

Economy Groups	Real GDP at Current Prices, in billion $		Growth in Global and Regional Real GDP in current prices from 2011 to 2021	Growth Component of Change in GDP	Domestic Inflation Effect 2021/2011	PPP Change Effect 2011/2021	Combined Price Effect 2021/2011
	2011	2021					
(1)	(2)	(3)	(4) = (3)/(2)	(5)	(6)	(7)	(8) = (6)*(7)
ADB Regional Members	37,225	68,203	1.832	1.620	1.343	0.844	1.134
Rest of the World	55,991	84,156	1.503	1.197	1.422	0.884	1.257
World	**93,215**	**152,359**	**1.634**	**1.361**	**1.388**	**0.867**	**1.203**

$ = United States dollars, ADB = Asian Development Bank, GDP = gross domestic product, ICP = International Comparison Program, PPP = purchasing power parity.

Note: The table uses ADB estimates based on available data for 169 economies (comprising approximately 95% of the world's population in 2021) that participated in the 2021 ICP cycle and for which GDP, PPPs, and National Accounts Deflators were available for both 2011 and 2021.

Sources: World Bank. World Development Indicators Database, https://databank.worldbank.org/source/world-development-indicators# (accessed 15 April 2025). For Taipei,China, data for GDP and PPP in 2021, World Bank. DataBank: ICP 2021. https://databank.worldbank.org/source/icp-2021# (accessed 4 June 2024). For Taipei,China, data for GDP and PPP in 2011, World Bank. DataBank: ICP 2017. https://databank.worldbank.org/source/icp-2017 (accessed 4 June 2024). For Taipei,China, data for GDP deflator, Directorate General of Budget, Accounting and Statistics (DGBAS). Statistics from DGBAS: Statistical Tables.

3 Rao, D.S. Prasada, A.N. Rambaldi, G. Hajargasht, D. Chotikapanich, and W.E. Griffiths. 2022. University of Queensland International Comparisons Database: UQICD V3.0. https://uqicd.economics.uq.edu.au (accessed on 20 May 2025).

The first component captures actual growth of output, while the latter two reflect shifts in relative price structures across economies and together can be interpreted as the price effect between 2011 and 2021.

Decomposing the 2011–2021 change of 63.4% in real GDP (in current PPP terms) of the world into the actual growth component and the combined price effect of the two price components, the main contribution is attributed to 36.1% actual growth in economies of the world (equivalent to the growth in constant price terms in local currency units). The effect of domestic prices and PPP movements between 2011 and 2021 for the world represented a 20.3% increase in real GDP growth.

Global growth is the result of growth in the Asia and Pacific region and in the rest of the world in constant prices between 2011 and 2021. From 2011 to 2021, real GDP (in current PPP terms) in Asia and the Pacific increased by 83.2%, largely driven by a 62.0% growth in output, 34.3% domestic inflation, and a downward effect on real GDP due to changes in PPPs in 2011 and 2021. By contrast, real GDP (in current PPP terms) in the rest of the world increased by 50.3% over the same period, with 19.7% accounted for by the growth component for economies in this grouping.

Attributing Growth to Individual Economies and Groups of Economies

The analytical framework developed by Balk, Rambaldi, and Rao (2022) not only enables detailed decomposition of global economic growth by separating its core components but also by attributing contributions to individual economies and economy groupings. This offers a clearer picture of the principal drivers of global expansion and the shifting dynamics of economic growth across the world.

Figure 4.11 offers an insightful visual interpretation of the contributions of select economies and groups of economies to global growth from 2011 to 2021.

Figure 4.11: Contribution to Global Growth by Region and Select Economies, 2011–2021

(%)

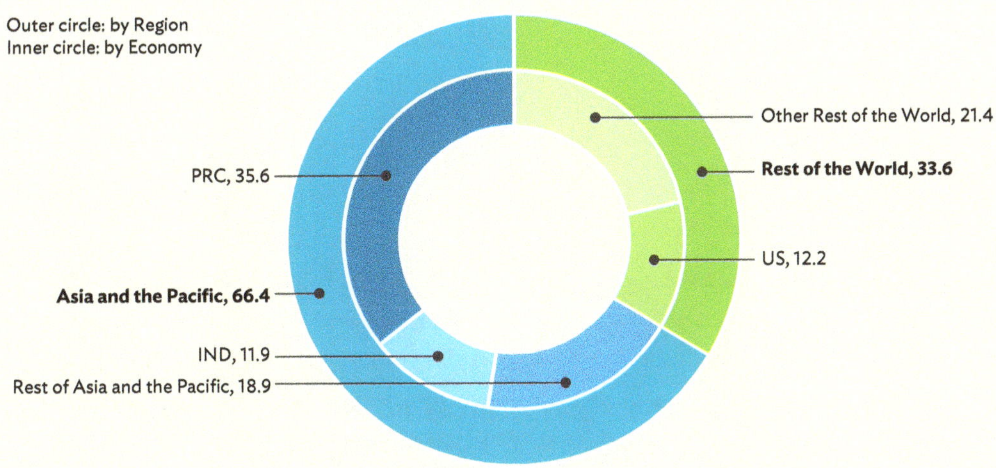

ICP = International Comparison Program, IND = India, PRC = People's Republic of China, US = United States.

Note: The table uses Asian Development Bank estimates based on available data for 169 economies (comprising approximately 95% of the world's population in 2021) that participated in the 2021 International Comparison Program cycle and for which gross domestic product, purchasing power parities, and National Accounts Deflators were available in both 2011 and 2021. It uses the methodology in: B. M. Balk, A. N. Rambaldi, and D. S. P. Rao. 2022. Macro- Economic Measures For A Globalized World: Global Growth And Inflation. *Macroeconomic Dynamics*. Cambridge University Press. 26 (2). pp. 314–360.

Data Sources: World Bank. World Development Indicators Database, https://databank.worldbank.org/source/world-development-indicators# (accessed 18 July 2025). For Taipei,China, data for gross domestic product and purchasing power parity in 2021, World Bank. DataBank: ICP 2021. https://databank.worldbank.org/source/icp-2021# (accessed 4 June 2024). For Taipei,China, data for gross domestic product and purchasing power parity in 2011, World Bank. DataBank: ICP 2017. https://databank.worldbank.org/source/icp-2017 (accessed 4 June 2024). For Taipei,China, data for gross domestic product deflator, Directorate General of Budget, Accounting and Statistics (DGBAS). Statistics from DGBAS: Statistical Tables.

Key Findings:

- Of all global growth in GDP for 2011–2021, 66.4% or two-thirds of expansion was contributed by just 33 economies in the Asia and Pacific region.
- The remaining 136 economies—encompassing much of Europe, Africa, and the Americas—collectively accounted for just only one-third or 33.6% of global growth over the period.
- The PRC alone contributed 35.6% of global growth for 2011–2021, underscoring its status as the world's largest economy (in PPP terms) since 2017.
- India's contribution of 11.9% is particularly striking, given its relatively smaller economic size in relation to the PRC and the US (essentially matching the 12.2% contribution from the US, the world's second-largest economy).

These findings provide empirical evidence on the growing importance of the Asia and Pacific region and its contribution to global growth.

Comparing Growth and Inflation by Geographic Region

Table 4.4 shows the growth performance of the major geographic groupings. Columns (2) and (3) of the table present estimates of GDP in PPPs for 2011 and 2021, respectively, expressed in current international dollars using 2011 and 2021 price levels. The observed change in GDP in PPPs is decomposed into two components: the growth component, which captures the actual expansion in economic activity in constant prices (Columns 6 and 7); and the combined price effect, reflecting the effects of domestic inflation and changes in PPPs over time (Columns 8 and 9).

Figure 4.12, meanwhile, differentiates the annualized global and regional growth and price effects over the 10-year period from 2011 to 2021.

Key Findings:

- Asia and the Pacific was the fastest-growing region of the world for 2011–2021, recording a remarkable 62.0% growth in comparison to the world average of 36.1%.
- Africa was the second-fastest-growing region, with its growth matching the global average of 36.1% over the period.
- Annualized growth in GDP (local currency units at constant 2011 prices) for 2011–2021 was highest for Asia and the Pacific at 4.95%, with the world average at 3.13%.
- In driving the growth of GDP in PPP terms at current prices from 2011 to 2021, the actual growth component was higher than the price effect for Asia and the Pacific, the US, and Africa region, and for the world as a whole. Due to its very high growth, Asia and the Pacific drove the overall global expansion during this period. For Europe and economies in "the rest of the world", the price effect played a greater role than the growth component in driving the expansion of GDP in PPP terms between 2011 and 2021.

This analysis reaffirms the position of Asia and the Pacific as the engine of global growth. The region's dynamic economic expansion not only contributed most to the increase in global output for 2011–2021, this expansion has also had far-reaching social implications globally. Most important among these was the substantial reduction in extreme poverty that enabled the global community to halve the proportion of people living in absolute poverty by 2015 (section on Asia and the Pacific's role in Fighting Global Poverty offers more on this). In this and other ways, the economic momentum within the Asia and Pacific region has been both transformative and inclusive, shaping the trajectory of global development.

Table 4.4: Real Growth and Price Effects in Different Regions and Globally, 2011 and 2021

Economy Groups	Real GDP at Current Prices, in billion $		Growth in Global and Regional Real GDP at Current Prices		Growth in Global and Regional GDP at Constant 2011 Prices		Global and Regional Price Effect 2021/2011	
	2011	2021	2021/2011	Annualized (%)	2021/2011	Annualized (%)	2021/2011	Annualized (%)
(1)	(2)	(3)	(4)	(5)	(6)	(7)	(8)	(9)
Asia and the Pacific	37,225	68,203	1.832	6.24	1.620	4.95	1.134	1.26
United States	15,600	23,681	1.518	4.26	1.261	2.34	1.204	1.88
Africa	4,272	7,248	1.696	5.43	1.361	3.13	1.256	2.31
Europe	18,646	28,128	1.509	4.20	1.141	1.33	1.322	2.83
Rest of the World	17,472	25,098	1.436	3.69	1.161	1.50	1.238	2.15
World	**93,215**	**152,359**	**1.634**	**5.04**	**1.361**	**3.13**	**1.203**	**1.87**

$ = United States dollars, GDP = gross domestic product, ICP = International Comparison Program.

Note: The table uses Asian Development Bank estimates based on available data for 169 economies (comprising approximately 95% of the world's population in 2021) that participated in the 2021 International Comparison Program cycle and for which GDP, purchasing power parities, and National Accounts Deflators were available for both 2011 and 2021.

Source: World Bank. World Development Indicators Database. https://databank.worldbank.org/source/world-development-indicators# (accessed 18 July 2025). For Taipei,China, data for GDP and purchasing power parity in 2021, World Bank. DataBank: ICP 2021. https://databank.worldbank.org/source/icp-2021# (accessed 4 June 2024). For Taipei,China, data for GDP and purchasing power parity in 2011, World Bank. DataBank: ICP 2017. https://databank.worldbank.org/source/icp-2017 (accessed 4 June 2024). For Taipei,China, data for GDP deflator, Directorate General of Budget, Accounting and Statistics (DGBAS). Statistics from DGBAS: Statistical Tables.

Figure 4.12: Annualized Growth and Price Effects in Different Regions and Globally, 2011–2021

(%)

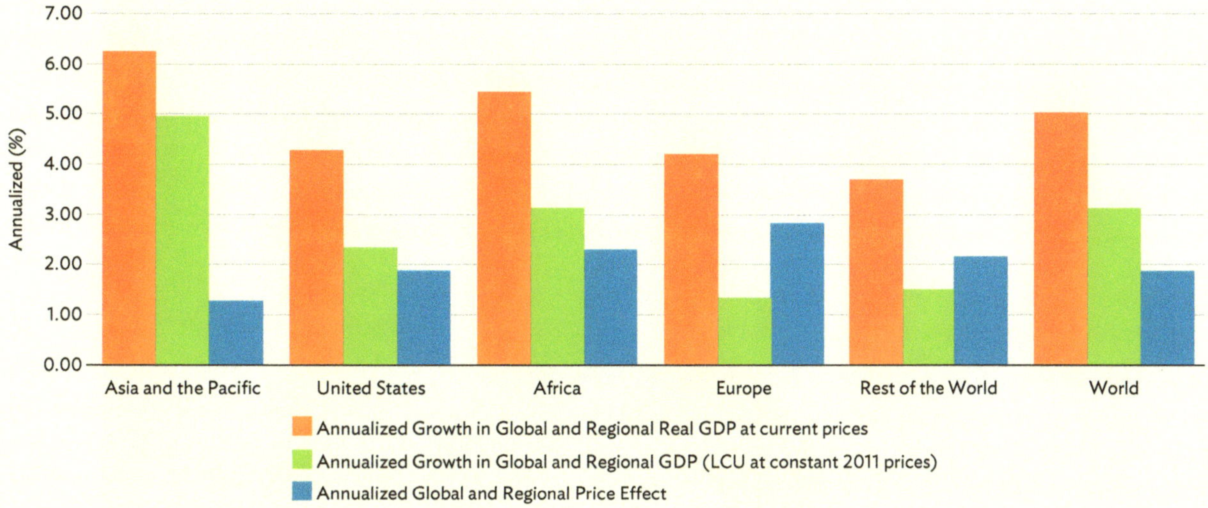

GDP = gross domestic product, LCU = local currency unit.

Note: The figure uses Asian Development Bank estimates based on available data for 169 economies (comprising approximately 95% of the world's population in 2021) that participated in the 2021 International Comparison Program cycle and for which GDP, purchasing power parities, and National Accounts Deflators were available in both 2011 and 2021.

Source: World Bank. World Development Indicators Database. https://databank.worldbank.org/source/world-development-indicators# (accessed 18 July 2025). For Taipei,China, data for GDP and purchasing power parity in 2021, World Bank. DataBank: ICP 2021. https://databank.worldbank.org/source/icp-2021# (accessed 4 June 2024). For Taipei,China, data for GDP and purchasing power parity in 2011, World Bank. DataBank: ICP 2017. https://databank.worldbank.org/source/icp-2017 (accessed 4 June 2024). For Taipei,China, data for GDP deflator, Directorate General of Budget, Accounting and Statistics (DGBAS). Statistics from DGBAS: Statistical Tables.

Asia and the Pacific Dominates Global Investments

Gross capital formation plays a vital role in economic growth and development as it reflects an economy's level of investment in productive assets. High values of gross capital formation indicate that an economy is expanding its productive capacity, leading to higher levels of output and employment and higher standards of living over time. Investment is a key driver of long-term growth, particularly in developing economies where investment in physical and human capital is essential for structural transformation and poverty reduction.

Under the System of National Accounts, gross capital formation includes the total value of gross fixed capital formation (GFCF), changes in inventories, and acquisitions less disposals of valuables. GFCF is the biggest component of gross capital formation. It includes construction of residential and nonresidential buildings, construction of civil engineering works such as roads, and purchases of machinery and equipment and other products during an accounting period.

Figure 4.13 outlines shares of global GFCF in 2021 for key regions and economies. The outer circle shows nominal (exchange-rate-adjusted) GFCF shares while the inner circle shows real (PPP-based) shares.

Key Findings:

- In 2021, the global value of GFCF in real terms was $37.962 trillion, of which $20.608 trillion or 54.3% was from economies of the Asia and Pacific region. The region also accounted for 49.1% of nominal GFCF.
- The US contributed 13.2% of GFCF in real terms and Africa just 2.9%, with the remaining 29.6% coming from economies in Europe and the rest of the world.
- Five of the world's top 10 economies with respect to the size of real GFCF in 2021 are in the Asia and Pacific region: the PRC, with $11.381 trillion, ranked first globally; followed by India (third), Japan (fourth), Indonesia (sixth), and the Republic of Korea (ninth). Among individual economies, the US had the second-highest value of real GFCF in 2021.

Figure 4.13: Share of Global Real and Nominal Gross Fixed Capital Formation, 2021

(%)

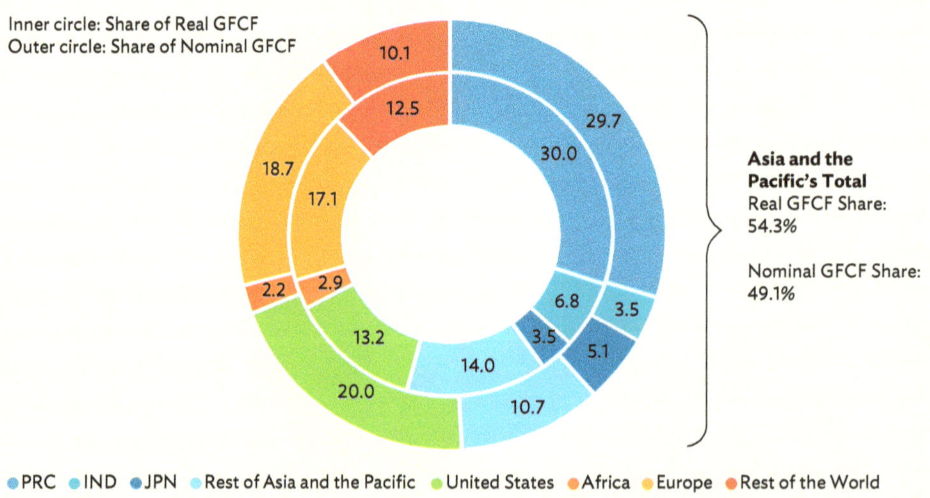

GFCF = gross fixed capital formation, ICP = International Comparison Program, IND = India, JPN = Japan, PRC = People's Republic of China.

Note: The outer circle refers to nominal GFCF while the inner circle shows real GFCF shares.

Source: Asian Development Bank estimates using World Bank data. DataBank: ICP 2021. https://databank.worldbank.org/source/icp-2021# (accessed 4 June 2024).

Since the turn of the millennium, Asia and the Pacific has emerged as a major destination for global investments, driven by its sustained economic growth, expanding consumer markets, and deepening integration into global value chains. With robust infrastructure development, favorable demographic trends, and ongoing policy reforms, the region continues to position itself as an investment destination amid an increasingly uncertain global economic environment.

Table A1.7 in Appendix 1 offers full results for GFCF for the 33 economies of Asia and the Pacific that participated in the 2021 ICP cycle, including comparisons with other major regions of the world.

Intereconomy Income Inequality

Measuring global inequality is fundamental to understanding disparities in income, consumption, and living standards, both across and within economies. It offers a quantitative basis for evaluating the inclusiveness of economic growth and for determining whether the benefits derived from globalization, technological progress, and broader development initiatives are equitably distributed.

Reliable inequality indicators are indispensable in identifying the extent and underlying causes of economic divergence across economies of the world. These indicators drive international policy development and coordination and they inform targeted policies around social protection schemes, tax reform programs, and international aid distribution strategies. In addition, the continuous monitoring of global inequality is crucial for assessing progress toward international development targets, most notably the Sustainable Development Goals, with particular emphasis on Sustainable Development Goal 10 to "reduce inequality within and among countries."

The analysis in this section specifically examines inequality between economies. This intereconomy inequality is assessed using the population-weighted Gini measure. It may be noted that the results from ICP are available at the national level only and not provide any insights on inequalities within economies.

In a hypothetically equal society, the poorest 10% of the population would receive 10% of an economy's total income, the poorest 50% would receive 50% of income, and so forth. The Gini coefficient summarizes how income is distributed across the population, reflecting cumulative shares of both population and income. It takes into account the relative population sizes of economies, thereby providing a more accurate representation of inequality in per capita incomes across economies.

Table 4.5 features estimates of the Gini measure of intereconomy income inequality for per capita real (PPP-adjusted) GDP in 2011, 2017, and 2021, covering various geographic subsets. Figure 4.14 presents a visual interpretation of these data, establishing the influence on intereconomy inequality of Asia and the Pacific and its major economies such as the PRC and India.

Key Findings:

- Global and regional inequality trends: The Gini measures show a consistent decline in income inequality over time for both the world (all economies) and the Asia and Pacific region.

- Regional versus global disparities: Inequality in Asia and the Pacific was significantly lower than global levels across 2011, 2017, and 2021.

- Global inequality excluding the PRC and India: For 2011 onwards, excluding the PRC and India from the analysis resulted in consistently higher and rising global inequality. This reflects the rapid, sustained, and inclusive economic growth of these two Asian powerhouses.

Table 4.5: Gini Measure of Income Inequality Between Economy Groupings

	Gini Coeffcients		
Economy Groups	2011	2017	2021
All economies	0.4859	0.4681	0.4610
All economies excluding the People's Republic of China and India	0.4935	0.4970	0.5017
All economies excluding Asia and the Pacific	0.4788	0.5009	0.5096
Asia and the Pacific	0.3635	0.3393	0.3273
Asia and the Pacific excluding the People's Republic of China and India	0.4807	0.4425	0.4302

$ = United States dollars, ICP = International Comparison Program.

Note: The term "All economies" pertains to the 176 economies that participated in the 2021 ICP cycle. The term Asia and the Pacific relates to the 33 Asian Development Bank members that participated in the 2021 ICP cycle. Data for the 2021 ICP participating economies that did not participate in previous ICP cycles were sourced from the estimates available in the World Development Indicators.

Source: For 2021 and 2017, Asian Development Bank estimates using World Bank data. DataBank: ICP 2021. https://databank.worldbank.org/source/icp-2021# (accessed 4 June 2024). For 2011, DataBank: ICP 2017. https://databank.worldbank.org/source/icp-2017 (accessed 4 June 2024). For economies not participating in 2011 and 2017 ICP cycles, World Bank. World Development Indicators Database, https://databank.worldbank.org/source/world-development-indicators# (accessed 15 April 2025).

Figure 4.14: Trends in Inequality Between Economy Groupings

ICP = International Comparison Program, IND = India, PRC = People's Republic of China.

Note: The term "All economies" pertains to the 176 economies that participated in the 2021 ICP cycle. The term Asia and the Pacific relates to the 33 Asian Development Bank members that participated in the 2021 ICP cycle. Data for the 2021 ICP participating economies that did not participate in previous ICP cycles were sourced from the estimates available in the World Development Indicators.

Source: For 2021 and 2017, Asian Development Bank estimates using World Bank data. DataBank: ICP 2021. https://databank.worldbank.org/source/icp-2021# (accessed 4 June 2024). For 2011, DataBank: ICP 2017. https://databank.worldbank.org/source/icp-2017 (accessed 4 June 2024). For economies not participating in 2011 and 2017 ICP cycles, World Bank. World Development Indicators Database, https://databank.worldbank.org/source/world-development-indicators# (accessed 15 April 2025).

- Global inequality excluding economies of Asia and the Pacific: Higher levels of global inequality are observed for 2017 and 2021 when all economies of Asia and the Pacific are excluded from the analysis, indicating the region's substantial role in reducing poverty and other inequities over time.

- Regional inequality: The Gini measure for Asia and the Pacific in 2021 was 0.3273, almost 29% lower than the global figure, suggesting relatively equitable income distribution within the region.

- Significance of the PRC and India in the region: Without the PRC and India, regional inequality in 2021 would have been 31% higher, highlighting the importance of these economies in the context of results for Asia and the Pacific.

Taken together, these findings highlight the significant contribution of the Asia and Pacific region—and particularly its two largest economies, the PRC and India—in enhancing global economic well-being. By moderating intereconomy disparities and improving the distribution of income across populations, the region and its economies have helped reduce global inequality. As economic well-being depends jointly on the size of economies, per capita income levels, and the degree of inequality, the strong and inclusive growth trajectory of Asia and the Pacific plays an increasingly important role in driving the convergence of incomes across economies and shaping a more equitable world.

The Role of Asia and the Pacific in Fighting Global Poverty

The PPPs for individual consumption expenditure by households produced as part of the ICP are critical inputs in the estimation and periodic updating of the international poverty line. By providing PPPs that are used to convert household expenditures into a common currency, which is also adjusted for differences in price levels across economies, it has been possible to consistently and accurately track the fight against regional and global poverty.

In 2000, the United Nations member states proclaimed eight Millennium Development Goals (MDGs), with the first goal to halve global poverty, i.e., people living on less than $1.25 per day, by 2015 (MDG 1). The measurement of poverty using a common yardstick at the national, regional, and global levels was at the center of MDG 1. The $1.25 extreme poverty line was based on the PPPs from the 2005 ICP cycle. The World Bank played a major role in the calibration of an international poverty line and in providing regular estimates of the incidence of absolute poverty in different regions and globally. These estimates became vital to monitoring global progress on MDG 1 over time.

MDG 1, which had a timeline from 1990 to 2015, was achieved at the global level ahead of schedule. This marked a significant milestone in international development. It reflected the combined effects of economic growth, improved access to education and health services, and targeted poverty reduction strategies in many low-income and middle-income economies. Nonetheless, progress was uneven across regions, with some parts of the world experiencing slower improvements and continued vulnerability, highlighting the need for sustained efforts beyond 2015.

Figure 4.15 presents trends in absolute poverty in terms of the proportion of the population living below the current extreme poverty line of $3.00 per day (2021 PPP). The figure's estimates for $3.00 per day poverty since 1990 are based on the PPPs for individual consumption expenditure from the 2021 ICP cycle. Table 4.6, meanwhile, provides insights on the number of people in each region who were living below the current poverty line.

Figure 4.15: Proportion of Population Living Below the $3.00 per Day Poverty Line
(%)

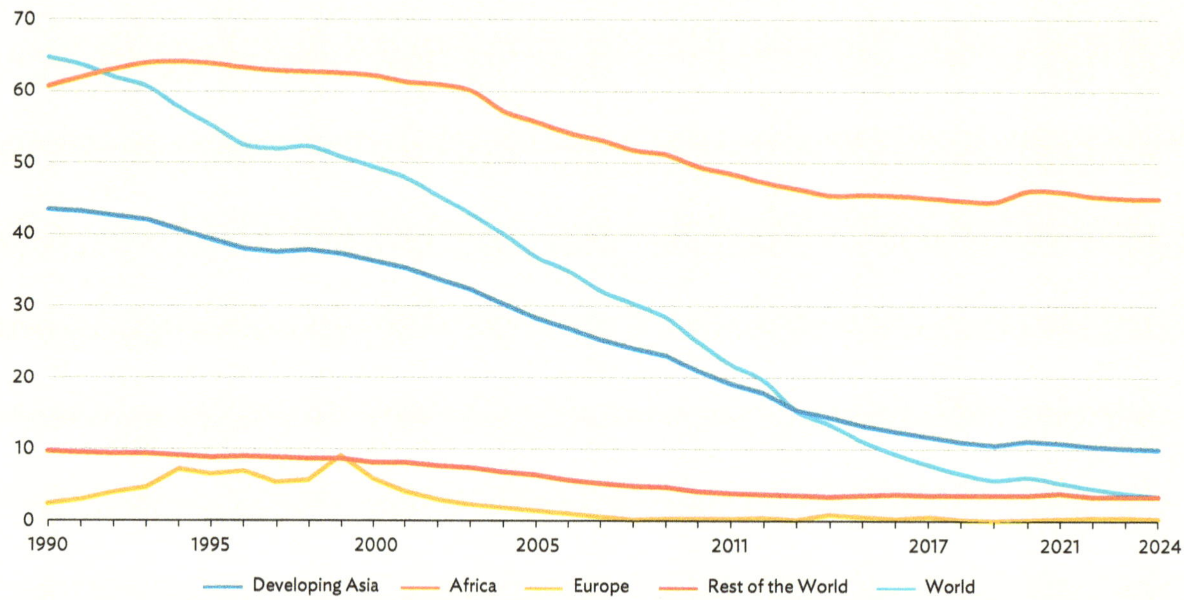

$ = United States dollars.

Note: Data refer to $3.00 a day poverty line at 2021 purchasing power parity terms. "Developing Asia" is composed of 37 Asian Development Bank developing member economies with available data: Armenia, Azerbaijan, Bangladesh, Bhutan, the People's Republic of China, Fiji, Georgia, India, Indonesia, Kazakhstan, Kiribati, the Kyrgyz Republic, the Lao People's Democratic Republic, Malaysia, Maldives, the Marshall Islands, the Federated States of Micronesia, Mongolia, Myanmar, Nauru, Nepal, Pakistan, Papua New Guinea, the Philippines, Samoa, Solomon Islands, Sri Lanka, Tajikistan, Thailand, Timor-Leste, Tonga, Türkiye, Turkmenistan, Tuvalu, Uzbekistan, Vanuatu, and Viet Nam.

Source: Asian Development Bank estimates using data from World Bank. Poverty and Inequality Platform. https://pip.worldbank.org (accessed 10 June 2025).

Table 4.6: Number of Population Living Below the $3.00 per Day Poverty Line (million)

Year	Population Living Below $3.00 per Day Poverty Line				
	Developing Asia	Africa	Europe	Rest of the World	World
1990	1,828.97	317.25	8.77	156.73	2,311.72
1995	1,695.01	381.69	22.79	154.94	2,254.44
2000	1,637.42	424.42	20.51	151.87	2,234.22
2005	1,301.40	435.18	5.22	127.46	1,869.26
2011	825.96	446.53	1.26	82.82	1,356.58
2017	318.44	488.97	2.18	83.05	892.64
2021	225.77	552.80	1.26	88.91	868.74
2024	150.36	582.71	1.53	82.14	816.74

$ = United States dollars.

Note: "Developing Asia" is composed of 37 Asian Development Bank developing member economies with available data: Armenia, Azerbaijan, Bangladesh, Bhutan, the People's Republic of China, Fiji, Georgia, India, Indonesia, Kazakhstan, Kiribati, the Kyrgyz Republic, the Lao People's Democratic Republic, Malaysia, Maldives, the Marshall Islands, the Federated States of Micronesia, Mongolia, Myanmar, Nauru, Nepal, Pakistan, Papua New Guinea, the Philippines, Samoa, Solomon Islands, Sri Lanka, Tajikistan, Thailand, Timor-Leste, Tonga, Türkiye, Turkmenistan, Tuvalu, Uzbekistan, Vanuatu, and Viet Nam.

Source: Asian Development Bank estimates using data from World Bank. Poverty and Inequality Platform. https://pip.worldbank.org (accessed 10 June 2025).

Key Findings:

- From Figure 4.15, it can be seen that the Asia and Pacific region and Africa both recorded similarly high poverty incidences, i.e., more than 60%, in 1990. However, their trajectories diverged markedly thereafter. By 2024, absolute poverty in Asia and the Pacific had plummeted to just 3.6%—an extraordinary achievement. Conversely, Africa continued to experience persistently high poverty incidences above 45% through to 2024.

- Populous economies of Asia and the Pacific—such as Bangladesh, the PRC, India, Indonesia, and Pakistan—contributed significantly to the reduction in the region's numbers for absolute poverty.

- As of 2024, Asia and the Pacific had an estimated 150 million people living below the international extreme poverty line of $3.00 per day (down from nearly 1,829 million in 1990). By contrast, Africa had almost 583 million living in absolute poverty in 2024 (up from 317 million in 1990) and the region is now home to the largest number of the world's poor.

These findings highlight the pivotal role of sustained economic growth in lifting large segments of the population out of poverty. Although the Asia and Pacific region has made substantial progress in reducing poverty, interpreting trends solely in terms of incidence can be misleading given the size of the region's population and economies. While the gains reflect major advances, the persistence of large absolute numbers highlights the continuing challenge. Eradicating poverty in its entirety will require sustained economic momentum and targeted social and policy initiatives across the region.

Asia and the Pacific is Driving Down Consumer Prices in Advanced Economies

The price level index (PLI) is a measure of relative price levels between economies and is obtained by dividing the PPP of an economy with its exchange rate relative to the reference economy and multiplying the result by 100. With the US as the reference economy for ICP global results, the US dollar is the reference currency for PPPs in global comparisons. The PLI for the US is 100 and the PLIs for each other economy are then expressed as a number relative to the US.

Before examining how economies of Asia and the Pacific influence consumer prices in high-income economies, it is useful to examine the most recent evidence from the ICP on price levels. To this end, Table 4.7 shows PLIs—the ratio of PPP to the market exchange rate (relative to the US)—for GDP and specific commodity groupings across the 33 economies of Asia and the Pacific that participated in the 2021 ICP cycle.

Key Findings:

- At the GDP level, all economies other than Australia and New Zealand had price levels below the US in 2021. Many economies had PLIs below 30, indicating price levels less than one third of the US.

- When food is considered, several economies—including the PRC and the Republic of Korea, along with high-income economies such as Singapore—had higher price levels than the US.

- For clothing and footwear, price levels were low in Bangladesh, India, and Viet Nam, indicating a price advantage that may be reflected in the export performance of these economies. However, high price levels for clothing and footwear in the PRC may appear counterintuitive as the economy is a major exporter of clothing.

- For machinery and equipment, all the economies with the exception of Tajikistan had price levels higher than the US in 2021. As PPPs for machinery and equipment are based on prices paid by purchasers, and as these items are traded freely, the general expectation is that PPPs would be close to exchange rates. Higher PPPs could be partly due to mark-ups and transport costs involved in importing machinery in the economies of Asia and the Pacific.

The relatively lower price levels in the lower- and upper middle-income economies of Asia and the Pacific, as reflected in their PPPs, are central to these economies being instrumental in lowering consumer prices in high-income economies. Lower domestic production costs—arising from more affordable labor, energy, and raw materials—enable producers to offer competitive prices in international markets. These cost advantages are often passed on in export prices, resulting in a supply of goods to global markets at levels below those prevailing in higher-cost economies. As these exports enter developed markets, they exert deflationary pressure by displacing more-expensive domestic alternatives and expanding the range of affordable consumer choices.

Table 4.7: Price Level Indexes (US = 100) for Selected Aggregates and Economies, 2021

Economy	Gross Domestic Product	Food	Clothing and Footwear	Furnishings, Household Equipment and Routine Household Maintenance	Transport	Restaurants and Hotels	Recreation and Culture	Machinery and Equipment	Construction
Developing ADB Member Economies									
Armenia	29.4	62.5	74.7	62.9	53.6	37.4	46.9	107.1	13.3
Azerbaijan	26.9	51.3	69.8	59.0	44.8	34.5	39.3	101.3	13.5
Bangladesh	33.3	73.1	51.5	44.4	63.6	27.8	44.6	136.2	14.6
Bhutan	26.5	66.1	44.1	52.1	53.2	19.8	36.1	135.0	14.3
Brunei Darussalam	39.6	86.8	61.6	55.9	55.3	46.5	62.6	126.4	17.0
Cambodia	34.8	76.2	47.1	55.3	75.8	32.8	44.4	119.0	12.4
China, People's Republic of	61.8	111.0	135.0	102.6	70.8	59.7	67.1	153.8	30.0
Fiji	44.0	79.4	55.2	74.7	65.1	61.6	56.3	130.4	18.8
Georgia	26.8	69.6	73.2	62.4	52.2	36.0	48.5	113.9	12.3
Hong Kong, China	75.5	145.7	81.0	101.0	109.8	65.2	72.4	125.9	46.1
India	28.0	49.5	30.1	41.4	53.2	27.6	36.7	113.8	12.2
Indonesia	33.6	76.1	57.0	56.8	54.0	31.5	44.3	127.3	12.1
Kazakhstan	30.3	53.9	70.7	57.9	44.2	33.1	38.3	101.8	15.4
Korea, Republic of	72.3	177.7	137.2	102.6	98.7	99.8	96.0	127.3	41.4
Kyrgyz Republic	23.5	56.6	70.2	60.7	48.2	35.4	41.0	101.4	8.7
Lao People's Democratic Republic	31.3	75.4	44.0	52.3	71.9	33.8	38.3	125.8	14.9
Malaysia	36.6	70.7	47.9	55.7	54.1	21.5	49.6	126.2	14.5
Maldives	53.4	88.1	101.5	75.2	87.2	48.6	72.5	133.3	23.0
Mongolia	30.5	63.9	48.9	63.9	49.4	30.7	44.4	122.4	15.7
Nepal	27.5	56.6	35.5	45.7	73.6	25.8	31.3	117.5	13.6
Pakistan	26.7	50.5	34.6	39.1	47.0	24.9	29.3	118.0	13.0
Philippines	39.3	79.3	61.5	56.2	65.4	33.8	50.0	119.5	16.0
Singapore	60.3	111.3	77.0	92.2	149.1	49.1	65.3	140.6	31.7
Sri Lanka	27.9	64.7	31.1	48.6	56.5	24.4	29.8	128.9	13.1
Taipei,China	51.4	120.8	61.3	85.7	74.7	43.8	62.3	142.1	27.8
Tajikistan	22.5	60.0	65.9	62.2	52.8	35.3	36.1	94.3	9.4
Thailand	34.9	71.7	54.2	69.1	59.0	29.3	48.5	128.9	13.5
Türkiye	30.7	63.6	48.4	53.7	78.2	48.5	44.9	106.0	18.3
Uzbekistan	24.4	61.9	68.2	58.6	46.1	37.2	36.2	108.4	11.2
Viet Nam	30.7	67.6	41.9	53.9	60.3	25.3	36.7	120.0	13.9
Developed ADB Member Economies									
Australia	106.4	126.4	93.8	112.1	117.2	132.0	115.4	131.2	85.8
Japan	89.9	169.8	109.5	118.6	129.7	104.1	123.5	119.7	81.5
New Zealand	103.0	121.3	96.5	114.0	113.7	122.1	111.9	130.2	117.6
United States	**100.0**	**100.0**	**100.0**	**100.0**	**100.0**	**100.0**	**100.0**	**100.0**	**100.0**

ADB = Asian Development Bank, ICP = International Comparison Program, US = United States.

Note: The table shows price level indexes relative to the US.

Source: World Bank. DataBank: ICP 2021. https://databank.worldbank.org/source/icp-2021# (accessed 4 June 2024) and Asian Development Bank estimates using data supplied by the participating economies.

The deflationary price mechanism is particularly evident in the strong trade linkages between exporters in Asia and the Pacific and their high-income markets such as the European Union, Japan, and the US. The sustained inflow of competitively priced goods—from consumer durables to intermediate manufactured products—has had a moderating effect on inflation across these economies. Over time, these trade flows have reinforced the downward pressure on the overall consumer price index and for the importing economies, the result has been increased real incomes and household purchasing power. Meanwhile, at the global level, supply chains have increasingly reoriented towards lower-cost producers in the Asia and Pacific region.

In attempting to find evidence to support the notion of an "Asia and Pacific price effect," it is important to understand that export prices in the region's economies are shaped by domestic cost structures, but may not always correspond directly to prices in local markets. In many smaller or open economies, domestic consumption is modest compared to export production, and domestic price levels tend to influence export pricing through labor and input costs. Lower domestic prices for tradable goods often translate into lower export prices, reinforcing these economies' positions as competitive suppliers in global markets. This is particularly the case in economies such as Bangladesh, Indonesia, and Viet Nam, where production of certain consumer goods is heavily export-oriented and domestic consumption has limited bearing on overall pricing strategies.

Nevertheless, for a broad array of manufactured goods, economies of Asia and the Pacific continue to supply low-cost exports that play a central role in anchoring inflation in developed markets.

Asia and the Pacific as a Competitive Tourist Destination

The region's generally low PLIs for food, clothing, transport, restaurants and hotels, and recreation and culture may explain why economies in Asia and the Pacific continue to be price-competitive destinations for tourists from all over the world. In the case of Japan, although price levels for most GDP aggregates are high relative to the US, the economy has become an attractive tourist destination due to relatively low domestic inflation coupled with a significant depreciation (over 40%) of the yen against the US dollar from January 2021 to June 2024.

This chapter's analysis of PPPs and PPP-based macroeconomic indicators shows that Asia and the Pacific has emerged as the principal engine of global economic growth, contributing more than any other region to global GDP, consumption, and investment. The region has also led the reduction in global poverty since 1990. Its rapid and inclusive development has not only narrowed income disparities across economies but also has played a pivotal role in shaping a more equitable and dynamic global economy.

CHAPTER 5

Regional Program Participation, Governance, and Partnerships

In 2003, the Asian Development Bank (ADB) took on the role of regional coordinating agency (now known as regional implementing agency) for Asia and the Pacific under the International Comparison Program (ICP). The invitation, made ahead of the 2005 ICP cycle,[1] came in view of ADB's strong working relationships with national statistics offices in the region; relationships that had been nurtured over a long period through support for statistical capacity building.

The ICP was a natural extension of ADB's ongoing work to strengthen official statistics across Asia and the Pacific. ADB also had the means to raise the crucial financial resources required to implement a complex program of this size in a geographically and economically diverse region. It assumed responsibility as the regional implementing agency for the 2005 ICP cycle, and has continued in this role for subsequent cycles, successfully implementing the 2011, 2017, and 2021 cycles and leading the current 2024 cycle in the region.

The successful implementation of successive ICP cycles in Asia and the Pacific reflects ADB's sustained commitment to the program. The bank's leadership has been evident not only in bringing about operational efficiencies but also in its ability to foster participation, regional cooperation, and creating a sense of ownership of the program among a diverse group of economies. ADB has been instrumental in establishing effective regional structures, promoting technical innovation, and addressing methodological challenges inherent in applying complex ICP procedures across a region that is home to economies of wide-ranging income status and statistical capacity.

Fostering Participation by Economies of Asia and the Pacific

Only 13 current ADB members from across Asia and the Pacific participated in the 1985 ICP cycle. This number rose significantly to 25 in the 1993 cycle. However, despite this near doubling of the number of participating economies, the percentage of the world population covered by the ICP increased only marginally from 50% in 1985 to 51% in 1993. This was because India, which participated in the 1985 cycle, did not participate in the 1993 cycle. The People's Republic of China (PRC) did not participate in any ICP cycle until 2005.

One of the responsibilities of the implementing agencies is to foster participation of economies within their ICP regions. With ADB taking over as the regional implementing agency for Asia and the Pacific, a major achievement of the 2005 ICP cycle was the participation of both India and the PRC. With the two largest economies of the world joining the regional program under an ADB technical assistance program associated with ICP operations, the ICP's coverage of the world population went up from 51% in 1993 to 95% in 2005. India participated in the 2005 ICP conducting nationally representative price surveys, while the price surveys in the PRC were conducted in 11 cities and surrounding rural areas. The prices for this coverage were then suitably adjusted to estimate national average prices required by the ICP. Since then, both India and the PRC have participated in all ICP cycles (Box 5.1).

1 The ICP benchmarks until the 2011 ICP were referred to as a 'round'. With the decision of the United Nations Statistical Commission to transition ICP to a global statistical program to be conducted regularly every three years, the ICP benchmarks from 2017 are referred to as cycles. In this publication, the term cycle is generally used to refer to an ICP benchmark exercise.

Box 5.1: A Lasting Contribution of ADB to the International Comparison Program

A major and enduring contribution of the Asian Development Bank (ADB) to the International Comparison Program (ICP) has been securing program participation by the People's Republic of China (PRC) and India, which together account for more than a third of the global population.

India participated in the 2005 ICP cycle, undertaking nationally representative price surveys. The PRC's participation in the 2005 cycle, while partial with respect to geographical coverage of price surveys, marked a significant breakthrough with the economy's first-time participation in the global program.

The National Bureau of Statistics of China (NBS), as the national implementing agency for the ICP, agreed to participate in the 2005 ICP cycle and collected price data in 11 major cities, including Beijing, Shanghai, Guangzhou, and Xi'an, along with their surrounding rural areas. For comparisons across economies, and to produce purchasing power parities (PPPs) using comparable price data, the ICP requires nationally representative price surveys, which can provide reliable national average prices of the items. To produce national PPP estimates from the data collected in the 11 cities and surrounding areas, the ADB Regional Office, in collaboration with the ICP Global Office at the World Bank, worked closely with the NBS. Average prices for the 11 cities were used and weights were developed in consultation with the NBS to generate correction factors to approximate national averages. For government consumption, national-level data from the *China Statistical Yearbook* were used. Price data for construction were collected in three cities, while data for machinery and equipment were obtained from cities where appropriate items could be sourced. National accounts data were disaggregated into the 155 basic headings as required by the ICP, using household expenditure surveys and administrative sources (ADB 2007). This work was supported by a technical mission conducted jointly with the NBS in mid-2006.

Both the PRC and India have participated in subsequent ICP cycles in 2011, 2017, 2021, and 2024, with nationally representative surveys to estimate national average prices, and each economy has contributed to the ongoing success of the program in the Asia and Pacific region and globally. PPPs from the ICP are critical inputs for estimating the extreme poverty line and for calculating the number of poor people in the economies of the world. As such, participation by the PRC and India in the ICP was significant in tracking progress towards the goal of reducing the global extreme poverty rate to half its 1990 value by 2015 under the Millennium Development Goals and currently continues in the tracking of global and regional poverty under the Sustainable Development Goals era.

Securing the participation of both the PRC and India stands as a key achievement of ADB's leadership in Asia and the Pacific, and is a major milestone in enhancing the global coverage and credibility of the ICP.

Reference: Asian Development Bank (ADB). 2007. *2005 International Comparison Program in Asia and the Pacific: Purchasing Power Parities and Real Expenditures*. https://www.adb.org/sites/default/files/publication/29145/ppp-real-expenditures.pdf.

Source: Asian Development Bank compilation and analysis.

The 2005 ICP cycle, with a regionalized governance framework introduced, saw the participation of 32 current ADB members spread across three ICP regions (Table 5.1). Of these 32 members, the following 21 economies (CoreAP21) participated via the ICP's regional program for Asia and the Pacific, with ADB as the regional implementing agency and have since participated in each of the subsequent ICP cycles of 2011, 2017, 2021, and 2024: Bangladesh; Bhutan; Brunei Darussalam; Cambodia; the PRC; Fiji; Hong Kong, China; India; Indonesia; the Lao People's Democratic Republic; Malaysia; Maldives; Mongolia; Nepal; Pakistan; the Philippines; Singapore; Sri Lanka; Taipei,China; Thailand; and Viet Nam.

Among the 11 remaining ADB member economies taking part in the 2005 ICP cycle, Australia, Japan, New Zealand, the Republic of Korea, and Türkiye participated via Organisation for Economic Co-operation and Development (OECD) comparisons, while six ADB members in Central Asia—Armenia, Azerbaijan, Georgia, Kazakhstan, the Kyrgyz Republic, and Tajikistan—participated under the ICP's regional program for the Commonwealth of Independent States (CIS) under the leadership of Interstate Statistical Committee of the CIS (CIS-STAT).

Additionally, two economies who are not ADB members, the Islamic Republic of Iran and Macau, China, joined the ICP's regional program for Asia and the Pacific in 2005.

While the 32 ADB regional members remained through the ensuing cycles of the ICP, there were minor differences in overall participation in the subsequent benchmarks. ADB member Myanmar participated via the ICP's regional program for Asia and the Pacific only in the 2011 and 2017 cycles. The Islamic Republic of Iran did not participate after 2005 under the Asia and Pacific regional program, while Macau, China did not participate in the ICP after 2011. Uzbekistan joined in 2021 under the ICP's regional program for the CIS.

The 2024 ICP cycle has the same participation from ADB members as in 2021, but is augmented by the participation of Timor-Leste as a first-time entrant under the ICP's regional program for Asia and the Pacific. This means there are a total of 34 ADB member economies participating in the 2024 ICP cycle distributed across different ICP regions and contributing significantly to the success of the global program.

Table 5.1 presents the list of the current ADB regional members participating in ICP benchmark cycles since 2005 by ICP regional programs.

Table 5.1: Participation by ADB Members in the International Comparison Program, 2005–2024

ICP Year	ADB Member Economies Participating Under:			Total ADB Regional Members in ICP
	ICP's Asia and Pacific Regional Program led by ADB	OECD PPP Program led by the OECD	ICP's CIS Regional Program led by CIS-STAT	
2005	Bangladesh; Bhutan; Brunei Darussalam; Cambodia; the PRC; Fiji; Hong Kong, China; India; Indonesia; the Lao PDR; Malaysia; Maldives; Mongolia; Nepal; Pakistan; the Philippines; Singapore; Sri Lanka; Taipei,China; Thailand; and Viet Nam. (CoreAP21)	Australia, Japan, New Zealand, the Republic of Korea, and Türkiye (CoreOECD5)	Armenia, Azerbaijan, Georgia, Kazakhstan, the Kyrgyz Republic, and Tajikistan (CoreCIS6)	32
2011	CoreAP21 + Myanmar	CoreOECD5	CoreCIS6	33
2017	CoreAP21 + Myanmar	CoreOECD5	CoreCIS6	33
2021	CoreAP21	CoreOECD5	CoreCIS6 + Uzbekistan	33
2024	CoreAP21 + Timor-Leste	CoreOECD5	CoreCIS6 + Uzbekistan	34

ADB = Asian Development Bank, CIS = Commonwealth of Independent States, CIS-STAT = Interstate Statistical Committee of the CIS, GDP = gross domestic product, ICP = International Comparison Program, Lao PDR = Lao People's Democratic Republic, OECD = Organisation for Economic Co-operation and Development, PPP = purchasing power parity, PRC = People's Republic of China.

Notes: Two economies who are not ADB members have participated in ICP cycles under the Asia and Pacific regional program administered by ADB: the Islamic Republic of Iran (2005) and Macau, China (2005 and 2011). In the 2011 ICP cycle, 13 ADB members from Pacific Islands participated only for the household consumption expenditure component of GDP, with the Australian Bureau of Statistics playing the role of regional implementing agency for Pacific island economies.

Source: Asian Development Bank compilation.

Establishing the Regional Implementation and Governance Framework

The successful implementation of a statistical initiative with the scale and complexity of the ICP requires a well-designed governance and organizational framework. Coordinating geographically widespread data collection on nationally representative survey activities for a large number of national statistics offices requires careful planning and structured oversight to ensure coherence, consistency, and adherence to international standards. Given the logistical demands involved—particularly in managing price and expenditure data collection across a very diverse set of economies—the governance structure must be capable of delivering timely and reliable estimates of purchasing power parities (PPPs), price levels, and real expenditures.

These objectives, in turn, require the establishment of clear institutional arrangements and well-defined responsibilities at various levels. The framework must also promote efficient allocation and use of the limited financial and human resources that are available for the ICP, while ensuring that the data produced meet the methodological and quality standards set by the ICP Global Office. In this context, effective governance is not only a prerequisite for operational success but also essential for maintaining the credibility of the program and comparability of the results across participating economies.

ADB, as the ICP's regional implementing agency for Asia and the Pacific, has shown the capacity and expertise to deliver on the program's effective implementation and governance over five ICP cycles following a set of guiding principles for its successful implementation in the region (Box 5.2).

Establishing a Framework of Partnerships with Participating Economies

At the outset of each ICP cycle, partnerships are established between ADB and participating economies through a process of mutual agreement outlined in a nonlegal Framework of Partnership (FOP). The FOP clearly describes the roles and responsibilities of ADB as the regional implementing agency and those of the participating economies as the implementing agencies at the national level. The FOP is the foundation on which the trust between ADB and participating economies is developed through collective ownership and shared responsibilities. Key elements of the FOP are provided in the Box 5.3.

Box 5.2: Guiding Principles for the International Comparison Program in Asia and the Pacific

In its role as the regional implementing agency, the Asian Development Bank has guided the International Comparison Program (ICP) in Asia and the Pacific over five ICP cycles to date. Successful implementation has been achieved by adhering to a set of core principles that have underpinned the program's success. These four principles are:

(i) **ownership by the participating economies:** ensuring that participating economies take ownership and lead in implementing the program, thereby building capacity and accountability at the national level;
(ii) **fostering a strong sense of engagement:** encouraging active engagement and shared responsibility among national implementing agencies to strengthen regional cooperation and long-term commitment to the program;
(iii) **transparency:** promoting openness in methodological choices, data collection processes, and validation procedures to enhance trust and credibility; and
(iv) **commitment to data quality and integrity:** maintaining high standards in the generation, validation, and use of data to ensure that PPPs and real expenditure estimates are robust, consistent, and suitable for policymaking.

These principles have shaped a collaborative and well-functioning regional framework, enabling the successful delivery of the ICP across one of the most diverse and complex regions of the world.

Source: Asian Development Bank compilation and analysis.

Box 5.3: Key Elements of the Framework of Partnership in the International Comparison Program for Asia and the Pacific

The primary objective of the International Comparison Program (ICP) Framework of Partnership is to provide a structured collaborative arrangement between the Asian Development Bank (ADB) as the regional implementing agency and the implementing agencies at the economy level. The framework defines the roles and responsibilities for managing and implementing the ICP in Asia and the Pacific, ensuring effective implementation of the regional program. Established in the 2005 ICP cycle, it has been in place for all ICP cycles since then. The Framework of Partnership also outlines policies guiding data-handling at economy and regional levels.

Roles and Responsibilities of the Regional Implementing Agency

ADB, as the regional implementing agency, manages daily operations of the ICP's regional program for Asia and the Pacific. This includes fostering participation, aiding resource mobilization, coordinating with implementing agencies, and ensuring adherence to global ICP standards and timelines. ADB appoints a Regional Coordinator and forms a Regional Advisory Board to help identify priorities and provide guidance on objectives specific to Asia and the Pacific. ADB subdivides the region for analytical purposes, prepares regional product lists and survey operation guidelines for price surveys, organizes regular workshops for product list preparations, conducts training on concepts and operations of ICP surveys, and supports capacity building in participating economies. ADB undertakes rigorous validation of prices and national accounts data submitted by the individual economies and analyzes this data to calculate regional purchasing power parities. It then publishes regional reports and promotes dissemination for policy-oriented uses of ICP data. ADB also oversees data archiving and dissemination, ensures compliance with data access policies, and liaises with the ICP Global Implementing Agency at the World Bank and other Regional Coordinators through the Inter-agency Coordination Group to share best practices, discuss timetables, address data quality issues, and finalize regional results.

Roles and Responsibilities of the Implementing Agencies in Participating Economies

At the economy level, each implementing agency is responsible for implementing ICP price surveys following the regional product lists and timelines and compilation of gross domestic product (GDP) expenditures and other support data required for calculation of purchasing power parities. The implementing agency appoints a National Coordinator and a Deputy National Coordinator to manage communications with ADB and to coordinate a national ICP team of experts in price surveys and national accounts following the System of National Accounts standards and ICP classifications. The national implementing agencies join regional workshops, help finalize regional product lists, create national survey work plans, conduct ICP price surveys to collect price data, and submit validated national average prices and GDP expenditures data to ADB as scheduled, following ICP standards and classifications. The implementing agencies in participating economies ensure data quality through rigorous validation, responding to diagnostic queries from ADB, and maintaining national ICP databases for archiving and dissemination.

Source: Asian Development Bank compilation and analysis.

Additionally, at the beginning of each ICP cycle, each participating economy signs a formal "no objection" letter, acknowledging its participation under the ADB technical assistance program that finances ICP activities in the Asia and Pacific region. To operationalize this partnership, a regional workshop is organized at the outset to (i) present the objectives of the ICP and its implementation plan to the heads of the implementing agencies of the participating economies, (ii) clarify institutional arrangements, and (iii) define the respective roles and responsibilities of ADB as the regional implementing agency and of the national implementing agencies. This process ensures a shared understanding of the program's objectives, data requirements, and roles and responsibilities of regional and national implementing agencies, thus laying the foundation for effective collaboration throughout the ICP cycle.

Other Arrangements for Strong Regional Governance and Quality Assurance

Following its appointment as the regional implementing agency in 2003, ADB formed two advisory bodies—the Regional Advisory Board (RAB) and the Expert Group—to help institutionalize ICP regional governance and quality assurance specific to Asia and the Pacific. These bodies aim to provide strategic oversight and reliability of the ICP results produced by ADB according to established policies, protocols, and methods.

Such regional governance arrangements were envisaged and established in the 2005 ICP cycle and have played a significant role not just in successfully implementing various ICP cycles but also in identifying the region's priority issues and providing innovative tools and methods to address them. The RAB and the Expert Group have helped further ensure the integrity, quality, and reliability of ICP results in Asia and the Pacific. Figure 5.1 illustrates where the RAB and the Expert Group each sit in the context of regional governance of the ICP in Asia and the Pacific.

Figure 5.1: Regional Governance of the International Comparison Program for Asia and the Pacific

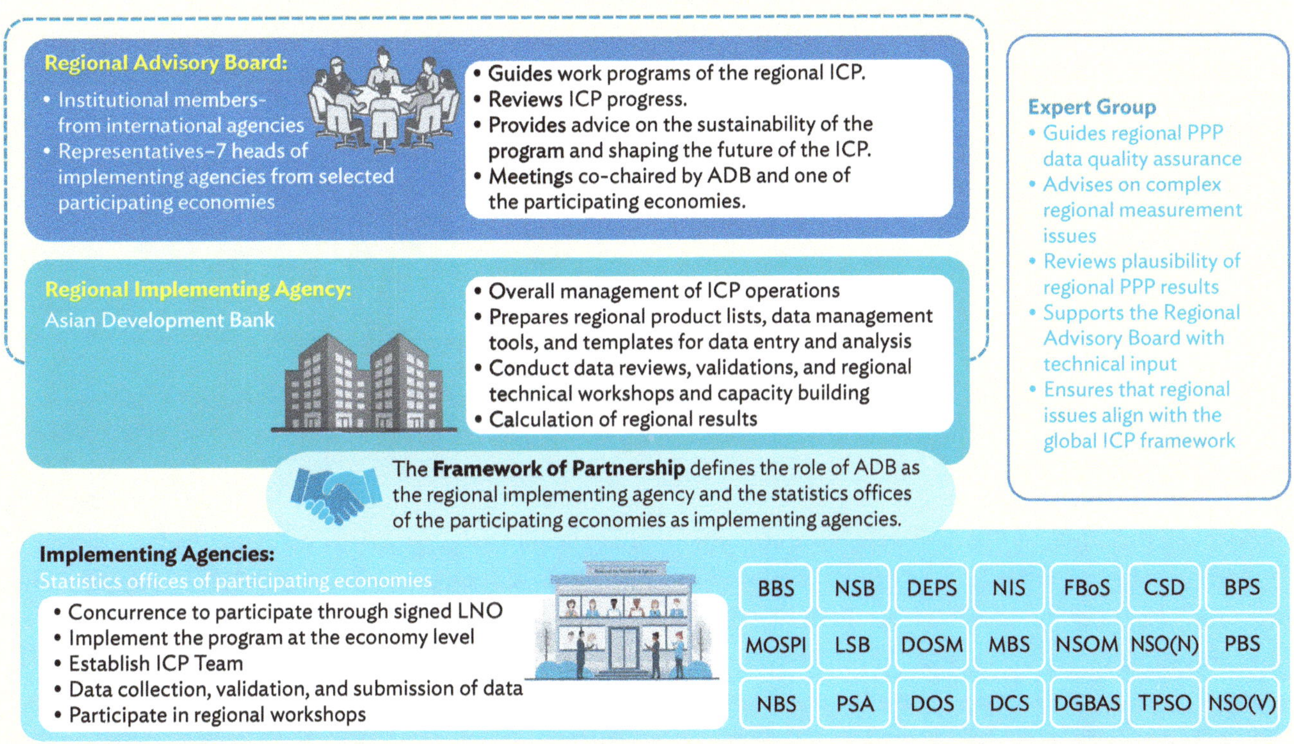

ADB = Asian Development Bank; BBS = Bangladesh Bureau of Statistics, Bangladesh; BPS = Badan Pusat Statistik, Indonesia; CSD = Census and Statistics Department, Hong Kong, China; DCS = Department of Census and Statistics, Sri Lanka; DEPS = Department of Economic Planning and Statistics, Brunei Darussalam; DGBAS = Directorate General of Budget, Accounting and Statistics, Taipei,China; DOS = Department of Statistics, Singapore; DOSM = Department of Statistics Malaysia, Malaysia; FBoS = Fiji Bureau of Statistics, Fiji; ICP = International Comparison Program; LNO = letter of no objection; LSB = Lao Statistics Bureau, the Lao People's Democratic Republic; MBS = Maldives Bureau of Statistics, Maldives; MOSPI = Ministry of Statistics and Programme Implementation, India; NBS = National Bureau of Statistics of China, the People's Republic of China; NIS = National Institute of Statistics, Cambodia; NSB = National Statistics Bureau, Bhutan; NSO(N) = National Statistics Office, Nepal; NSO(V) = National Statistics Office, Viet Nam; NSOM = National Statistics Office of Mongolia; PBS = Pakistan Bureau of Statistics, Pakistan; PSA = Philippine Statistics Authority, the Philippines; PPP = purchasing power parity; TPSO = Trade Policy and Strategy Office, Thailand.

Source: Asian Development Bank compilation.

Regional Advisory Board

The RAB provides advice to the Regional Coordinator of the ICP for Asia and the Pacific. It is not an executive body and is not involved in the day-to-day management of the ICP.

The RAB's terms of reference are to:

(i) provide guidance in setting up regional goals, priorities, and objectives;
(ii) guide the work program prepared by the Regional Coordinator who is responsible for the day-to-day management of the regional program;
(iii) review ICP progress in the Asia and Pacific region;
(iv) advise on the sustainability of the program; and
(v) assist in shaping the ICP's future direction.

The RAB includes representatives of statistics offices of the participating economies and regional and global stakeholders. The chair of the RAB is selected on a rotational basis from one of the participating economies for meetings of the board. The co-chair of the RAB is the Chief Economist and Director General within the Economic Research and Development Impact Department at ADB or his/her designated representative. The board includes seven members from participating economies, each represented by the head or director of respective statistics offices. Hong Kong, China—being the reference economy for regional comparisons—has always been included on the RAB, along with the PRC and India as the region's two largest economies. The other four regional members of the RAB represent different subregions of Asia and the Pacific on a rotational basis. The RAB also includes the following institutional members: Chief Economist, ADB; Director, Statistics Division, United Nations Economic and Social Commission for Asia and the Pacific; while the Director, Development Data Group of the World Bank; and Director, Data Division of ADB are ex-officio members. The RAB's meetings and functions are assisted by the Regional Coordinator of the ICP for Asia and the Pacific and ADB as the Member Secretary. ADB's ICP team serves as the RAB secretariat.

Since the 2005 ICP cycle, when the RAB was first established, it has played a pivotal role in establishing and advancing the regional program. It has provided essential guidance, contributed to methodological innovations, and offered recommendations and solutions tailored to the specific needs and capacities of economies across Asia and the Pacific.

Expert Group

ADB convenes a regional Expert Group to provide guidance on regional data quality assurance, review the overall quality of regional PPPs and results, and ensure transparency of regional ICP results. The group also provides technical advice on important data and measurement issues, taking into consideration region-specific situations and the varying statistical capacities of economies across Asia and the Pacific. It further advises ADB's ICP team on identifying technical issues to be raised with the RAB for their consideration.

Functioning similarly to the Technical Advisory Group to the ICP at the global level, the Expert Group for Asia and the Pacific is comprised of specialists in the fields of PPP comparisons, index number methods, and national accounts.

The Expert Group in the past has been tasked with advising on complex areas such as the estimation of PPPs and real expenditures for housing services, the application of productivity adjustments for government compensation, and guidance on the measurement of prices and volumes in sectors such as construction and machinery and equipment. The group also plays an important role in reviewing the data quality and assessing the plausibility and consistency of preliminary regional PPPs and PPP-based regional results prepared by the Regional Coordinator in each ICP cycle.

Members of the Expert Group contribute actively to the work of the RAB, offering technical input and supporting decision-making on challenging methodological issues. Their engagement ensures that complexities specific to Asia and the Pacific are adequately understood and addressed while maintaining alignment with the broader ICP global framework.

The establishment of a robust regional governance framework—anchored by clear institutional arrangements, collaborative partnerships, and specialist advisory and expert bodies—has been fundamental to the enduring success, credibility, and innovation of the ICP in Asia and the Pacific since 2005.

CHAPTER 6

Asia and the Pacific's Contributions to Methodological Advancements

Background

The International Comparison Program (ICP) operates within a global governance framework (Chapter 3) established by the United Nations Statistical Commission. This framework ensures that all participating regions around the world adhere to standardized methodologies for estimating purchasing power parities (PPPs) under the program. At the center of the framework is the ICP Technical Advisory Group, a collection of international experts who assure methodological soundness and endorse PPP estimation methodologies and protocols for the global program.

The concepts, classifications, data protocols, and methods of estimation of regional and global PPPs have evolved over time and are now well established for all regions to follow. The broad framework and methodology for the ICP are documented in detail in *Measuring the Real Size of the World Economy: The Framework, Methodology, and Results of the International Comparison Program (ICP)* (World Bank 2013) and in *Operational Guidelines and Procedures for Measuring the Real Size of the World Economy* (World Bank 2015). The Asian Development Bank (ADB) publication *2017 International Comparison Program for Asia and the Pacific: Purchasing Power Parities and Real Expenditures—Results and Methodology* also provides a comprehensive overview of the methods and framework (ADB 2020).

Adherence to methodologies endorsed by the ICP Technical Advisory Group for compiling regional PPPs and real expenditures is an essential requirement for establishing robust and high-quality international economic comparisons. However, to allow for effective operationalization of the guidelines, and to ensure the quality of the regional data and results, the governance structure of the ICP offers regional implementing agencies sufficient flexibility and independence to resolve region-specific issues arising during the implementation of the ICP in their regions.

Operationalizing the ICP and implementing its procedures in Asia and the Pacific since the 2005 ICP cycle has posed significant operational and methodological challenges for ADB as the regional implementing agency. These challenges have been largely due to the diversity of the economies participating in the ICP.

The Asia and Pacific region of the ICP encompasses high-income economies such as Brunei Darussalam; Hong Kong, China; Singapore; and Taipei,China to lower-middle-income economies such as Cambodia and Nepal. It also includes some of the world's most populous economies, including the People's Republic of China, India, and Indonesia, which are among the top 10 economies globally by size of gross domestic product (GDP) in PPP terms. This diversity is further accentuated by significant contrasts in urbanization and geography: highly urbanized and densely populated economies such as Hong Kong, China and Singapore stand in stark contrast to landlocked and predominantly rural economies such as Bhutan, the Lao People's Democratic Republic, and Mongolia. Adding to this complexity are the varying levels of statistical capacity and resources of the region's implementing agencies of the participating economies.

This diversity has presented significant challenges in operationalizing ICP methods and ensuring high data quality for intereconomy comparisons in the region. At the same time, this also opened opportunities to explore innovative approaches and tailored solutions that take into consideration the region's specific situations.

ADB, together with participating economies of the region, has undertaken important initiatives to overcome the practical challenges faced in operationalizing the ICP's globally approved methods across Asia and the Pacific. These initiatives have produced methodological advancements for measuring PPPs in comparison-resistant categories such as government compensation and housing expenditure; research on PPP-based comparisons in key areas of international development, such as poverty-specific PPPs; alternative approaches to generating PPP estimates more frequently but with reduced burden on economy resources; and measures to address other operational and technical challenges. The outcomes of some of these ADB initiatives have, in turn, fed back into consideration for updating the ICP's global methods and standards.

Methodological Advancements for Comparison-Resistant Services

International comparisons of services such as health, education, housing, and government services present significant difficulties in applying standard methods within the framework of the ICP. Health and education services are often provided by the government and, like other government services, they lack observable prices. This makes direct price comparisons across economies difficult. As a result, comparisons rely on an "input approach" that uses the prices of inputs—such as compensation paid to the teachers, healthcare workers, or other government employees—as proxies for the price of these services. Comparing dwelling services consumed by households introduces further complications, especially in economies with high proportions of informal housing and owner-occupied dwellings, resulting in underdeveloped rental markets. Factors such as housing quality, tenure structure, urban density, and land-use regulation vary widely across economies, influencing the cost and nature of housing services in ways that standard price surveys cannot easily capture.

ADB grappled with this problem of comparison-resistant services in implementing the ICP program for Asia and the Pacific in its very first cycle as the regional implementing agency in 2005. Through successive ICP cycles, ADB introduced practical methods to tackle the two most-difficult-to-measure areas, namely government services and housing, faced by the region in its comparisons. These approaches, tailored to regional conditions and data availability, were rigorously reviewed and endorsed by the ICP Technical Advisory Group highlighting the contribution of ADB to the advancement of ICP methodology. These are briefly discussed in the following subsections.

Contribution to Comparisons of Government Final Consumption Expenditure

In the system of national accounts, government final consumption expenditure (GFCE) comprises individual consumption expenditure by government (ICEG) and collective consumption expenditure by government (CCEG). ICEG relates to government expenditure on services to individuals, primarily in health care and education and, to a lesser extent, on housing, recreation and culture, and social protection. CCEG relates to expenditure incurred by the government to provide services that collectively benefit households but cannot be identified with specific households. Examples of CCEG expenditure include defense, law and order, and other general activities of the government.

Compensation of employees is the biggest component of general government expenditure. In the 2021 ICP cycle, this component ranged from 32% to 72% of total government expenditure in the 21 participating economies of Asia and the Pacific. The average across these economies was 43.4%, accounting for 6.3% of the total GDP of the region.

The ICP classification divides ICEG into 21 basic headings for which PPPs are to be estimated. PPPs for 19 of these 21 basic headings are compiled using "reference PPPs."[1] The only two basic headings of ICEG for which prices are collected are (i) "compensation of employees working in the production of health services," and (ii) "compensation of employees working in the production of education services" of the government. For these two basic headings, PPPs are compiled using standard ICP methods by comparing data on compensation paid to the employees for selected government occupations in the health and education sectors.

Under CCEG, reference PPPs are used for four of the five basic headings in the ICP classification. The only basic heading for which PPPs are compiled using prices (in the form of compensation paid to the government employees) by standard ICP methods is for the basic heading "compensation of employees" providing collective services of the government.

In other words, of the 26 basic headings comprising the general government expenditure, PPPs for government final consumption expenditure are compiled with the PPPs for three basic headings (compensation of employees in health, education, and collective services) by comparing compensation paid to select government occupations, and the PPPs for other 23 basic headings are reference PPPs.

As per standard ICP procedures and recommendations, data on total compensation paid to employees for a representative list of government occupations in health, education, and collective services are the price paid by the government for providing these services. In recent ICP cycles, this list comprised 34 well-defined occupations: 9 for health, 5 for education, and 20 for collective services. The different occupations in each category generally reflect the skill sets of employees providing these services.[2] Data on the compensation paid to government employees in these occupations are then used to derive PPPs for the three basic headings of compensation of employees in health, education, and collective services using country-product-dummy (CPD) method, which are then aggregated with other respective reference basic heading PPPs and expenditure as weights to produce PPPs for ICEG and CCEG using the Gini-Eltetö-Köves-Szulc or GEKS method.

The Problem: Implausible Purchasing Power Parities and Real Expenditures for the Government Sector

Problems in comparing the compensation of government employees in different economies came to fore at the beginning of ADB's involvement as the regional implementing agency in Asia and the Pacific during the 2005 ICP cycle. Preliminary analysis and results from compensation data collected during this cycle highlighted several comparability issues (ADB 2007).

Firstly, there were huge disparities in hourly compensation (based on exchange rates) for the same government occupations across economies. For example, the hourly compensation rate in the government health sector of Hong Kong, China was about 120 times that of the Lao People's Democratic Republic (ADB 2007).

Secondly, PPPs based on compensation data were very low for economies such as Bangladesh, Cambodia, Nepal, and Viet Nam, which had relatively very low government compensation rates, resulting in low PPPs and relative price levels for government services. As real expenditures are obtained by dividing the expenditures in local currency units by the corresponding PPPs, very low PPPs resulted in relatively high per capita real consumption of government services in such economies (ADB 2007).

1 For some basic headings, it is difficult to specify products and collect product prices. For such basic headings, PPPs of other basic headings (or a combination of basic headings for which price data were collected and are considered similar or related) are used as proxies or reference PPPs.

2 Examples of occupations include general practitioners, nurses, etc., for health services; primary school teachers, university teachers, etc., for education services; and judges, custom inspectors, statisticians, prison guards, etc., for general government services.

Thirdly, per capita real expenditure of government final consumption expenditure (GFCE) was found to be higher than per capita real individual consumption expenditure by households (ICEH) for some economies. These results seemed implausible considering that, in 2005, the average share of ICEH to GDP (in local currency units) across Asia and the Pacific was about 51% while the average share of GFCE to GDP was much lower at around 10%.

The Solution: Adjusting Labor Productivity Differentials Between Economies

During the 2005 ICP cycle, ADB set up an Expert Group to examine the discrepancies observed in the PPPs and per capita real GFCE. The group's mission was to devise an approach that would result in meaningful PPPs and per capita real expenditures.

Having reviewed the compensation data submitted by economies, as well as the PPPs and per capita real expenditures based on those data, the Expert Group concluded that this approach of comparing services of government employees assumes constant productivity across economies and does not account for differences in service quality, institutional efficiency, or intensity of capital use, leading to a low level of reliability for price comparisons between some of the participating economies.

At the core of this finding is the fact that, even though each of the listed occupations to be priced were well defined in terms of skills and education (thus assuming similar quality of labor) and the data on compensation levels were accurately measured, differences in productivity levels reflect low levels of capital intensity or capital per unit of labor in low-income economies. Thus, a government worker in an economy with low capital intensity is less productive than an employee with similar functions in an economy with high levels of capital per unit of labor.

The Expert Group therefore recommended that adjustments for productivity differences be made to the PPPs for government compensation so that estimated real expenditures reflect true differentials in the prices paid to government employees in different economies.

The methodology recommended for the computation of productivity adjustment factors by the Expert Group was based on some practical assumptions. The first assumption is that the productivity of government employees approximates the average labor productivity of the overall economy. This assumption was made due to the data limitations for estimating productivity adjustment factors for the government sector only. The second assumption is that the aggregate production function follows a Cobb-Douglas form with constant returns to scale. This functional form facilitates a straightforward relationship between labor productivity and the capital–labor ratio, thereby enabling a simplified analytical framework.

Productivity adjustments for government compensation PPPs were introduced by ADB in the regional comparisons in the 2005 ICP cycle for Asia and the Pacific. The ICP Technical Advisory Group endorsed the methodology proposed by ADB, making it an integral part of the methodology for estimating PPPs for government compensation in the Asia and Pacific region.

In the 2011 ICP cycle, similar problems of implausibly low PPPs were observed, confirming the problems attributed to productivity differentials, and the ADB methodology was again used (with some minor refinements).

For the 2017 ICP cycle, on the initiative of the World Bank, a uniform methodology (Inklaar 2019) for productivity adjustment across all regions was considered and endorsed by the ICP Technical Advisory Group. This global methodology was a further refinement of the ADB methodology (ADB 2020) and it was also used in the subsequent 2021 ICP cycle and has since become an established method for estimating PPPs for GFCE.

A timeline for the development of productivity adjustment methodologies since the 2005 ICP cycle is shown in Figure 6.1.

Figure 6.1: Productivity Adjustment Methodologies Developed Since 2005

The Problem

There is a significant variation in the wages and salaries of government employees across low-income and high-income economies. Typically, low-income economies have lower salaries, resulting in low PPPs and Price Level Indexes (PLIs). This data results in unusually high per capita real government expenditures in some low-income economies that do not appear plausible to the experts. The method does not account for differences in intensity of capital used by economies in the production of government services which lead to implausible results. The problem was observed in the very first ICP cycle of 2005 led by ADB as the regional implementing agency.

The Solution

Expert Group Recommendation: Adjust PPPs for government compensation calculating Productivity Adjustment Factors (PAFs) relative to the reference economy to account for differences in labor productivity based on differences in capital-labor ratios. The 'Adjusted PPP', for compensation BH would then be calculated as 'Unadjusted PPP', divided by the PAF.

Methodology Recommended by the ADB Expert Group to calculate PAF (used for 2005 and 2011 ICP)
The method starts with a simple Cobb-Douglas Production Function with constant returns to scale for each economy

$$Y_c = A{L_c}^{\alpha_c}{K_c}^{1-\alpha_c}$$

$$\Rightarrow Labor\ Productivity = \frac{Y_c}{L_c} = A_c\left(\frac{K_c}{L_c}\right)^{1-\alpha_c} \ where\ \frac{K_c}{L_c} = \frac{Y_c}{L_c} \times \frac{K_c}{Y_c}$$

where Y denotes output, K is Capital, L is Labor, and α is labor share. Subscript c refers to economy "c".

Under some simplifying assumptions, following productivity adjustment factors (PAFs) for economy "c" with Hong Kong, China as reference economy was recommended to adjust the PPPs for government compensation.

$$PAF_{HKG,C} = \frac{{k_C}^{1-\alpha_C}}{{k_{HKG}}^{1-\alpha_{HKG}}} where\ k = \frac{K}{L}\ and\ \alpha = share\ of\ labor$$

2005 ICP:
PAF's calculated assuming:

1. Capital-output ratios of 2.5 for low income and 3.5 for high income.
2. Labor shares: 0.5 for low income and 0.7 for high income.
3. The efficiency term A_c is assumed to be the same for all economies.
4. Relative labor productivity levels in the government sectors across economies are proportional to those observed for the whole economy.

2011 ICP:
PAF's calculated using:

1. Capital-output ratios were calculated using data from World Development Indicators.
2. Labor shares: 0.5 for low income; 0.6 for middle and 0.7 for high income.
3. The efficiency term A_c is assumed to be the same for all economies.
4. Relative labor productivity levels in the government sectors across economies are proportional to those observed for the whole economy.

Inklaar Methodology endorsed by the ICP Technical Advisory Group (used for 2017 and 2021 ICP)
The Inklaar approach first measures productivity of an economy relative to an average economy:

$$PROD_C = \left(\frac{k_C}{\bar{k}}\right)^{1-\frac{1}{2}(\alpha_C+\bar{\alpha})} \quad where k_C = \frac{K_C}{L_C}$$

where $\bar{k}$ is geometric mean of $k's$ and $\bar{\alpha}$ is the average labor share

Then the PAF for an economy relative to Hong Kong, China is defined as:

$$PAF_{HKG,C} = \frac{PROD_C}{PROD_{HKG}} = \frac{\left(\frac{k_C}{\bar{k}}\right)^{1-\frac{1}{2}(\alpha_C+\bar{\alpha})}}{\left(\frac{k_{HKG}}{\bar{k}}\right)^{1-\frac{1}{2}(\alpha_{HKG}+\bar{\alpha})}}$$

PAF's from this method are both transitive and base invariant.

2017 ICP:
PAF's calculated using:

1. Capital and labor data provided by the World Bank sourced from the Penn World Tables and International Labour Organization databases.
2. Technical Advisory Group for ICP recommended that productivity adjustments be applied uniformly by all regions using Inklaar methodology.
3. PAFs were made transitive and invariant to reference economy.

2021 ICP:
PAF's calculated using:

1. Same methodology as used in 2017 ICP cycle.
2. Same data sources (provided by the World Bank sourced from the Penn World Tables and International Labour Organization databases) as used in 2017 ICP.

BH = basic heading; HKG = Hong Kong, China; ICP = International Comparison Program; PAF = productivity adjustment factor; PPP = purchasing power parity.

Source: Asian Development Bank compilation and analysis.

The Outcomes: Productivity Adjustments Used in Economy Comparisons

Figure 6.2 shows the productivity adjustment factors relative to the reference economy Hong Kong, China, estimated using the Inklaar method and used in calculating PPPs for government compensation and per capita real GFCE in the 2021 ICP cycle for the Asia and Pacific region.

The productivity adjustment factors for the economies in Figure 6.2 are shown relative to the reference economy Hong Kong, China, for which the productivity adjustment factor equals 1.00. Thus, an adjustment factor of 0.25 implies that labor productivity in the nominated economy is one fourth of that in Hong Kong, China.

Figure 6.2: Productivity Adjustment Factors for Government Compensation in the Asia and Pacific Region, 2021

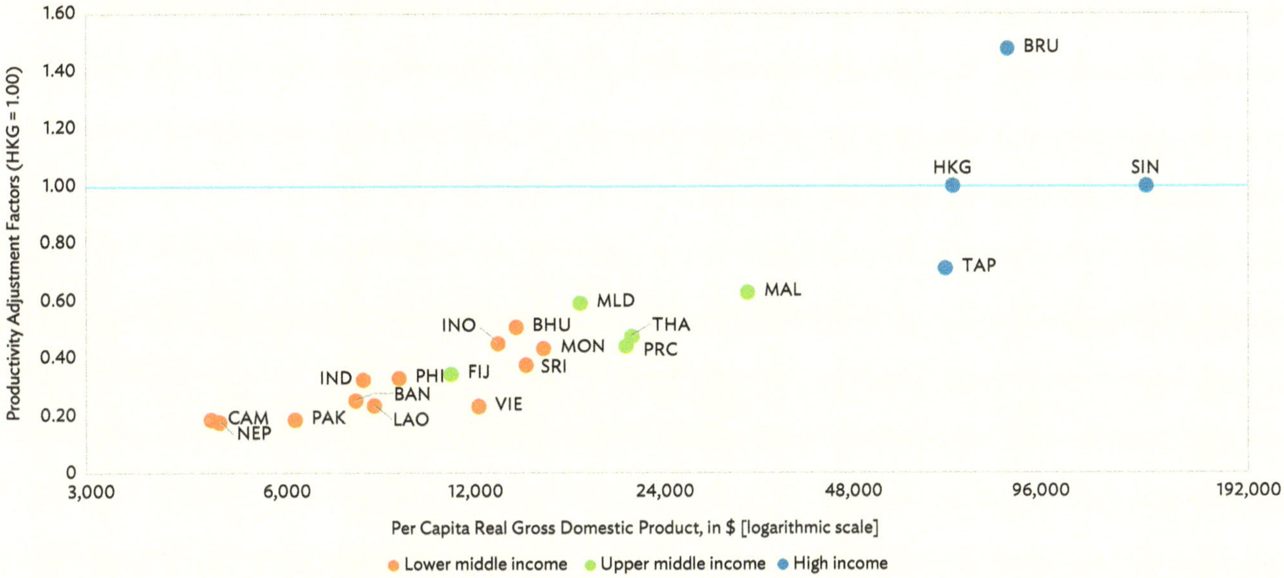

$ = United States dollars; BAN = Bangladesh; BHU = Bhutan; BRU = Brunei Darussalam; CAM = Cambodia; FIJ = Fiji; GDP = gross domestic product; HKG = Hong Kong, China; IND = India; INO = Indonesia; LAO = Lao People's Democratic Republic; MAL = Malaysia; MLD = Maldives; MON = Mongolia; NEP = Nepal; PAK = Pakistan; PHI = Philippines; PPP = purchasing power parity; PRC = People's Republic of China; SIN = Singapore; SRI = Sri Lanka; TAP = Taipei,China; THA = Thailand; VIE = Viet Nam.

Source: Asian Development Bank compilation and analysis.

For the 2021 ICP cycle, lower-middle- and upper-middle-income economies of Asia and the Pacific generally exhibited low productivity levels and vice versa. Except for Brunei Darussalam, whose productivity adjustment factor was above 1.0, all economies had productivity levels lower than that of Hong Kong, China, with Singapore close to 1.0 and therefore exhibiting similar productivity levels to Hong Kong, China. The lowest adjustment factors were for Cambodia and Nepal, economies which also have the lowest per capita incomes. The factor for the People's Republic of China was 0.44 compared to 0.33 for India.

These productivity adjustment factors are applied to obtain the productivity-adjusted PPPs of the three basic headings of government compensation by dividing an economy's unadjusted PPPs by the corresponding adjustment factors. As a result, economies in Asia and the Pacific with productivity levels below that of Hong Kong, China will have their government compensation PPPs adjusted upward. For instance, the adjustment factor for Cambodia is 0.19 and the adjusted PPPs and corresponding price level index for Cambodia would be approximately five times higher than the unadjusted values. These productivity-adjusted PPPs lead to lower and more plausible estimates of per capita real GFCE in comparison with the unadjusted PPPs.

With productivity adjustment factors now applied uniformly by all regions, including by the ICP Global Office in linking regional ICP results for compiling global ICP results, the adoption of this methodology as standard practice across all regions represents a lasting contribution by ADB to the ICP.

Contribution to Comparisons of Real Expenditure on Housing

Persistent Challenges in Housing Comparisons Globally

Comparing prices and real expenditures for housing services across economies has long posed significant methodological challenges, and housing services remain among the most comparison-resistant components of international comparisons.

Housing is classified as a comparison-resistant service primarily due to the diversity in housing markets across economies—especially the varying mixes of owner-occupied and rented dwellings. As Heston (2013) contends, this diversity complicates efforts to develop a standardized approach to housing comparisons, prompting the exploration of alternative methods.

The two methodologies recommended by the ICP Technical Advisory Group for measuring housing services are the "rental approach" and the "quantity or volume approach," with the choice largely dependent on the presence and reliability of rental markets within the economy being assessed (Box 6.1).

Box 6.1: Recommended Approaches to Housing Expenditure Comparisons

There are two recommended approaches that provide frameworks for housing comparisons in the International Comparison Program (ICP).

The Rental Approach:
This method estimates purchasing power parities (PPPs) directly from data on average annual rents collected in a given economy for a standardized list of dwellings. Real expenditure on housing is then derived by dividing the expenditures on dwelling services in local currency units by the PPPs estimated from the rental prices of the economies. The expenditures by households on dwelling services in an economy comprise expenditures made on actual rentals paid and imputed rents for the owner-occupied dwellings. The rental approach is most appropriate in economies with a well-established and representative rental market, where observed rents accurately reflect the value of the broader housing stock, including owner-occupied dwellings.

The Quantity (Volume) Approach:
In economies where rental markets are underdeveloped or unrepresentative, the quantity approach offers a viable alternative. In these economies, the expenditures on dwelling services are largely comprised on the imputed rents for owner-occupied dwellings. The quantity approach estimates the volume of housing services in a given economy using physical indicators such as the number of dwellings, rooms, or total floor area. These volumes are typically adjusted by quality indicators on the availability of basic amenities (e.g., water supply, sanitation, and electricity). Under this method, PPPs are estimated indirectly by dividing expenditures on housing services in local currency units by the corresponding volume measures of dwelling services. This approach requires the availability of reliable data on housing indicators and housing expenditures from national accounts.

Choice of Method:
Under the ICP, one of the two methods is generally used by the regional implementing agencies in compiling PPPs for housing. The choice of approach depends on data availability, data quality, and the structure of the housing market in each economy of each region. The rental approach is preferred where rental data are reliable, broadly reflective of national housing conditions, and estimate the PPPs directly. The quantity approach is recommended where rental data are limited or where rents are not representative of national conditions due to a prevalence of owner-occupied dwellings, which dominate housing in many economies.

Both approaches are endorsed for use by the ICP Technical Advisory Group.

Source: Asian Development Bank compilation and analysis.

Challenges and Evolving Approaches to Housing Comparisons in Asia and the Pacific

The Asia and Pacific region comprises economies with highly diverse rental markets ranging from about 3% to almost 50%, with low-income economies having limited rental markets mainly confined to the capital city. Considering this, since the 2005 ICP cycle, systematic data collection for both the rental and volume approaches has been undertaken across Asia and the Pacific in an attempt to produce robust PPPs and real expenditure estimates for housing.

However, despite these consistent and well-structured efforts, both approaches have produced implausible PPPs and per capita real expenditures for housing across all ICP cycles in the region since 2005. As discussed in ADB's 2020 publication, *2017 International Comparison Program for Asia and the Pacific: Purchasing Power Parities and Real Expenditures—Results and Methodology*, the plausibility of housing PPPs calculated using either of the two recommended approaches is broadly assessed using the ratio of an economy's "per capita real expenditure on housing" to "per capita real household expenditure excluding housing" (ADB 2020; ADB 2024a). This ratio was observed to fall within the range of 0.05 to 0.40 for most economies in regions of the world other than Asia and the Pacific.

For the Asia and Pacific region, however, irrespective of which approach (rental or quantity) was used, the ratio of "per capita real expenditure on housing" to "per capita real household expenditure excluding housing" has exceeded 0.40 and reached close to 1.00 for many economies consistently in all ICP cycles. The red dots in Figure 6.3 represent these ratios from the two approaches (volume approach on the y-axis and rental approach on the x-axis)

Figure 6.3: Ratios of Per Capita Real Expenditure on Housing to Per Capita Real Household Expenditure Excluding Housing, 2021

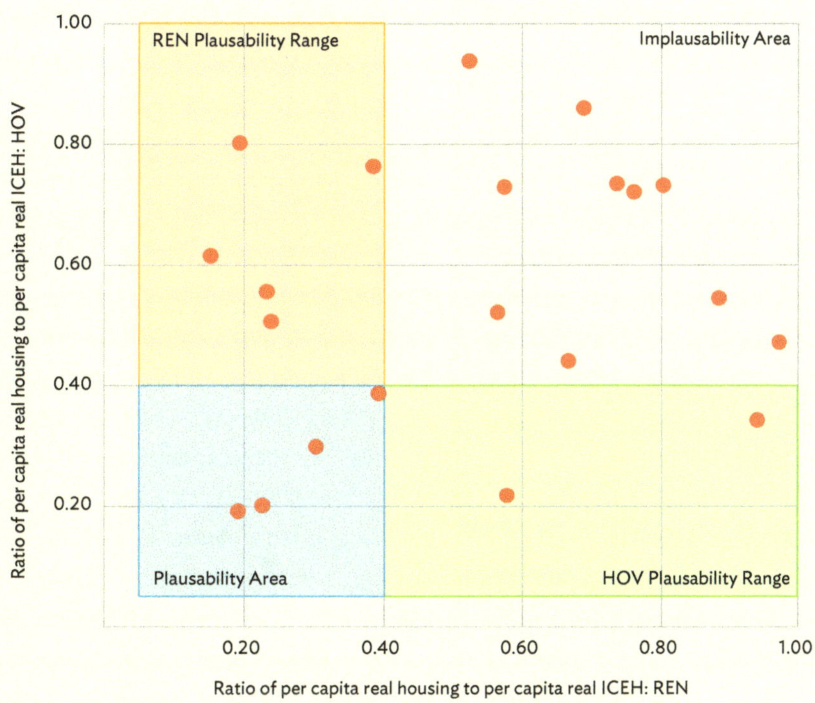

HOV = housing volume, ICEH = individual consumption expenditure by households, REN = housing rental.

Source: Asian Development Bank compilation and analysis.

for each economy in the 2021 ICP cycle. Except for four economies for which the ratios were below 0.40 from both approaches, for others the ratios exceeded 0.40 for both or either of the approaches. For 10 economies, the ratio exceeded 0.40 from both approaches, making these results unreliable for any meaningful intereconomy comparisons from either approach.

These outcomes from the 2021 ICP cycle, which were similar to the outcomes observed since the 2005 ICP cycle, raised concerns about the plausibility of the housing PPP estimates calculated from either method. Considering these implausible results, in consultation with the Expert Group, PPPs produced from either of the approaches were not used for housing comparisons in the Asia and Pacific region. Consequently, in the 2005 ICP cycle, alternative approaches were considered to resolve these limitations and fill the gaps in the estimates for housing PPPs in Asia and the Pacific, while ADB continued to explore improved methods that could overcome the specific problems faced by the region.

Use of the Reference Volume Approach

Due to the implausibility of results from the two standard approaches of measuring housing PPPs, neither rental nor quantity approaches could be used during the 2005, 2011, and 2017 ICP cycles. However, to estimate the PPPs for individual consumption expenditure by the households (which includes expenditures on housing), PPPs for housing were required. To fill the gap for housing PPPs the approach referred to as the "reference volume approach" was adopted (with some reservations) to estimate PPPs for housing services during the 2005 ICP cycle and was also used in the 2011 and 2017 ICP cycles because the challenges faced remained unresolved (ADB 2020).

The reference volume approach assumes that the ratio of "per capita real housing expenditure" to "per capita real household expenditure excluding housing" is identical across all economies. Note that housing is a component of household expenditure, so its PPPs affect the PPPs for overall household consumption. The reference volume approach is, however, neutral in the sense that using PPPs from this approach for housing does not change the volume relatives for overall household expenditure.

While this neutral and simplified assumption was applied for the 2005, 2011, and 2017 ICP cycles, in the absence of reliable PPPs for housing, it was clearly a pragmatic workaround rather than a methodological solution.

Despite its operational simplicity and neutrality, the reference volume approach has two major shortcomings. Firstly, it discards all the rental and volume indicator data that were meticulously collected by the participating economies for housing comparisons, resulting in artificially derived PPPs in the region. Secondly, and more significantly, it imposes a uniformity in housing expenditure patterns that fails to capture actual intereconomy differences. This assumption risks distorting the underlying reality of housing consumption and weakens the comparability and accuracy of real expenditure estimates across economies.

Refining Housing Comparisons: The Evolution of a Hybrid Methodology

During the 2017 ICP cycle, when both the approaches—rental and quantity—again produced unreliable estimates of real housing expenditure, an Expert Group constituted by ADB conducted a detailed review of input data and results for the Asia and Pacific region. After extensive data reviews and deliberation, the experts concluded that the failure of both recommended approaches was largely due to their inability to properly capture differences in dwelling quality across economies of the region.

The enormous diversity of Asia and the Pacific, in terms of income levels and other factors across economies, makes the challenge of capturing the vast differences in the quality of dwellings using the standard approaches impossible. At one end of the spectrum, the region includes highly urbanized, high-density, high-income economies such as Singapore and Hong Kong, China, where houses are equipped with modern conveniences. At the other end of the spectrum, there are much poorer economies with large rural populations, where dwellings are often traditional, built with lower-quality materials, and lacking many modern amenities. Varying rates of urbanization across economies further contribute to this contrast. The Expert Group concluded that adjusting for these vast quality differences is therefore essential for making any meaningful housing comparison across the region.

With this conclusion of the Expert Group, ADB explored and developed a new "hybrid" methodology that incorporates data from both housing rental surveys and housing volume surveys. This methodology combines the strengths of both rental and volume data while introducing quality adjustments to housing PPPs obtained from the rental and quantity approaches. Additionally, this methodology adjusts the PPPs calculated from the recommended rental and quantity approaches to account for the differences in the housing quality across economies. For quality adjustment, it uses an income-based adjustment factor that is expected to suitably capture quality differentials in housing services between high-income and low-income economies. This quality adjustment assumes that the average quality of dwellings increases with the average incomes of the general population, measured in this instance by per capita real household expenditure excluding housing. The process of calculating PPPs from the "hybrid methodology" is described in Figure 6.4.

The approved hybrid methodology that was used in the 2021 ICP cycle involves first calculating PPPs independently using the standard recommended approaches—one set of PPPs for the rental approach and other set for the quantity approach. As a second step, PPPs obtained for each approach are then adjusted using an adjustment factor that captures relative housing quality with Hong Kong, China as the reference economy. A final single housing expenditure PPP for each economy is obtained as the geometric mean of the quality-adjusted PPPs from both the rental and quantity approaches. Figure 6.4 presents the key steps in the methodology.

Figure 6.4: A Hybrid Approach of Quality-Adjusted Purchasing Power Parities from the Rental and Quantity Approaches

The Problem

- Comparison of housing across economies is difficult because of the varying range of mix of owner-occupied versus rented dwellings.
- In Asia and the Pacific, housing comparisons challenge is further amplified due to the wide heterogeneity between participating economies.
- Recommended standard approaches namely "Rental Approach" and "Quantity or Volume" Approach yielded implausible results.

The Solution

- Expert Group recognized that the housing comparisons must account for the enormous differences in quality of dwellings across very diverse economies of Asia and the Pacific in terms of per capita gross domestic product.
- A hybrid approach combining both the approaches was devised, that introduced quality adjustments to PPPs using an income-based factor and making full and efficient use of the data collected by the economies.

Collect Housing Rental (REN) Data

- National annual average rents per m^2 for 20 dwelling types

Collect Housing Volume (HOV) Data

- Housing Quantity Index (QN) Indicators: Number of dwellings per 100 persons ($QN_{Dwellings}$), number of rooms per 100 persons (QN_{Rooms}),
- Housing Quality Index (QL) Indicators: % of households with access to electricity ($QL_{Electricity}$), % of households with access to inside water (QL_{Water}), % of households with access to private toilets ($QL_{Sanitation}$)

REN PPPs

Calculated using the CPD method

HOV Index

Calculated as a product of **QN** and **QL**

$$HOV_{index} = \left(QN_{Rooms}^{\frac{2}{3}} \times QN_{Dwellings}^{\frac{1}{3}}\right) \times \left(QL_{Electricity}^{\frac{1}{3}} \times QL_{Water}^{\frac{1}{3}} \times QL_{Sanitation}^{\frac{1}{3}}\right)$$

Quality adjustment REN PPP calculated using square root of relative per capita ICEH without Housing with HKG as reference economy as adjustment factor

$$Adjusted\ REN\ PPP_j = REN\ PPP_j \times \sqrt{\frac{Per\ Capita\ Real\ ICEH\ without\ Housing_{HKG}}{Per\ Capita\ Real\ ICEH\ without\ Housing_j}}$$

Quality adjusted HOV PPP calculated using square root of relative per capita ICEH without Housing with HKG as reference economy as adjustment factor

$$Adjusted\ HOV\ PPP_j = HOV\ PPP_j \times \sqrt{\frac{Per\ Capita\ Real\ ICEH\ without\ Housing_{HKG}}{Per\ Capita\ Real\ ICEH\ without\ Housing_j}}$$

Select Reliable PPPs from the REN Approach

(For quality adjusted PPPs, reject the PPP for economies for which ratio of per capita real housing to per capita real ICEH is outside the range 0.05 to 0.40.)

Select Reliable PPPs from the HOV Approach

(For quality adjusted PPPs, reject the PPP for economies for which ratio of per capita real housing to per capita real ICEH is outside the range 0.05 to 0.40.)

Compute Linking Factor

Using the PPPs of economies that have reliable PPPs from both the approaches

use Linking Factor to gapfill PPPs considered not reliable from quality adjusted PPPs from either approach

Compute Hybrid Housing PPPs as the square root of the product of quality-adjusted rental PPPs and quality-adjusted housing volume PPPs (geometric mean)

% = percent; ADB = Asian Development Bank; CPD = country-product-dummy; HKG = Hong Kong, China; HOV = housing volume; ICEH = individual consumption expenditure by households; m^2 = square meter; PPP = purchasing power parity; REN = housing rental.

Source: Asian Development Bank compilation and analysis.

The first iteration of the methodology was developed during the 2017 ICP cycle. This iteration proposed different quality adjustment factors for the rental and quantity approaches. It proposed an indicator based on per capita expenditure of households without housing for adjusting the PPPs derived from the rental approach, while proposing relative urbanization rates as an adjustment factor to estimate quality-adjusted PPPs from the quantity approach. Using these quality adjustments, the results obtained from the two approaches were found to be very promising and plausible (ADB 2024a).

The results from this approach were presented by ADB to the Regional Advisory Board for Asia and the Pacific and to the ICP Technical Advisory Group in 2019. Both advisory bodies agreed that the hybrid methodology showed great potential in providing plausible PPPs based on innovative ways of combining the rental and quantity approaches. However, they recommended continued use of the reference volume approach for the 2017 ICP cycle with further testing of the robustness of the hybrid methodology during the 2021 ICP cycle.

During the 2021 ICP cycle, a second iteration of the hybrid methodology—a refinement of the first iteration—was developed. It proposed using same income-based adjustment factor for adjusting the PPPs calculated from the rental as well as quantity approaches to account for the differences in the quality of dwellings. The methodology was extensively tested using both 2021 and 2017 data collected for the program. These tests gave consistent and robust results for both reference years. The quality-adjusted PPPs from the rental and quantity approaches were again tested based on the plausibility criteria, i.e., the ratio of "per capita real expenditure on housing" to "per capita real household expenditure without housing." It was observed that these ratios lie within the plausibility range of 0.05 to 0.40 for all economies, except for only one economy from each approach for whom the ratio exceeded 0.40. These outlier PPPs were excluded from the computations and were gap-filled by multiplying the PPP estimated from the other approach by a linking factor derived from the ratio of the "geometric mean of the PPPs from the rental approach" and the "geometric mean of PPPs from the quantity approach" calculated for the common set of economies for which the PPPs were considered plausible under both approaches. This resulted in quality-adjusted PPPs available for each economy from the rental approach and the quantity approach with both satisfying the plausibility criteria.

In Figure 6.5, the red dots represent the ratios obtained using PPPs not adjusted for quality, while the green dots represent these ratios calculated using quality-adjusted PPPs. While the unadjusted PPPs exceed 0.40 for several economies, the quality-adjusted and gap-filled PPPs from both the rental and quantity approaches for all economies lie within the range of 0.05 to 0.40. The final PPPs for each economy were then calculated as the geometric mean of the PPPs from the rental approach and the quantity approach; hence the methodology is termed as "hybrid" or "mixed."

Following rigorous evaluation, the hybrid methodology was formally endorsed by both the Regional Advisory Board for the Asia and Pacific region and the ICP Technical Advisory Group at the global level for implementation in the 2021 ICP cycle and for the retrospective revision of PPPs for the 2017 ICP cycle. The ICP Technical Advisory Group advised that a reference to the methodology be included in the ICP's 2021 global report and suggested testing the new hybrid methodology in other regions of the world (World Bank 2023).

Figure 6.5: Ratios of Per Capita Real Expenditure on Housing to Per Capita Real Household Expenditure Excluding Housing, 2021

(Before and After Quality Adjustments)

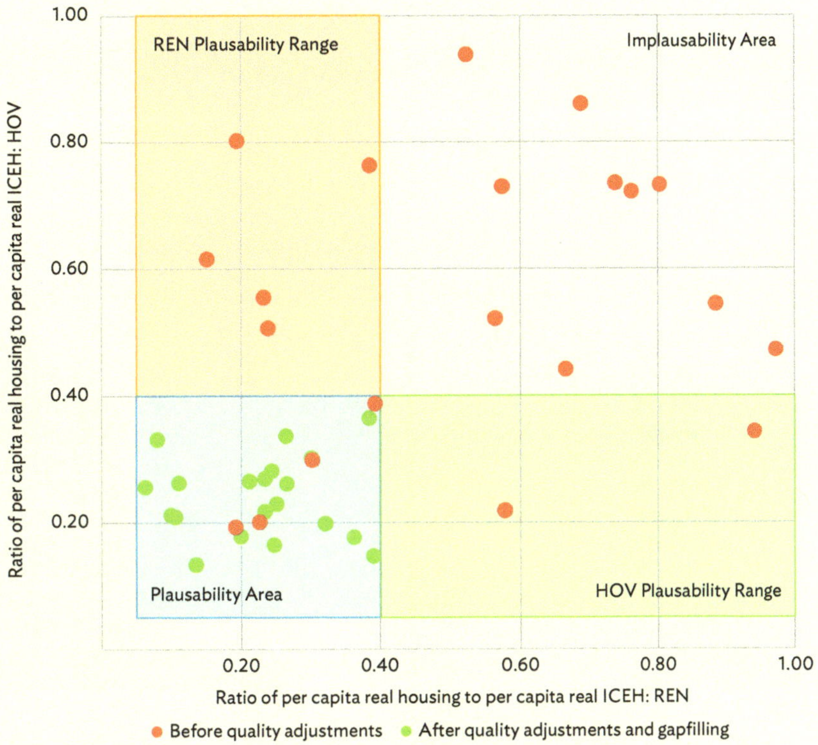

HOV = housing volume, ICEH = individual consumption expenditure by households, REN = housing rental.

Source: Asian Development Bank compilation and analysis.

Quantifying the Impact of Switching to the Hybrid Methodology

The impact of the hybrid methodology on PPPs for GDP and for individual consumption expenditure by households (ICEH) has been systematically quantified. Figure 6.6 shows the percentage change in PPPs for GDP and ICEH due to the shift from the reference volume approach to the hybrid methodology for the 2021 ICP cycle in Asia and the Pacific.

The differences shown in Figure 6.6 reflect the extent to which estimates based on the reference volume approach, which produces artificially derived PPPs under certain assumptions, diverge from those derived using the hybrid methodology, which incorporates real-world rental and quantity data reported by participating economies. The results indicate that, for most economies, the PPPs for both GDP and ICEH were revised downward under the new methodology, implying higher expenditures for housing using the hybrid methodology compared to the reference volume approach. Exceptions to this trend included Cambodia, Fiji, Indonesia, Mongolia, the Philippines, and Viet Nam, where upward revisions in the PPPs suggested corresponding decreases in real housing expenditures captured by the hybrid methodology.

The hybrid methodology is now recommended by the ICP Technical Advisory Group for testing in other ICP regions where significant differences exist in the quality of dwellings. This practical solution to one of the most persistent challenges in international price comparisons marks the culmination of 2 decades of sustained effort and methodological innovation by ADB and participating statistics offices across the Asia and Pacific region. It will strengthen and shape global ICP methodology for estimating housing PPPs in the future.

Figure 6.6: Impact on Purchasing Power Parities for Gross Domestic Product and Individual Consumption Expenditure by Households, 2021
(%)

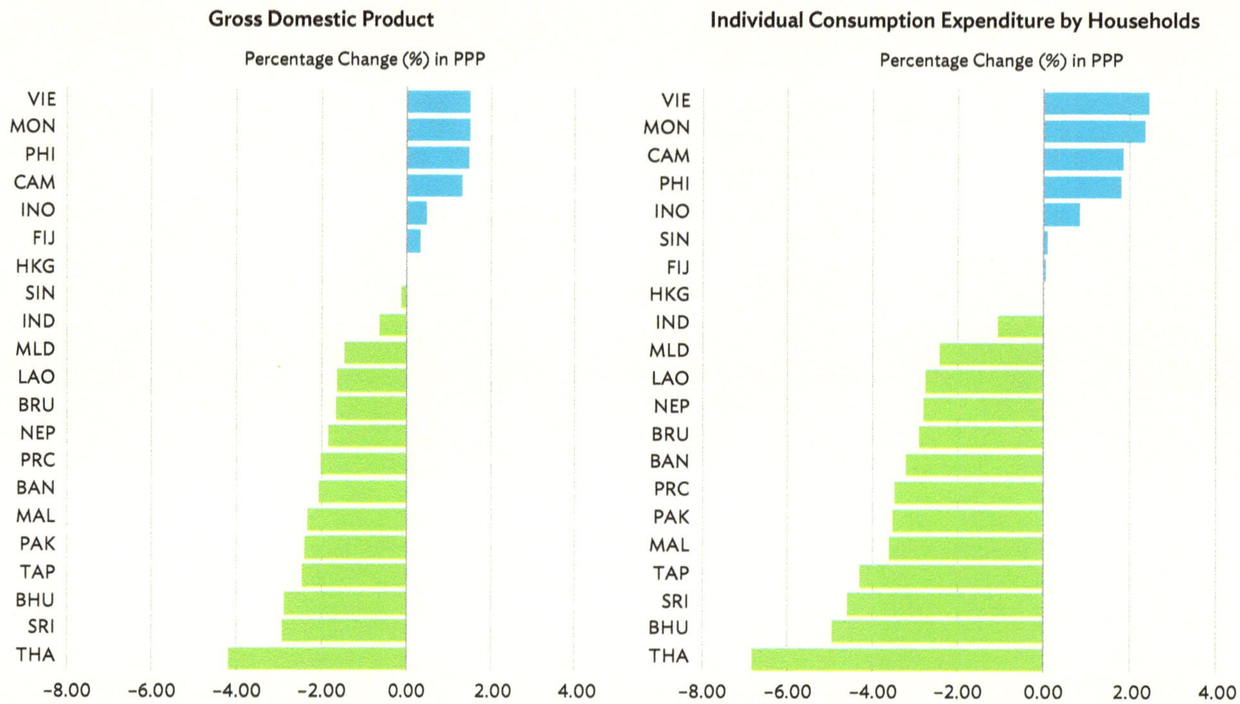

BAN = Bangladesh; BHU = Bhutan; BRU = Brunei Darussalam; CAM = Cambodia; FIJ = Fiji; HKG = Hong Kong, China; IND = India; INO = Indonesia; LAO = Lao People's Democratic Republic; MAL = Malaysia; MLD = Maldives; MON = Mongolia; NEP = Nepal; PAK = Pakistan; PHI = Philippines; PPP = purchasing power parity; PRC = People's Republic of China; SIN = Singapore; SRI = Sri Lanka; TAP = Taipei,China; THA = Thailand; VIE = Viet Nam.

Source: Asian Development Bank estimates.

Contribution to Poverty-Specific Purchasing Power Parities

Recognizing that the Asia and Pacific region was home to more than 50% of the world's poor, halving the incidence of extreme poverty (from the 1990 baseline) by 2015 was a critical ambition under the Millennium Development Goal agenda (2000–2015). ADB, with poverty reduction in the region as an overarching goal, conducted a special research project on poverty-specific PPPs by integrating the topic into the 2005 ICP cycle for Asia and the Pacific.

Key Issues for the Research Project

The motivation for the research project stemmed from critical concerns surrounding the methodology employed by the World Bank to determine international poverty lines. These global poverty thresholds such as the widely used extreme poverty line—earlier referred to as $1-a-day poverty line (currently set a $3.00 at 2021 PPPs)—are calibrated using PPPs for ICEH produced by the ICP. This approach involves converting national poverty lines, expressed in local currency units, into a common currency (typically United States dollars) using PPPs for household consumption derived from the ICP. While this method provides a uniform framework for measuring the incidence of extreme poverty, it raises some methodological concerns, which the ADB research study (ADB 2008) sought to answer.

Limitations of Household Consumption Purchasing Power Parities Used for Poverty Measurement

A central issue lies in the nature of price data used to compile household consumption PPPs within the ICP. The ICP price data are collected with the primary objective of facilitating international comparisons of household consumption expenditures for the entire economy. As such, the selection of items for price collection prioritizes both comparability across economies and representativeness of the national household consumption of individual economies. However, this design implies that the price data collected for the items as a part of the ICP reflects the consumption patterns of the general population rather than those of the poor. Consequently, the ICP prices may not accurately capture the cost of goods and services typically consumed by low-income households, thereby potentially introducing bias when such PPPs are applied to poverty analysis.

Incompatibility of Expenditure Weights with Consumption Patterns of the Poor

A second concern involves the expenditure weights used in aggregating item-level prices to derive consumption PPPs. In the ICP, these weights are sourced from household expenditures in the national accounts statistics and are intended to reflect the relative importance of different groups of goods and services in total household consumption. However, because they are based on average national expenditure patterns, they may significantly diverge from the actual consumption behaviors of poor households or communities. The use of more specific expenditure patterns of the poor as weights was recommended by the Poverty Advisory Group set up by the ICP Global Office at the World Bank during the time when the 2005 ICP cycle was in progress.

Scope of the Research Project

The research project on poverty-specific PPPs of ADB had two primary objectives:

(i) to implement the recommendation of the Poverty Advisory Group that expenditure patterns of the poor, as opposed to national accounts household expenditure weights, be used in the aggregation of ICP-collected price data for PPP calculations; and
(ii) to conduct separate surveys to collect price data of items representative of the consumption baskets of the poor, and assess use of such prices in calculating PPPs.

Project Participation

The study benefited from participation by 16 of the 21 ADB member economies engaged in the 2005 ICP cycle for Asia and the Pacific. Importantly, this group included Bangladesh, India, Indonesia, and Pakistan—four of the eight most populous economies globally—whose involvement lent weight to the study's findings. Upper-middle-income and high-income economies Brunei Darussalam; the People's Republic of China; Hong Kong, China; Singapore; and Taipei,China did not participate in the project.

Implementation of the Project

To help determine the target population for price survey purposes and to establish expenditure patterns for those considered poor, the ADB research project made use of an iterative scheme originally developed by Deaton (2004). Figure 6.7 outlines various steps involved in the project's implementation, with further detail provided in the ADB report on this project (ADB 2008).

Key Conclusions from the Research Project

The Poverty Advisory Group Methodology Yielded Distinct Results

The application of the Poverty Advisory Group methodology, which recommended the use of expenditure patterns of the poor as weights instead of national accounts weights, resulted in poverty-specific PPPs that differed from the standard consumption PPPs used in the

Figure 6.7: Key Steps to Implementing Research on Poverty-Specific Purchasing Power Parities

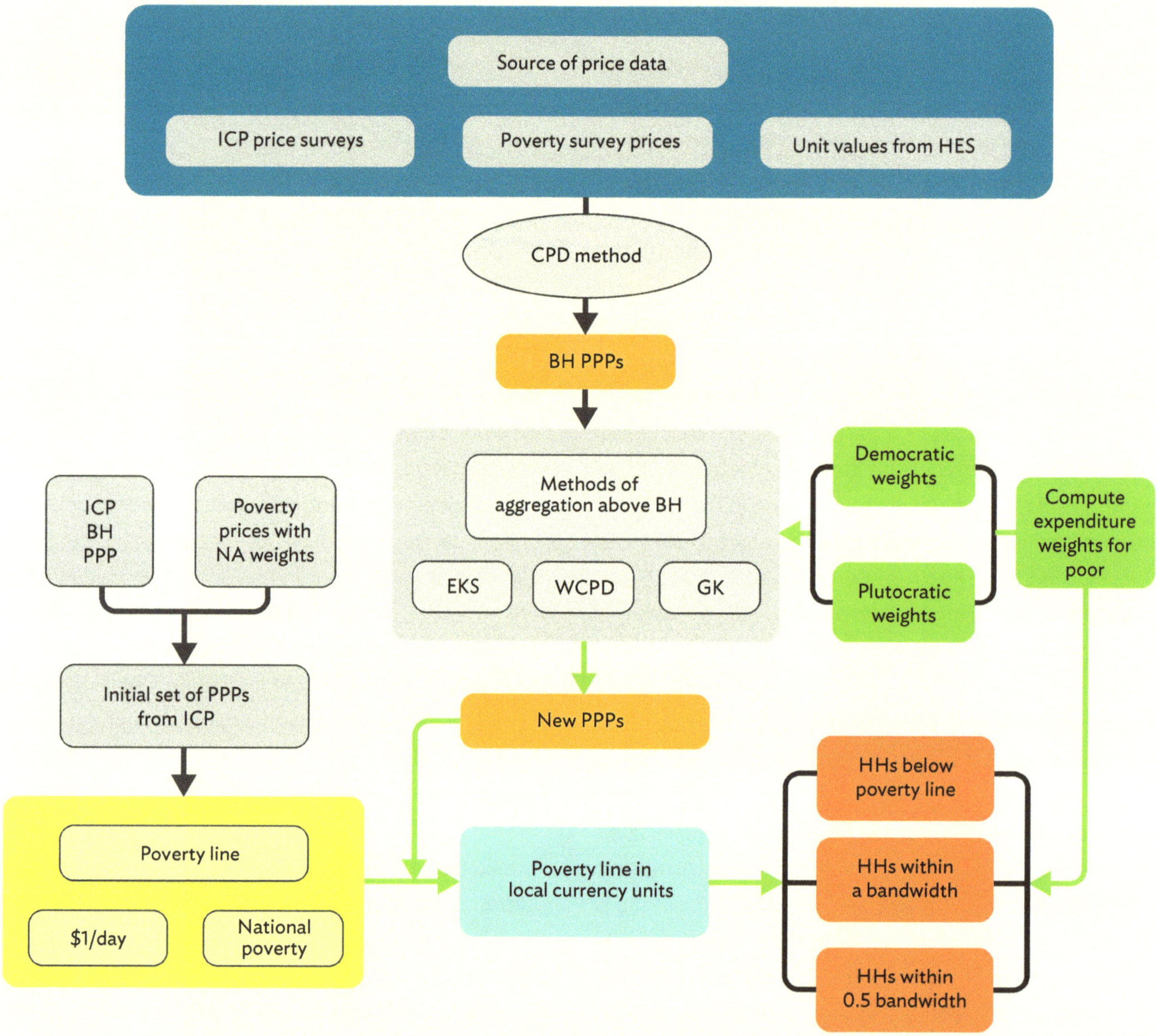

$ = United States dollars, BH = basic heading, CPD = country-product-dummy, EKS = Èltetö-Köves-Szulc, GK = Geary-Khamis, HES = household expenditure survey, HH = household, ICP = International Comparison Program, NA = national accounts, PPP = purchasing power parity, WCPD = weighted country-product-dummy.

Source: Asian Development Bank. 2008. *Research Study on Poverty-Specific Purchasing Power Parities for Selected Countries in Asia and the Pacific*. p. 58. https://www.adb.org/sites/default/files/publication/29130/poverty-specific-ppp.pdf.

2005 ICP cycle for Asia and the Pacific. This confirms the relevance of tailoring PPPs to reflect the expenditure patterns of the poor.

Poverty-Specific Price Data Have Greater Impact

The most significant outcome of the research project was that the introduction of price data collected specifically to reflect the consumption habits of the poor resulted in even more pronounced changes in poverty PPPs. Importantly, this can help deliver more accurate estimates of poverty incidence across economies. It suggests that identifying consumption items of relevance to the poor, and conducting targeted surveys to capture prices paid by the poor for those items, would yield PPPs more relevant to poverty measurement.

Price Data Drive Larger Revisions Than Methodology Alone

The magnitude of change in poverty PPPs was greater when poverty-specific price data were used than when only the Poverty Advisory Group methodology was applied with standard ICP data. This underscores that *what* prices are collected may matter more than *how* they are aggregated when estimating poverty with accuracy. This approach, however, requires additional resources to design and conduct price surveys specific to the items consumed by the poor from the markets and outlets popular to this group of population.

Although differences in economy coverage and timing of the survey in this research study make it difficult to directly compare PPPs resulting from this study with the PPPs from the 2005 ICP cycle, the conclusions highlight the importance of further methodological research into whether poverty estimates are grounded in price data that reflect the realities faced by poor households and communities.

Other studies on the topic include the one by Deaton and Dupriez (2011), based on 2005 ICP data for 62 poor economies around the world, and another by Dikhanov et al. (2017) for 28 African economies using 2011 ICP data. Both these studies concluded that use of poverty-specific weights, i.e., using the Poverty Advisory Group methodology, gave similar results to the PPPs generated by the ICP. Both studies, however, were based on prices collected in the ICP household surveys, rather than being based on specific prices paid by the poor. The ADB study, however, went a step further than these studies by collecting the prices for items consumed by the poor.

Contribution to Methods for Estimating Purchasing Power Parities for Non-Benchmark Years

ICP benchmark PPPs are available only once every few years (1993, 2005, 2011, 2017, and 2021, with the 2024 cycle currently in progress). This infrequency is largely due to the fact that the ICP is an extensive statistical exercise that poses a substantial burden on the financial and human resources of national statistics offices and regional implementing agencies. However, more frequent data and related PPPs are often needed, especially for policymaking in a rapidly changing world.

Between the benchmark years, PPPs for GDP and ICEH are estimated through extrapolation methods by the World Bank. However, large divergences have been observed between the extrapolated results and actual ICP benchmarks, so that more frequent and reliable PPPs are being demanded by users.

To meet this gap in PPPs for non-benchmark years, ADB explored an alternative approach—the "reduced information approach"—for compiling such PPPs. This approach was developed after the 2005 ICP cycle and at a time when the interval between ICP benchmarks was 6 years.

ADB first introduced the reduced information approach in its 2012 study *Purchasing Power Parity Update for Selected Economies in Asia and the Pacific* (ADB 2012a). The purpose of this study was to provide interim PPP estimates for the reference year 2009, i.e., between the 2005 and 2011 ICP cycles. A follow-up study was conducted after the 2011 ICP cycle, to provide interim PPPs for the reference year 2016. The results of this study were later detailed in the ADB publication *Constructing Purchasing Power Parities Using a Reduced Information Approach* (ADB 2021).

Box 6.2 summarizes the methodological steps in operationalizing the reduced information approach for the 2016 reference year and describes the PPP calculations under this approach.

Box 6.2: The Reduced Information Approach to Constructing Purchasing Power Parities for 2016

The objective of the reduced information approach was to explore methods of estimating purchasing power parities (PPPs) that are less burdensome for participating economies and can provide reliable PPPs for non-benchmark years, based on price surveys instead of extrapolations from the International Comparison Program (ICP) benchmark. The Asian Development Bank (ADB) developed the "reduced information" or "core list" approach. The key steps used in this approach for 2016 estimates are outlined below.

1. **Core Product List Developed:**
   - (i) From the benchmark 2011 ICP product list for household consumption price surveys, a subset of products was identified as the "core list" of household consumption products. The core list of products was prepared for each basic heading for price surveys in 2016.
   - (ii) The selected products in the core list minimized the root mean square error for the PPPs calculated based on the core list versus PPPs calculated in the benchmark cycle based on the full list.
   - (iii) The core list of 2016 comprised a minimum of one-third of the items in the 2011 ICP full list for each basic heading. Overall, the core list for the 2016 study (ADB 2021) was about two-fifth of the full 2011 product list.
2. **Survey Coverage Established:**
   - (i) Price data for the core list were collected in 2016 only in capital cities, unlike national level surveys in the ICP benchmark.
   - (ii) The frequency of collecting prices for household items was minimized to once every quarter for four quarters to cover the 12-month period. However, some economies collected prices monthly, especially for food items.
   - (iii) The average prices from the capital city were extrapolated to the national average price using the adjustment factor to generate "derived national average prices" that were calculated as the ratio of capital city average prices to national average prices from the 2011 ICP benchmark. This assumes that the ratio of capital city average prices to national average prices for the items remains unchanged.
3. **Basic Heading Purchasing Power Parities Generated:**
   - (i) Basic-heading-level PPPs for core list products were generated using the "derived national average prices" (from step 2 above) for 2016.
   - (ii) PPPs for each basic heading from the core list were then adjusted to the full list using PPP adjustment factors generated from the ratio of basic heading PPPs for the core list and the full list from the 2011 ICP as shown below for basic heading "Rice" as an illustration. This assumes that the ratio of PPPs derived from the core list to the PPPs derived from the full list in 2011 remains constant over time. PPPs for the core list or the full list are calculated using the "country-product-dummy" method.

$$ADJ_j^{Rice,2011} = \frac{PPP_j^{Rice,Core,2011}}{PPP_j^{Rice,Full,2011}} \text{ for } j = 1,2,\ldots,20 \text{ and } ADJ_{HKG}^{Rice,2011} = 1$$

   - (iii) The derived PPP for a basic heading (e.g., Rice) would be represented as below. The adjustment factor for rice for the core list and the full list in the formula below are derived from the 2011 ICP results:

$$PPP_j^{Rice,Full,2016} = \frac{PPP_j^{Rice,Core,2016}}{ADJ_j^{Rice,2011}}$$

   - (iv) These basic heading PPPs adjusted from the core list to the full list were then used to calculate higher-level PPPs for all categories and individual consumption expenditure by households using standard ICP aggregation methods. The PPPs at any level of aggregation above the basic heading level are then estimated using the standard Gini-Éltető-Köves-Szulc method.

Reference: Asian Development Bank (ADB). 2021. *Constructing Purchasing Power Parities Using a Reduced Information Approach.* https://www.adb.org/sites/default/files/publication/674276/purchasing-power-parities-reduced-information-approach.pdf.

Source: Asian Development Bank compilation and analysis.

Through the "core list" methodology described in Box 6.2, ADB explored a method that could potentially produce PPPs for an interim year between the benchmark years of ICP cycles. With the decision of the United Nations Statistical Commission in 2016 to implement the ICP every 3 years, the limitations in the availability of more frequent PPPs over time have been substantially resolved.

However, despite moving to an ICP cycle every 3 years, there are demands from the users to move to production of annual PPPs globally because the ICP results from each benchmark currently become available with a 3-year lag. The results of the 2021 ICP cycle, for example, were available only by May 2024, and the 2024 ICP results are likely to become available only by early 2027. The rolling survey approach used in PPP comparisons by Eurostat and the Organisation for Economic Co-operation and Development offers a way forward to producing annual PPPs, but this would require suitable adaptations for a diverse region such as Asia and the Pacific. The reduced information approach, with suitable modifications, can be one of the alternative approaches that can be considered by the region while examining alternative ways of generating annual PPPs.

Innovative Measures to Address Other Technical and Operational Challenges

As the regional implementing agency for Asia and the Pacific, ADB has pioneered and developed solutions tailored to address specific ICP issues experienced in the region. The bank has taken a structured and considered approach to such solutions, forming expert groups to review technical issues and develop region-specific recommendations. These innovations have helped deliver a high-quality dataset of average annual prices for calculating PPPs.

Achieving Representativity and Comparability in Price Surveys

Achieving comparability and representativity in price surveys is crucial to ICP objectives. Comparability ensures that products priced by economies have the same quality and specifications, while representativity means that product lists for price surveys are comprehensive and representative of GDP expenditures in participating economies.

ADB and statistics offices across Asia and the Pacific have taken important measures to balance comparability and representativity in price surveys through regional cooperation and expert consultations on ICP protocols.

As an example of innovation in this area, ADB developed an online interactive tool for the 2024 ICP cycle to review the household product list. The tool enabled easy submission and consideration of suggestions from implementing agencies of the participating economies on product specifications, new items, and deletion of obsolete products. These suggestions were then discussed in subsequent regional workshops to finalize the draft household product list.

A more detailed account of ADB measures to achieve representativity and comparability in price surveys is provided in Appendix 2 of this report.

Achieving Price Comparability via Additional Data Validation Tools

The participating economies of Asia and the Pacific vary greatly in statistical capacity and resources required for ICP price collection and validation. Consequently, significant resources are invested in data validation and quality assurance at the regional level by ADB.

Using Visual Charts For Price Validation Discussions

During price data validation, large variations are observed in average prices reported by economies. Standard methods and tools such as Quaranta tables and Dikhanov tables, developed by the ICP Global Office, are used by the regional implementing agencies for intereconomy price validation and to identify outliers for further clarification from implementing agencies.

ADB has developed additional data validation tools to supplement the ICP's standard solutions. Used in regional validation workshops, these supplementary tools include charts that visualize item prices across all economies, and comparing current cycle prices with previous ICP cycle prices, as shown in Figure 6.8. These charts make it simpler to compare prices across economies as well as over two ICP cycles (for items common across the two cycles). The charts offer invaluable insights when assessed in conjunction with Dikhanov tables, which highlight outlier prices (based on residuals from "country-product-dummy" regressions) and provide intereconomy comparisons for the current ICP cycle (Figure 6.9). Together, these tools deliver powerful visual evidence for assessing price quality over time and across economies, identifying potential errors, and taking appropriate actions. Through their visual appeal, these tools greatly facilitate intereconomy data validation discussions among the representatives of all participating economies in regional data validation workshops organized by ADB with the objective of identifying outlier prices and ensuring high data quality.

Comparing Price Movements to Validate Household Price Data

Price data validation for household surveys in the ICP includes nearly 1,000 items in the regional list, spread across 91 basic headings for food and nonfood items and services consumed by households. Standard tools such as Quaranta tables, Dikhanov tables, and exchange-rate-based visual price graphs are integral to identifying price outliers within and across economies.

Figure 6.8: Visual Chart Comparing Prices for Two Cycles of the International Comparison Program

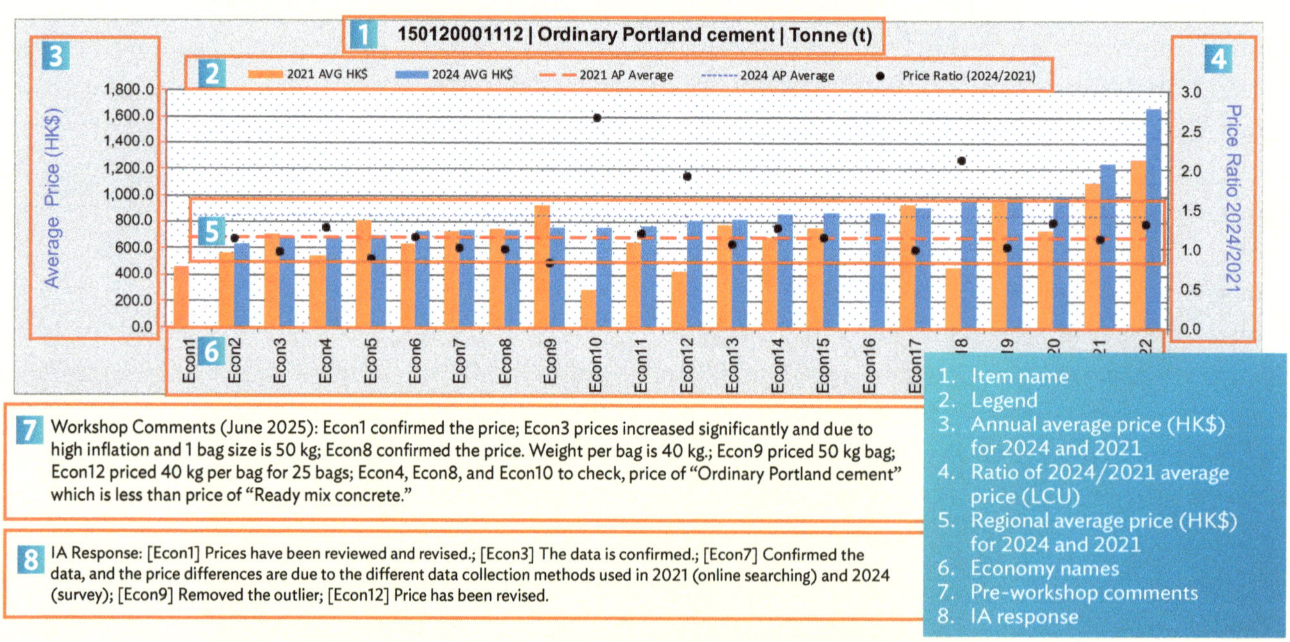

AP = Asia and the Pacific Product, AVG = average, Econ = economy, HK$ = Hong Kong dollar, kg = kilogram, IA = implementing agency, LCU =local currency unit.

Source: Asian Development Bank compilation and analysis.

Figure 6.9: Dikhanov Table with Country-Product-Dummy Residuals for Identifying Outlier Prices

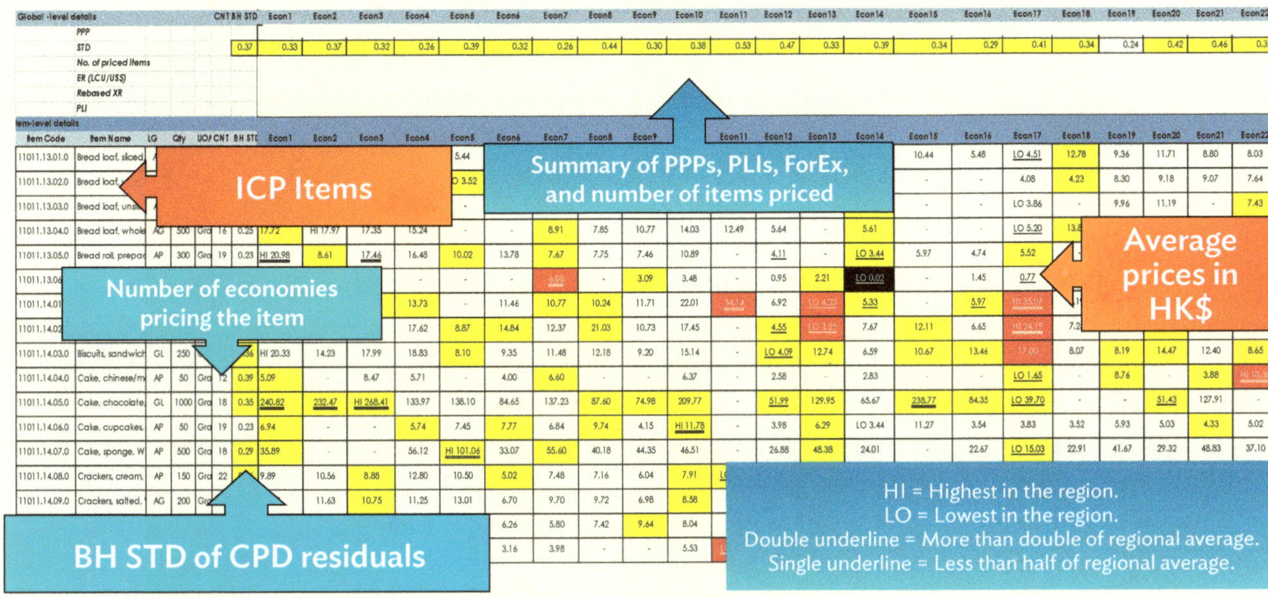

BH = basic heading, CPD = country-product-dummy, Econ = economy, ForEx = foreign exchange rates, HK$ = Hong Kong dollar, ICP = International Comparison Program, PLI = price level index, PPP = purchasing power parity, STD = standard deviation.

Source: Asian Development Bank compilation and analysis.

During the 2017 ICP cycle for Asia and the Pacific, ADB supplemented these tools with an additional validation method based on temporal price movements between the 2011 and 2017 ICP cycles and corresponding movements in the consumer price index (CPI) in participating economies. This approach relied on the fact that many household items had identical specifications in both ICP cycles, allowing for temporal price changes to be measured solely based on ICP prices, which enabled individual economy validation without reference to other economies.

ADB calculated ICP price changes from 2011 to 2017 for each basic heading, then compared these against CPI inflation for the same period. Given that both datasets reflect macroeconomic conditions, the expectation was that price movements would align reasonably well in both their direction and magnitude. Any systematic and/or significant differences between ICP-based and CPI-based inflation were flagged for further investigation by the implementing agencies for potential errors, such as misclassification of items, inconsistent quality, or data entry errors.

ADB has also strengthened its in-house quality assurance procedures in other ICP surveys. The validation methods are used in bilateral consultations between ADB and the implementing agencies in participating economies and in the technical reviews of data quality by the Expert Group constituted by ADB. These measures have helped validate and enhance the quality of price datasets and continue to complement existing validation tools. They reflect ADB's commitment to its role in advancing the global ICP agenda through technically grounded, regionally responsive innovations that ensure high-quality and comparable data for the calculation of regional PPPs and PPP-based macroeconomic measures.

CHAPTER 7

Initiatives to Enhance Statistical Capacity in Asia and the Pacific

The purchasing power parities (PPPs) compiled under the International Comparison Program (ICP) are based on two critical data streams to be provided by every participating economy: (i) prices of goods and services collected via surveys using specified lists for items of household consumption, housing rentals, government compensation, construction, and machinery and equipment; and (ii) gross domestic product (GDP) from the expenditure side, classified into 155 item groups known as "basic headings." With the United Nations System of National Accounts (SNA) as the underlying framework, the ICP also uses internationally established economic classifications to generate PPPs.

As the regional implementing agency for the ICP in Asia and the Pacific, the Asian Development Bank (ADB) has placed strong emphasis on building statistical capacity in participating economies. This capacity building remains a core objective alongside the technical implementation of the program. In the process of improving data quality and enhancing capabilities for statistical analysis in individual economies, ADB has played an important role in improving price statistics, harmonizing classifications, implementing the SNA, and institutionalizing the ICP and PPP compilation in the region.

At the end of each ICP cycle in the Asia and Pacific region, it has been a practice to document experiences of the national statistics offices in implementing the program. This assessment includes organization of survey operations, operational and technical challenges and lessons learnt, and capacity building gains from participation in ICP activities. While these economy experience reports for earlier ICP cycles are included as part of the Asia and Pacific ICP reports, for the 2021 ICP cycle, these reports prepared by the implementing agencies in participating economies are published online at https://icp.adb.org/economy. This chapter presents excerpts from the individual economy reports to demonstrate the capacity building aspects of regional ICP initiatives and how they have been beneficial to the participating economies.

Collaborative Learning and Training Approaches

Since its first involvement in the ICP for the program's 2005 cycle, ADB has prioritized strengthening the ability of economies in Asia and the Pacific to generate internationally comparable data on prices and real expenditures. Central to this effort has been the organization of regular regional training and data validation workshops, bringing together statisticians and experts in price data and national accounts from across the region. These workshops have provided intensive technical training, peer exchange, and a collaborative problem-solving and learning environment, supported by bilateral consultations and expert missions (Figure 7.1).

Through hands-on learning and direct interaction with ADB specialists, statistics offices in participating economies have been able to improve their capabilities in price statistics, national accounts, and methodologies underpinning international comparisons. A common technical framework and strong focus on data quality have guided collaboration and helped address technical challenges. Regional workshops on multiple topics of ICP processes have provided a platform to share knowledge and experiences, overcoming limited opportunities within

Figure 7.1: Workshops and Training to Build Statistical Capacity in Asia and the Pacific

ICP = International Comparison Program.

Source: Asian Development Bank compilation.

individual economies. These workshops have enhanced understanding of common issues in price collection and national accounts, fostered collaborative networks, and enabled economies to learn from each another.

ADB has consistently committed substantial financial and institutional resources to ensure workshops and training sessions are comprehensive, responsive, and aligned with the evolving needs of economies in the Asia and Pacific region. To illustrate this point, in the 2017 ICP cycle, the capacity building program included 20 face-to-face events—regional workshops, technical missions, and expert consultations—covering 74 working days. However, with the 2021 ICP cycle affected by the coronavirus disease (COVID-19) pandemic, preventing international travel and in-person workshops, ADB successfully shifted to a "virtual" mode for delivering regional workshops and training. From December 2020 to December 2022, 19 online training and data validation workshops were organized with participants from 21 economies in Asia and the Pacific. These virtual workshops often attracted over 100 attendees. Additional bilateral and small-group workshops were also held virtually to address economy-specific needs.

Although online sessions could not fully replicate the benefits of in-person engagement, they expanded participation within economies and maintained the continuity of the capacity building program. Face-to-face workshops resumed in November 2022 and are continuing under the 2024 ICP cycle.[1]

1 Details of ADB's workshop and training events for the ICP are available at https://icp.adb.org/events.

As a result of ADB's involvement across multiple ICP cycles, collaborative learning has become central to statistical capacity building across Asia and the Pacific, highlighting the importance of cooperation among individual economies and ADB as the regional implementing agency.

Selected excerpts from economy experiences during the 2021 ICP cycle are presented in Box 7.1:

Box 7.1: Collaborative Statistical Learning Activities: What Economies Say

Brunei Darussalam, Department of Statistics
"The knowledge and experience gained from the ICP improved the price collection activities in DOS. Furthermore, the project facilitated networking with regional counterparts, fostering communication on related issues."

Fiji, Bureau of Statistics
"The virtual workshops addressed issues, such as price variation and clarification of SPDs. Additionally, staff learned methodologies for compiling PPPs and its importance to the economy."

Hong Kong, China, Census and Statistics Department
"Participation in the ICP was a valuable experience as it provided a platform for statisticians to exchange experiences and views on price statistics, thereby increasing understanding of pricing surveys in other economies."

Nepal, National Statistics Office
"Experiences shared by economies during regional workshops played a crucial role in resolving challenges related to price data. Virtual and physical validation workshops facilitated by ADB were instrumental in identifying specific issues, particularly those concerning household consumption, machinery and equipment, construction, and rapidly evolving electronic items."

Singapore, Department of Statistics
"Participation in the ICP rounds helped enhance officers' understanding of PPP methodology and estimates. Various regional workshops were useful in raising awareness and understanding of issues and challenges encountered by different statistical offices of the participating economies in price collection and national accounts compilation."

Viet Nam, National Statistics Office
"ICP workshops provided a valuable platform for participating economies to share experiences, which improved the quality of price data. Meetings with international experts in different fields—such as machinery and equipment, construction, and housing—helped the GSO ICP team understand product specifications and price collection methods."

ADB = Asian Development Bank, CPI = consumer price index, DOS = Department of Statistics, GSO = General Statistics Office (now renamed as National Statistics Office), ICP = International Comparison Program, NSB = National Statistics Bureau, PPP = purchasing power parity, SPD = structured product description.

Source: The excerpts in this box are taken from reports on economy experiences in the ICP's 2021 cycle across Asia and the Pacific. The full economy experience reports are available at https://icp.adb.org/economy.

Integration of Price Data Across Statistical Programs

Scope and Benefits of Price Data Integration

The integration of household item price collection surveys for both consumer price index (CPI) and ICP activities has emerged as a valuable strategy for strengthening national price statistics and synergy between the two programs.

The CPI and ICP serve distinct purposes: the CPI tracks temporal changes in domestic prices and serves as a macroeconomic indicator for monitoring inflation in an economy, while the ICP focuses on spatial price comparisons between economies. Although the two rely on a similar data collection framework, their item baskets are not the same and the geographical coverage of their surveys may also differ. However, despite the differences in their primary objectives and some protocols, coordinated implementation of CPI and ICP activities can enhance the efficiency of data collection, improve the consistency and quality of data, and reduce the work burden and survey costs for national implementing agencies.

Economies are encouraged to identify items from the CPI that have matching specifications with ICP items, so that the price data collected can be used for both. A key area of divergence between the CPI and the ICP has been in the specification of goods and services: CPI items generally do not have detailed specifications, while ICP items have structured product descriptions (SPDs) as a standardized approach to describing items in detail. By providing clear identification and differentiation, applying SPDs to CPI items can improve the precision and comparability of price observations, especially for items with evolving quality or multiple varieties. Learning from the experience gained through participation in ICP, many economies are already incorporating SPDs into their CPI items while many other economies have been gradually integrating the ICP items deemed important for household consumption into their CPI item lists. This enhances not only domestic inflation estimates but also the quality of PPP calculations for ICP.

Integrated data collection also offers important resource efficiencies. In many developing economies with limited statistical capacity, aligning CPI and ICP price collection activities reduces duplication of fieldwork, training, and infrastructure. This makes better use of scarce resources while building institutional knowledge across both statistical programs.

Key Messages from Economy Surveys

As part of the 2017 and 2021 ICP cycles, two key surveys were conducted with statistical agencies in participating economies. The CPI-ICP Survey Questionnaire was initially prepared by the ICP Global Office at the World Bank and administered to the implementing agencies of the participating economies for the 2017 ICP cycle. ADB collected additional and updated CPI-ICP information for the 2021 cycle. The Household Consumption Survey Framework Questionnaire is part of the metadata requirements for each ICP cycle and filled by each participating economy. The information collected includes, but is not limited to, spatial coverage, outlets selected, items priced, data collection periods, and CPI-ICP item overlaps.

For the 2021 ICP cycle, 21 economies from across Asia and the Pacific responded to each of the two survey questionnaires from ADB. The information collected in the two questionnaires relates only to the household item price surveys. A summary of CPI-ICP integration in these economies is provided in Table 7.1, with some key outcomes detailed below.

Geographical Coverage of Price Surveys

Most (16) of the responding economies from the region conducted ICP price surveys nationally, covering both rural and urban areas. This rural and urban coverage aligns with ICP objectives to reflect national average prices. It contrasts with CPI surveys, which often focus on urban centers due to higher spending and market access.

Table 7.1: Price Data Integration in Surveyed Economies of Asia and the Pacific, 2021

	Yes	No	Some	Overlap products	Total
1. Price collection Infrastructure and Operations					
• CPI and ICP implementation by same organization	20	1			21
• Price collection staff for ICP is subset of the CPI price collection staff	13	2	6		21
• ICP survey collects prices from CPI outlets	19	2			21
• ICP price survey also incorporated price data from CPI survey	16	5			21
• Product catalogue available to assist field workers	21	0			21
• ICP and CPI price collection carried out at the same time	6	7		8	21
2. Data processing					
• ICP data captured in the same computer system as the CPI data	8	11		2	21
• Use the same editing/control procedures to ensure quality on CPI and ICP data	13	4		4	21
• ICP validation procedures help improve your processing of CPI data.	17	4			21
3. General					
• Any organizational plans to improve the integration of CPI and ICP price surveys and processes in the near future	17	4			21

CPI = Consumer Price Index, ICP = International Comparison Program.

Notes: The table above is derived from responses by 21 economies to the CPI-ICP Survey Questionnaire and the Household Consumption Survey Framework Questionnaire for the 2021 ICP cycle in Asia and the Pacific. The data in this table refers only to the household price surveys for 2021 ICP.

Sources: Asian Development Bank. CPI-ICP Survey Questionnaire for the 2021 ICP Cycle; and Household Consumption Survey Framework Questionnaire for the 2021 ICP Cycle.

Institutional Arrangements

In 20 of the 21 responding economies, the statistics offices of the participating economies implemented both the CPI and the ICP programs. This institutional alignment helped facilitate staff sharing, coordination, and operational efficiencies between the two programs. The arrangement differed only in Nepal, where the ICP is handled by the national statistics office and the CPI is under the responsibility of the Nepal Rashtra Bank.

Use of Staff in Price Surveys

ICP price data collection was conducted fully by CPI staff in 13 economies and partly by CPI staff in six economies. These staff were experienced in field operations for price surveys and could easily be trained to apply SPDs for ICP price collection. In two economies, however, the CPI and ICP price collection were undertaken by different sets of enumerators. While in one case, this was due to different organizations responsible for the two surveys, which led to different set of enumerators engaged for the ICP survey.

Use of Common Price Outlets and Products

For ICP data collection, 19 economies used CPI price outlets when appropriate. When the CPI item matched ICP specifications, 16 economies used CPI item prices for the ICP too. Use of CPI item prices for the ICP in 16 economies ranged from less than 20% of ICP items in some economies to over 40% in others, while in two economies this overlap through sustained efforts from previous ICP cycles has exceeded 60%.

Challenges in Item Mapping

Mapping CPI items to SPDs was difficult due to less-detailed or loose CPI product descriptions. Food items tended to be more compatible while nonfood items showed greater variation in specifications between the two programs.

Support Tools and Language Adaptation

All 21 economies used ADB-provided product catalogues with SPDs and reference images. The ADB provided catalogues, developed in English, are translated by implementing agencies into local language for price collectors' use.

Price Collection Timing

In terms of conducting ICP and CPI price collection at the same time, six economies did so fully, eight did so partially, and the remaining seven chose to keep the two operations completely separate. Timing choices depended on staffing availability and the frequency of CPI price updates.

Data Processing and Quality Control

Eight economies used the same computer system for processing both CPI and ICP data; 13 economies used the same editing and validation procedures for both datasets; 17 economies reported that ICP validation procedures improved CPI data validation processes.

Future Integration Plans

When asked about further aligning CPI and ICP activities, 17 economies expressed plans to further align these activities during the next CPI base-year revision. This includes enhancing CPI product descriptions and incorporating representative ICP items where appropriate for CPI purposes.

The survey findings outlined in this subsection are supported by statements from participating economies, as documented in the economy experience reports compiled and published at the end of the 2021 ICP cycle.[2] Box 7.2 offers selected observations on CPI-ICP integration from a few economies in the Asia and Pacific region.

Box 7.2: Integration of Price Data Across Statistical Programs: What Economies Say

Bhutan, National Statistics Bureau
"The NSB ICP team will incorporate ICP data validation checks into CPI surveys to improve data processing and validation and enhance data quality."

Indonesia, Badan Pusat Statistik
"Learning from ICP experiences, the CPI now uses standard units and volumes in its enumeration process."

Maldives, Maldives Bureau of Statistics
"The MBS ICP team gained useful knowledge regarding the importance of product specifications and effective data validation, which will further improve price statistics. Drawing from the ICP, a similarly structured product description is now used in the CPI."

Mongolia, National Statistics Office
"Significant efforts were made to improve the CPI surveys by incorporating the structured product descriptions from the ICP. The NSOM ICP team used the ICP basket to define the CPI basket for the 2022 rebase. The NSOM ICP team plans to further integrate the CPI and the ICP by using CPI prices for the same ICP items in the next cycle."

The People's Republic of China, National Bureau of Statistics of China
"Participation in the 2021 ICP and its implementation contributed to enhanced knowledge and statistical capability, which will significantly help other routine statistical activities."

Sri Lanka, Department of Census and Statistics
"The ICP's structured product descriptions, data validation procedures, and data processing methods were applied to CPI surveys to improve the CPI product list and data validations."

Taipei,China, Directorate-General of Budget, Accounting and Statistics
"Since the 2011 ICP, the integration of the CPI and ICP has been the DGBAS ICP team's direction for improvements because of limited staffing and resources. Drawing on experiences from the 2011 and 2017 ICP cycles, a relatively high CPI–ICP harmonization rate of 71% was achieved in Asia and the Pacific. High integration means that for most items, prices for the ICP can be reported without devoting additional effort and time from the routine CPI program."

CPI = consumer price index; DGBAS = Directorate-General of Budget, Accounting and Statistics; ICP = International Comparison Program; MBS = Maldives Bureau of Statistics; NSB = National Statistics Bureau; NSOM = National Statistics Office of Mongolia; PPP = purchasing power parity.

Source: The excerpts in this box are taken from reports on economy experiences in the ICP's 2021 cycle across Asia and the Pacific. The full economy experience reports are available at https://icp.adb.org/economy.

2 The full economy experience reports for the 2021 ICP cycle are available at https://icp.adb.org/economy.

A Case Study of Price Data Integration: Department of Statistics, Singapore

Statistical management in Singapore provides a compelling example of the synergies that can be achieved by integrating CPI and ICP activities at different stages; from product list development to the collection and processing of data. This integration was started with the 2017 ICP cycle by the Singapore's Department of Statistics. Figure 7.2 summarizes the status of CPI-ICP integration in Singapore's statistical system with reference to the integration of CPI and ICP surveys achieved for the 2021 ICP household consumption survey which had 990 items in the regional product list.

As illustrated in Figure 7.2, a substantial portion (more than half) of ICP item prices are directly sourced from CPI price surveys, with the remainder supplemented through targeted surveys where necessary. Notably, Singapore's national statistics office has institutionalized this integration by embedding ICP functionalities within the CPI system, including modules for data loading, item selection, and ICP-specific reporting. Even more significantly, Singapore has, where appropriate, reviewed and added items from the ICP 2024 product list into its latest 2024 CPI basket. This forward-looking approach demonstrates the operational and methodological benefits of aligning the two statistical programs and offers a model for leveraging synergies to improve efficiency, coverage, and consistency in price data collection.

Figure 7.2: Processes for Price Data Integration in Singapore's Statistical System

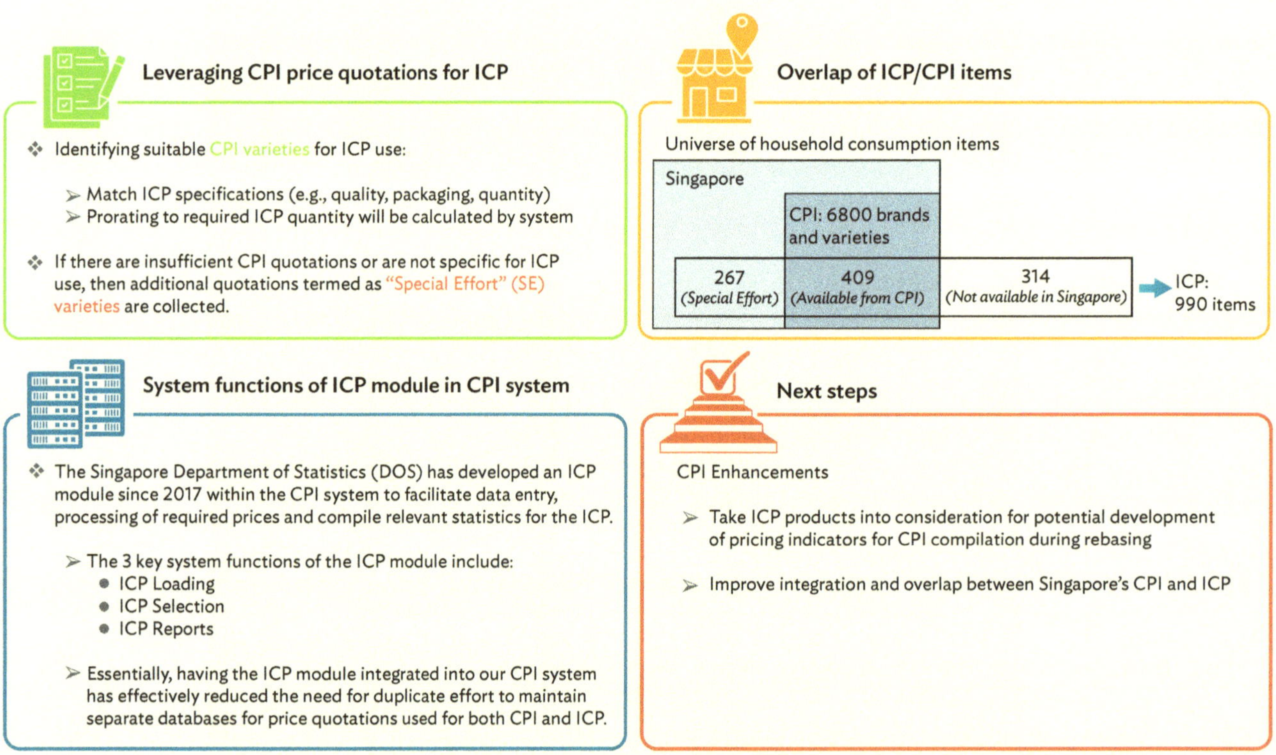

CPI = consumer price index, ICP = International Comparison Program.

Source: Singapore Department of Statistics. 2023. *Singapore's Integration of International Comparison Project (ICP) with Consumer Price Index (CPI)*. Presentation prepared for the ICP 2021 Workshop organized by the Asian Development Bank. 20–24 November.

Further Benefits of Advancing Price Data Integration

There is clear evidence that participating economies are increasingly recognizing the complementarities between CPI and ICP activities. Efforts to leverage synergies between the two programs are contributing to the development of more robust and reliable price measures at both the national and international levels.

The regularity of CPI surveys can support more frequent PPP updates, thereby increasing the relevance of PPPs for national and international policy use. More timely data allow for better monitoring of core development issues such as growth, inequality, and global poverty.

CPI-ICP integration also allows for the compilation of subnational PPPs by utilizing spatial price variations observed through CPI surveys. These subnational comparisons can provide valuable input for policy targeting and planning at provincial or district levels, particularly in large or economically diverse economies.

Technical Assistance to Improve Expenditure Estimates in National Accounts Statistics

The ICP provides internationally comparable measures of economic activity within the framework of the System of National Accounts (SNA). For ICP purposes, GDP is measured using the expenditure approach, which enables practical collection of price and expenditure data. GDP expenditures, stated in local currency and disaggregated into 155 "basic headings" by each economy, are an essential requirement for PPP estimation under the ICP.

It should be noted here that GDP estimates from the production side are generally more reliable for most economies and serve as the control GDP, while estimates from the expenditure side (as required for the ICP) are often weaker due to data source limitations, requiring the reporting of statistical discrepancies on the expenditure side to reconcile the two.

When ADB became the regional implementing agency for the 2005 ICP cycle in Asia and the Pacific, the bank observed weaknesses and data gaps in the national accounts of many economies, along with an inability to produce reliable GDP expenditure estimates.

Lessons learned from the 2005 ICP cycle shaped ADB's future capacity building initiatives and significantly influenced two phases of regional technical assistance by the bank. These two phases focused on **supply and use tables (SUTs)**, which provide a structured framework for estimating GDP consistently from both the production and expenditure sides to improve the overall consistency and accuracy of estimates. The ability to construct and apply SUTs is one of the steps required for an economy to comply with the SNA.

The two ADB regional technical assistance projects also supported economies of Asia and the Pacific in achieving the Minimum Requirement Data Set, as identified by the United Nations Statistics Division. This set—which includes key aggregates such as GDP by production and expenditure, value added by industry, final consumption by sector, and gross capital formation—is an important step toward full SNA compliance.

ADB's initiatives on SUTs not only provided participating economies with the capacity to produce one of the most technically demanding components of the SNA but also supported a strategic and phased approach toward SNA compliance and consistency in the production and expenditure sides of GDP estimates. By supporting economies in meeting the Minimum Requirement Data Set and establishing a sustainable framework for national accounts compilation, these technical assistance projects laid the groundwork for long-term improvements in macroeconomic statistics, enhanced evidence-based policy formulation, and promoted more effective participation in global statistical initiatives such as the ICP.

Regional Technical Assistance Phase 1, 2008–2012

From 2008 to 2012, ADB implemented Regional Technical Assistance 6483 to assist economies in adopting SUTs to achieve minimum compliance with the 1993 SNA.[3] This initiative supported 18 developing economies—Bangladesh; Bhutan; Brunei Darussalam; Cambodia; the People's Republic of China; Fiji; Hong Kong, China; India; Indonesia; Malaysia; Maldives; Mongolia; Nepal; Singapore; Sri Lanka; Taipei,China; Thailand; and Viet Nam—in compiling their first benchmark SUTs.

The project provided comprehensive technical assistance, including regional training workshops conducted in a phased manner (Figure 7.3), missions within each economy, and tailored training programs.

Figure 7.3: ADB Technical Assistance Workshops on Compiling Supply and Use Tables

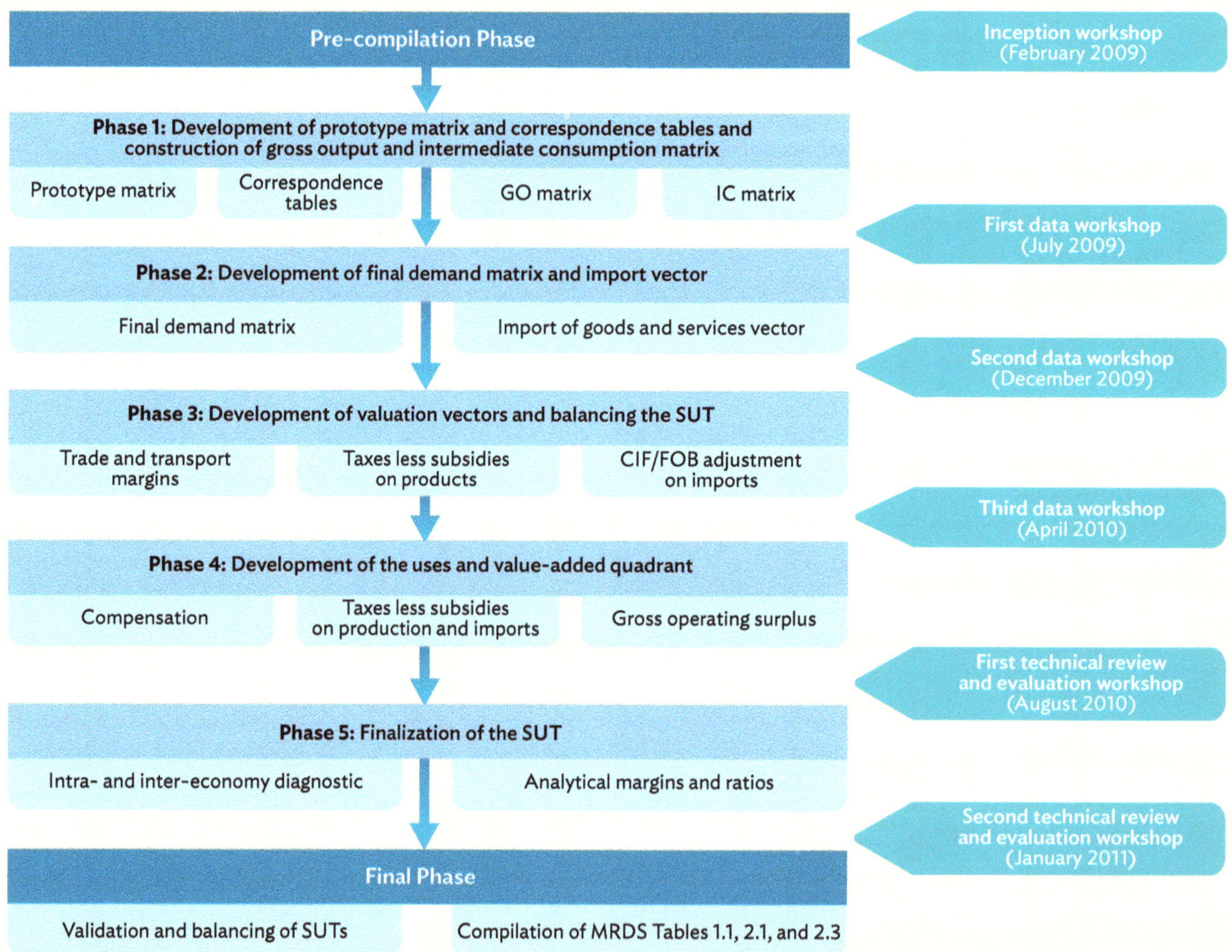

CIF = cost, insurance, and freight; FOB = free on board; GO = gross output; IC = intermediate consumption; MRDS = Minimum Requirement Data Set; SUT = supply and use table.

Source: Asian Development Bank. 2012b. *Supply and Use Tables for Selected Economies in Asia and the Pacific*. Figure 1, p. 15. https://www.adb.org/sites/default/files/publication/30121/supply-and-use-tables-research-study.pdf.

3 Full details of Regional Technical Assistance 6483 are available at https://www.adb.org/projects/42063-012/main.

The phased approach used in the SUT compilation was effective, combining learning with practical application. This strategy allowed for a better understanding of specific issues at each phase, enabling timely and appropriate solutions tailored to the topics addressed. The outcomes are documented in the 2012 ADB publication, *Supply and Use Tables for Selected Economies in Asia and the Pacific*, which presents the compiled SUTs and analyses of the economic structure in each participating economy (ADB 2012b).

For most participating economies, this was their first attempt to construct SUTs and the most significant achievement of ADB's technical assistance was building this statistical capacity simultaneously in the 18 economies. Regional workshops also became platforms for learning from the experiences of other economies, sharing knowledge, and establishing collaborative networks among statisticians and accountants. Box 7.3 presents some insights from individual economies on the benefits of participating in this regional capacity building exercise.

Box 7.3: Technical Assistance on Supply and Use Tables: What Economies Say

Bangladesh, Bangladesh Bureau of Statistics
"BBS appreciates the initiative of ADB on SUT compilation through RETA 6483, and in building the capacity of national statistics office that enabled BBS to construct SUTs on their own. The BBS has benefited immensely from RETA 6483 and it will make attempts to compile SUT independently and integrate it into the regular work program of national accounts compilation in the future."

Bhutan, National Statistics Bureau
"The compilation of the SUT 2007 was a challenging task for the NAPD team, as it was the first time it was undertaken in Bhutan. With constant guidance and feedback by ADB, SUT 2007 compilation was a good learning experience. More importantly, the NAPD felt that understanding and learning from the experiences of other economies in compiling SUTs was of immense help."

India, Ministry of Statistics and Programme Implementation
"There were many challenges encountered in the construction of the SUT FY2006. To begin with, the exercise was the first attempt by the CSO to compile on SUT. Therefore, the guidance, training, and capacity building provided by the ADB on the construction of the SUT were immensely helpful."

Maldives, Department of National Planning
"The Statistics Division of the Department of National Planning was exposed to SUT compilation through the SUTs 1997 and 2003, which were done by consultants. Compilation of SUT 2007 under RETA 6483 was a new experience for the staff because, unlike the previous SUTs which had extensive involvement of foreign consultants, the SUT under RETA 6483 was compiled by the national accounts unit."

Nepal, National Statistics Office
"ADB also provided a platform for interacting with other countries. Having learned from RETA 6483, the CBS established a mechanism to move toward compliance with the 1993 SNA."

Sri Lanka, Department of Census and Statistics
"For Sri Lanka, the SUT 2006 was its first attempted at compiling an SUT. The involvement of DCS in RETA 6483 provided an avenue for considerable knowledge and capacity building not only on the SUT construction, but also on the SNA, in general."

Thailand, National Economic and Social Development Board
"The workshop sessions held by the project facilitated better understanding of the SUT compilation procedures and SNA concepts, as well as in resolving issues faced in the compilation. In addition, the project provided an opportunity to share experiences on GDP compilation with other participating economies."

ADB = Asian Development Bank, BBS = Bangladesh Bureau of Statistics, CBS = Central Bureau of Statistics, CSO = Central Statistics Office, DCS = Department of Census and Statistics, FY = financial year, GDP = gross domestic product, NAPD = National Accounts and Price Division, RETA = regional technical assistance, SNA = System of National Accounts, SUT = supply and use table.

Source: The excerpts in this box are taken from the 2012 Asian Development Bank publication, *Supply and Use Tables for Selected Economies in Asia and the Pacific*, which is available at https://www.adb.org/sites/default/files/publication/30121/supply-and-use-tables-research-study.pdf.

Regional Technical Assistance Phase 2, 2014–2017

Building on the initial phase of assistance, ADB launched a second initiative from 2014 to 2017 under Regional Technical Assistance 8838.[4] This phase expanded support to 19 economies, including 17 from the first phase (Singapore did not continue) and adding the Lao People's Democratic Republic and Pakistan. The focus of this assistance shifted to aligning SUT compilation with the 2008 SNA recommendations, which became the basis for the ICP cycles of 2017, 2021, and 2024 (noting that the 2025 SNA has now been endorsed by the United Nations Statistical Commission and will serve as the foundation for future ICP cycles).

Key activities in the 2014–2017 phase encompassed an inception workshop, regional training sessions on the 2008 SNA, and training on updating and constructing benchmark national SUTs. This assistance culminated in the 2017 publication, *Compendium of Supply and Use Tables for Selected Economies in Asia and the Pacific* (ADB 2017). The compendium provides standardized SUTs for the participating economies, facilitating reliable, consistent, and internationally comparable estimates of key economic statistics such as GDP. The work accomplished under this technical assistance project was useful for many economies in providing the basic-heading level expenditure values required for the 2017 ICP cycle and subsequent benchmark years.

Subnational Purchasing Power Parities

While the PPPs generated by the ICP provide spatial comparisons of price levels, real output, and real consumption across economies of the world, subnational PPPs can serve a similar function within a given economy. They do so by adjusting for domestic variations in price levels to improve the comparability of income and expenditure data at, say, the provincial or district level.

The rationale for developing subnational PPPs is strongest in large and/or economically diverse economies, where geographic disparities in prices for food, housing, transport, and services can significantly impact income comparisons. By converting geographically granular expenditure data into a common price level, subnational PPPs allow for more accurate assessment of real living standards, poverty rates, and inequality across provinces or states. This, in turn, informs better-targeted policy interventions and resource allocation.

Methodologically, subnational PPP estimation draws on core principles of the ICP, particularly the use of matched product pricing and multilateral index methods. Where a national CPI system already collects price data domestically, these data can be leveraged to estimate spatial price indexes with relatively modest additional investment. However, key challenges include ensuring consistency in product specification across subnational localities, addressing differences in consumption patterns, and dealing with data sparsity in remote areas.

The benefits of subnational PPPs are both analytical and operational. They enhance the granularity of national accounts in real terms, provide evidence to improve the geographic targeting of fiscal transfers and social programs, and support subnational planning and monitoring of the Sustainable Development Goals. Subnational PPPs also support the integration of spatial economic analysis into national policy frameworks, including for issues such as urbanization, infrastructure shortfalls, and regional inequality.

Figure 7.4 provides an overview of the role of subnational PPPs for evidence-based policymaking within economies.

4 Full details of Regional Technical Assistance 8838 are available at https://www.adb.org/projects/48387-001/main.

Figure 7.4: Role of Subnational Purchasing Power Parities in Domestic Policymaking

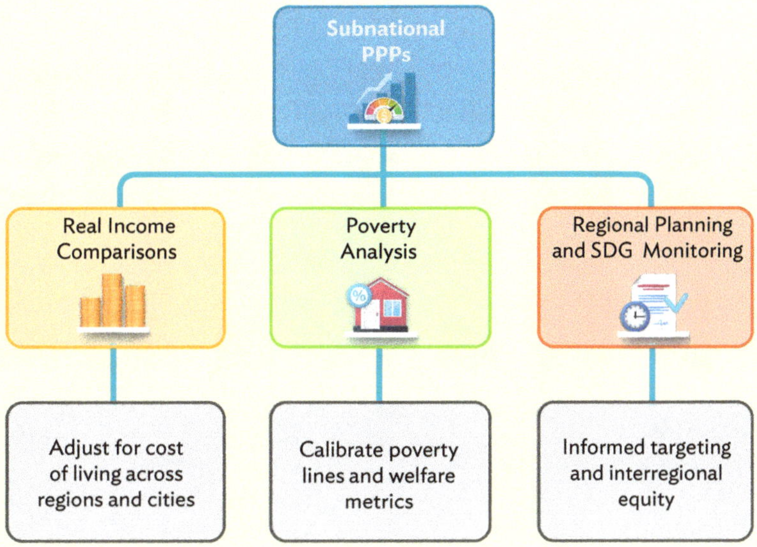

PPP = purchasing power parity, SDG = Sustainable Development Goal.
Source: Asian Development Bank compilation.

As economies continue to invest in statistical capacity, subnational PPPs offer a practical and policy-relevant extension of existing infrastructure for price statistics. Such PPPs bring the principles of comparability and measurement closer to the level at which development decisions are made.

ADB and the ICP Global Office at the World Bank realize the importance of subnational PPPs and, accordingly, have been adopting strategies to encourage economies of the Asia and Pacific region, to undertake experimental compilation of PPPs at the provincial or district level. With a view to creating awareness and building capacity, delegates from participating economies have been exposed to thematic presentations on this topic during ICP regional workshops organized by ADB.

Some economies in the region have been undertaking exploratory studies in producing subnational PPPs and one ADB member, Viet Nam, has institutionalized the construction of subnational PPPs in the economy's statistical program. Viet Nam's National Statistics Office publishes a Spatial Cost of Living Index comparing price levels for six economic zones within the economy, reflecting differences in the cost of living (Figure 7.5). The index is used to assess subnational differences in price levels, living standards, economic performance, general productivity, and price competitiveness (World Bank 2021).

The example presented for Viet Nam shows the feasibility of compiling subnational PPPs using price data available from national survey sources. Some economies of Asia and the Pacific have expressed interest in producing subnational PPPs in their economy experience reports for the 2021 ICP cycle (Box 7.4).

Figure 7.5: Spatial Cost of Living by Economic Zone in Viet Nam, 2020–2024

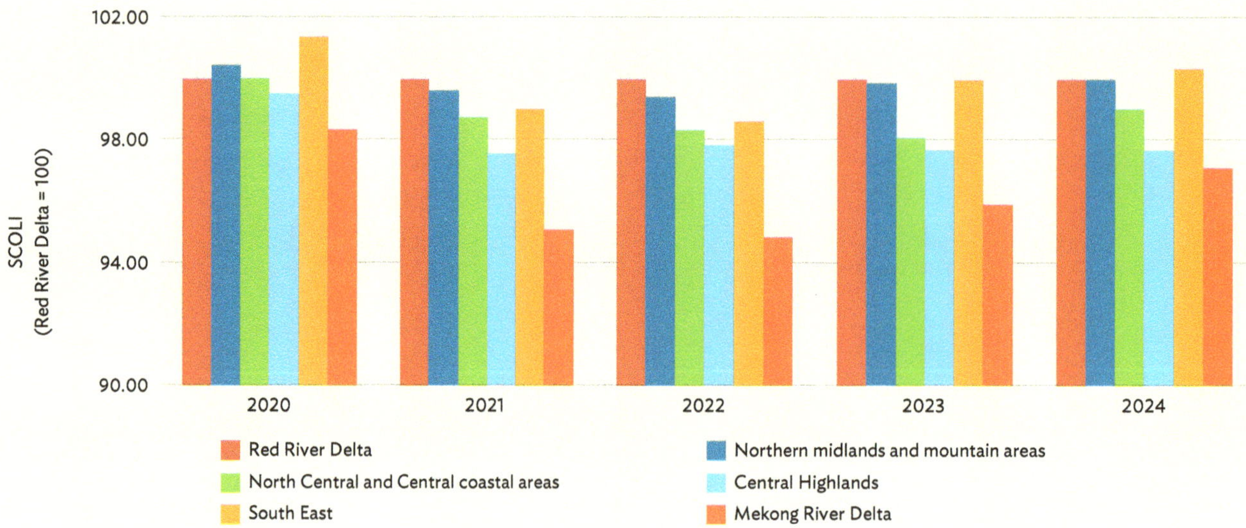

SCOLI = Spatial Cost of Living Index.

Source: National Statistics Office of Viet Nam. Spatial Cost of Living Index Among Regions (Red River Delta = 100) by Region and Year. Microsoft Excel file. https://pxweb.nso.gov.vn/sq/ded6d40c-b66f-49bd-8259-63a7336b62f1 (accessed 27 August 2025).

Box 7.4: Plans for Subnational Purchasing Power Parities: What Economies Say

Malaysia, Department of Statistics
"Adopting ICP concepts for PPP compilation and computation provided new ways for Malaysia to calculate comparative indexes between states."

Thailand, Trade Policy and Strategy Office
"The DTIEI will consider conducting subnational PPP following ICP regional implementation and guidelines, so support from ICP regional implementing agency will be advantageous."

Sri Lanka, Department of Census and Statistics
"With support from ADB, the DCS also intends to integrate similar methods to the ICP for calculating provincial (subnational) level PPPs into CPI activities."

Viet Nam, National Statistics Office
"The ICP helped price statisticians in Viet Nam improve their ability to analyze, review, and compare data between groups and localities. With new ICP tools and methods, the GSO improved its capacity to conduct price surveys in Viet Nam. These were especially helpful in laying the framework for estimating subnational PPPs."

ADB = Asian Development Bank; CPI = consumer price index; DCS = Department of Census and Statistics, DTIEI = Division of Trade Information and Economic Indices, GSO = General Statistics Office (now renamed as National Statistics Office), ICP = International Comparison Program, PPP = purchasing power parity.

Source: The excerpts in this box are taken from Asian Development Bank reports on economy experiences in the ICP's 2021 cycle across Asia and the Pacific. The full economy experience reports are available at https://icp.adb.org/economy.

Statistical Capacity and Data Management Tools

Each ICP cycle involves conducting large-scale surveys to simultaneously collect nationally representative prices of more than 1,200 items of goods and services in participating economies. In the 2021 cycle, 21 participating economies in the Asia and Pacific region conducted ICP price surveys and collected more than 3.2 million individual price quotations of items of household consumption, government consumption, and gross capital formation.

For these reasons, standardizing the processing and management of data is imperative for easing the workload of statisticians in participating economies and facilitating data reviews and further processing for comparisons at the regional level. Such standardization also helps ensure high data quality across a statistical exercise of the magnitude required for the ICP. ADB therefore continues to create and update data processing and management tools to support participating economies in maintaining the quality of ICP data.

The International Comparison Program Asia and the Pacific Software Suite (ICP APSS) is a software platform developed by ADB to assist national implementing agencies in managing the price data used to calculate PPPs. The ICP APSS has constantly evolved, with the goal of maintaining a simplified user experience that reduces the workload for data processing and quality control while strengthening data quality and comparability.

The system first took shape in Microsoft Excel, making use of an application that was already familiar to national statistics offices and was easy to deploy widely. For the 2011 ICP cycle, the ICP APSS was restructured as a Windows-based "visual basic application", which introduced greater automation and brought data entry and validation processes into a more controlled environment.

Building on this foundation, the ICP APSS transitioned into a web-based application in 2017, which provided more stable architecture, easier updates, and a modernized user interface. Until the 2017 ICP cycle, the platform was designed to cater only to the management of price surveys relating to household consumption, the biggest of all ICP price surveys.

By 2021, the ICP APSS had expanded into a modular structure covering all five ICP price surveys—household consumption, housing rentals, government compensation, construction, and machinery and equipment—making it a universal solution for the processing of all ICP survey data at the economy level.

The progression of the ICP APSS demonstrates a steady expansion in the suite's functionality and ease of use. Each development stage has enhanced system structure, introduced stronger validation protocols, and delivered broader domain coverage. Each module in the current suite is tailored to the product lists and data requirements of each survey, and each retains the core workflow of (i) configuration setting, (ii) product identification, (iii) data entry, (iv) data validation through statistical checks, and (v) generation of survey-specific summary reports, as shown in Figure 7.6.

Figure 7.6: Standard Workflow Using ADB's Price Data Software Suite

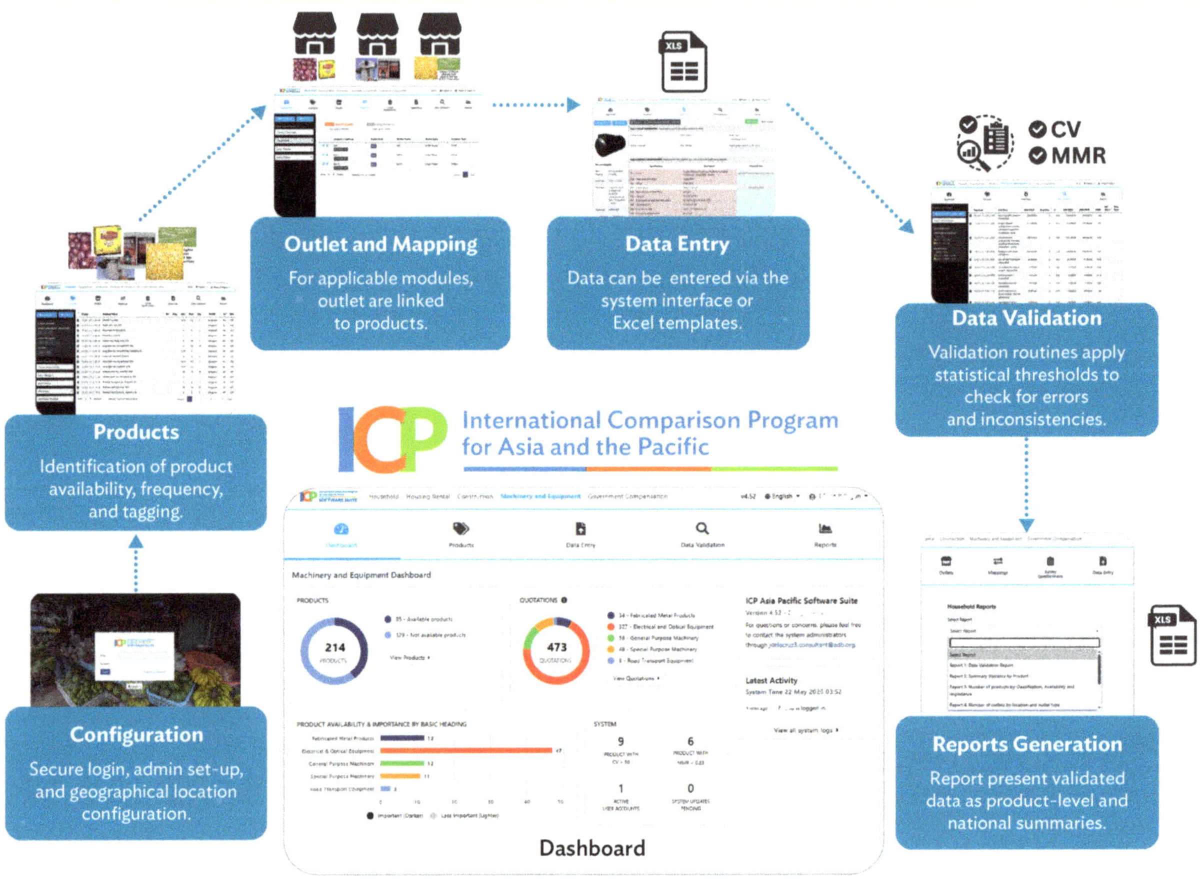

Source: Asian Development Bank visualization.

The modular design of the ICP APSS now allows multiple data systems to operate within a single framework, supported by an SQL database for reliable storage and processing, while standardized templates help users manage bulk data more efficiently. Furthermore, although the default interface is in English, ADB is supporting localized versions by enabling participating economies to upload translated product descriptions.

ADB provides regular ICP APSS training to users in implementing agencies of the participating economies, allowing them to make optimal use of the system for efficient data management and quality control. The suite has been widely adopted by economies participating in the ICP across Asia and the Pacific, with Box 7.5 presenting some feedback and experiences from the program's 2021 cycle.

Box 7.5: Using ADB's Price Data Software Suite: What Economies Say

Brunei Darussalam, Department of Economic Planning and Statistics
"Using the ICP APSS simplified price collection and data entry, efficiently generating summary statistics. As a result, price review and validation became more straightforward and precise. Utilizing the ICP Asia Pacific Software Suite allowed consistency checks using statistical criteria such as the coefficient of variation, standard deviation, and the minimum-to-maximum ratio."

Cambodia, National Institute of Statistics
"The ICP Asia Pacific Software Suite data validation feature enabled the NIS ICP team to address queries during workshops effectively."

The Lao People's Democratic Republic, Lao Statistics Bureau
"The LSB ICP team gained useful experience with the ICP APSS, particularly with the user-friendly price analysis tool. Data can be conveniently exported to Microsoft Excel for checking and validation and imported back to ICP APSS to update the database. The system allowed the database to be updated by uploading multiple Microsoft Excel files."

Mongolia, National Statistics Office
"The ICP APSS provided standardized templates that streamlined data entry for enumerators. The modules included simplified data input, automated checks for outliers and inconsistencies, and report generation for analysis and comparison, which helped identify errors and outliers."

Nepal, National Statistics Office
"The ICP APSS was highly user-friendly and effective for data entry and validation across various surveys, including household consumption, machinery and equipment, construction, housing rental, and government compensation. Enhancements have further facilitated database consolidation, validation, editing, and data sharing."

Taipei,China, Directorate General of Budget, Accounting and Statistics
"The ICP Asia Pacific Software Suite assisted the 2021 ICP in several ways. When validating quotations, the display showed information that allowed quick reference, such as the unit of measurement and a picture of the item. The identification of outliers was also made easier by the colored and tagged items. The overall view of the dashboard allowed a quick check for items priced and to see whether quotations were overlooked."

APSS = Asia and the Pacific Software Suite, ICP = International Comparison Program, LSB = Lao Statistics Bureau, NIS = National Institute of Statistics.

Source: The excerpts in this box are taken from Asian Development Bank reports on economy experiences in the ICP's 2021 cycle across Asia and the Pacific. The full economy experience reports are available at https://icp.adb.org/economy.

The ICP APSS serves as a reliable tool for implementing agencies of the participating economies to undertake rigorous validation of price quotations through inbuilt statistical tests, perform data consistency and completeness checks, and identify and correct outlier price quotations to ensure that the economy's price data inputs are of very high quality. The ICP APSS has significantly strengthened the ability of statistical systems of participating economies to undertake complex price data operations in line with ICP standards.

The ICP APSS is currently being developed into a fully online platform. This transition is aimed at further simplifying the user experience through centralized management, multi-user access, improved synchronization, and more efficient data consolidation.

CHAPTER 8

Summary and Conclusions

The Asia and Pacific region plays a pivotal role in driving global economic growth, contributing nearly 45% of the world's gross domestic product (GDP) when measured by purchasing power parities (PPPs). Home to about 55% of the global population, the region is marked by significant socioeconomic diversity. It encompasses affluent economies such as Singapore and Hong Kong, China; populous and fast-growing economies such as the People's Republic of China (PRC), India, and Indonesia; as well as numerous lower-middle-income and developing economies.

Given this diversity, it is essential for statisticians, economists, and policymakers to evaluate and compare the economic size and well-being of economies within the region against those in other parts of the world.

GDP remains the primary indicator of economic size and material well-being, especially when expressed as a per capita measure. National accounts aggregates, such as GDP and its expenditure components, are regularly compiled by statistics offices of the economies and expressed in local currency units. Effective comparisons across economies can only be made by converting these GDP figures in local currency units into a common currency. Such conversion can be achieved either by using market exchange rates or by generating PPPs to be used as currency converters. Here, PPPs prove the more reliable and accurate option because they account for differences in currency denominations and simultaneously adjust for price-level differences between economies.

The International Comparison Program and ADB

The International Comparison Program (ICP) has been the world's premier source of reliable PPPs for intereconomy comparisons. As one of the most ambitious and technically demanding statistical initiatives ever undertaken, the ICP today involves more than 175 economies globally and is conducted every 3 years.

The Asian Development Bank (ADB) took over as the ICP regional implementing agency for Asia and the Pacific in 2003, with the objective of implementing the program's 2005 benchmark cycle. Since then, ADB has played a crucial role in expanding program participation, contributing new statistical and operational methodologies, improving data quality, and building the capacity of statisticians from implementing agencies in the participating economies.

The governance framework established for Asia and the Pacific has enabled ADB to manage the program effectively at the regional level, in partnership with the participating economies. This partnership has encouraged collective ownership of the regional program, ensuring smooth and globally compliant implementation and completion of each cycle. ADB has now successfully overseen four ICP cycles (2005, 2011, 2017, and 2021) and is currently leading the 2024 cycle.

The Growing Global Influence of Asia and the Pacific

The empirical findings of this study from the results of the 2011 and 2021 ICP cycles demonstrate the significant contribution of Asia and the Pacific to the global economy since 2011. The analysis confirms that a majority of the world's largest economies by size, as measured in PPPs, are now located in the region. From 2011 to 2021, Asia and the Pacific accounted for a substantial share of global growth, outpacing other parts of the world. High and sustained levels of gross capital formation, underpinned by both public and private investment, have supported rapid structural transformation and rising standards of living across much of the region.

Analyzing results from the most recently completed ICP cycle for 2021, Asia and the Pacific now accounts for nearly 45% of global GDP in PPP terms and boasts the world's largest economy in real terms, with the PRC posting GDP of $28.822 trillion in 2021, while India with $10.963 trillion was the third largest economy globally. Four regional economies, namely the PRC, India, Japan, and Indonesia are among the top 10 economies of the world in terms of size of GDP and together accounted for 32.1% or close to a third of global GDP in PPP terms in 2021. As a major driver of global growth in GDP from 2011 to 2021, 66.4% of the world's economic expansion over this period was contributed by economies in the Asia and Pacific region. However, the region's largest economies still lag most others globally in terms of per capita real GDP. The Asia and Pacific region also exhibited large disparities in per capita incomes across its economies in 2021. However, the intereconomy income equality as seen from the Gini coefficient based on per capita real incomes from ICP results has been reducing since 2011 as seen from analysis of results of the 2017 and 2021 ICP cycles.

The study further establishes that the Asia and Pacific region has played a pivotal role in reducing intereconomy inequality and has contributed significantly to the global decline of poverty. Rapid income growth in large developing economies has aided in substantially narrowing international disparities in material well-being. Moreover, the region's integration into global production and trade has generated deflationary effects through the export of competitively priced goods, helping to moderate consumer prices in advanced economies. Taken together, the evidence highlights the region's role not only as a center of economic dynamism and investment but also as a major force for global equity, poverty reduction, and consumer welfare.

ADB's Notable Contributions to a Complex Statistical Undertaking

Since the 2005 ICP cycle, ADB has finely balanced strict adherence to ICP global guidelines with region-specific methodological refinements. Operating within the parameters set by the ICP Global Office and the ICP Technical Advisory Group, the bank has implemented innovations that enhance the quality, comparability, and policy relevance of the program's results. Key contributions include productivity adjustments in PPPs for government compensation and a new methodology for housing comparisons based on a hybrid of the quality-adjusted rental and quantity approaches. The first of these innovations, is now being applied in other regional comparisons under ICP and the latter is recommended for testing in other regions by the ICP Technical Advisory Group. This reflects ADB's contributions to advancing the global ICP agenda through technically grounded, regionally responsive solutions.

Over more than 2 decades as the ICP's regional implementing agency in Asia and the Pacific, ADB has significantly strengthened statistical capacity across the region, supporting sustained investments in training and technical assistance. These efforts have focused on building long-term capability in price statistics, national accounts, and broader economic measurement, tailored to meet economy-specific needs while adhering to global standards.

Through regional workshops, expert consultations, and hands-on guidance conducted by ADB as part of ICP implementation in the region, ADB has contributed to enhanced skills and knowledge of statisticians in the statistics offices in price collection, data validation, and the System of National Accounts. It has also supported the region's economies in compiling supply and use tables, which are foundational for sharpening estimates of GDP. The bank has additionally developed user-friendly data management systems which are utilized by the implementing agencies of the participating economies to manage ICP price surveys data to do validation and consistency checks for quality assurance. This includes ADB's development of the ICP Asia and the Pacific Software Suite to harmonize data practices by economies across the region (ICP IACG 2022).

ADB has also encouraged the integration of ICP and consumer price index activities to create resource efficiencies for statistics offices in the participating economies, while also supporting production of subnational PPPs to promote interprovincial price comparisons and policy applications. As an illustration of this work, Singapore has already demonstrated the synergies that can be achieved by integrating consumer price index and ICP activities (from product list development to the collection and processing of data) while Viet Nam is producing a Spatial Cost of Living Index comparing price levels for six economic zones i.e. subnational PPPs annually.

The Value of Commitment by Participating Economies

A key driver behind the successful implementation of the ICP in Asia and the Pacific has been the remarkable commitment and sense of ownership demonstrated by the implementing agencies of the region's participating economies.

Despite significant differences in statistical capacity, available resources, and competing statistical priorities, these agencies consistently supported the program. Their dedication was especially evident during the 2021 ICP cycle, when they completed price surveys and adopted innovative data collection methods in the face of the coronavirus disease pandemic. This has helped in implementing the vision of the United Nations Statistical Commission of establishing ICP as a permanent element of the global statistical program.

The region's ability to successfully carry out the ICP cycles in 2005, 2011, 2017, and 2021 highlights the tireless efforts and resilience of the staff within participating statistical agencies—efforts that are indispensable to the success of such a complex and exhaustive statistical exercise. This commitment has established a culture of methodological rigor, collaboration, and continuous improvement promoting regional cooperation for producing statistics of regional and global public value.

The Way Ahead for International Economic Comparisons

The Asia and Pacific region's economic dynamism, along with its resounding commitment to the ICP's success, has provided the foundations needed to consistently deliver robust and reliable economic comparisons in both the regional and global contexts. As this globally important region continues to grow and evolve, further innovation in statistical methodologies and advancements in digital solutions will be crucial to understanding and addressing the economic challenges and opportunities that lie ahead.

APPENDIX 1

Summary Tables on Purchasing Power Parities and Real Expenditures for 2021

The tables included in this appendix present summary results of the International Comparison Program (ICP) published by the World Bank for the 2021 ICP benchmark cycle. Globally, 176 economies from all regions of the world participated in the 2021 ICP cycle including 33 ADB member economies referred to as Asia and the Pacific in this publication. The results in these tables are organized by 33 economies of Asia and the Pacific as well as by other regional groupings: Africa, Europe, the Rest of the World, and the United States (US). The tables and figures presented in Chapter 4 of this publication also follow these regional groupings. The US is the reference economy and the US dollar ($) is the reference currency for the global ICP comparisons shown in the summary tables.

Seven expenditure aggregates are presented in the summary tables; namely gross domestic product and its six main aggregates: (i) individual consumption expenditure by households and nonprofit institutions serving households, (ii) actual individual consumption by households, (iii) individual consumption expenditure by government, (iv) collective consumption expenditure by government, (v) government final consumption expenditure, and (vi) gross fixed capital formation.

The summary tables A1.1 to A1.7 present data for the following indicators for gross domestic product and the six main aggregates:

(i) Purchasing Power Parity ($ = 1.00)
(ii) Exchange Rate ($ = 1.00)
(iii) Real Expenditure ($ billion)
(iv) Nominal Expenditure ($ billion)
(v) Shares of Nominal and Real Expenditure (World = 100)
(vi) Per Capita Real and Nominal Expenditure ($)
(vii) Per Capita Relative Real and Nominal Expenditure Index (US = 100)
(viii) Price Level Index (US = 100; World = 100)
(ix) Expenditure (LCU billion)
(x) Population (million)

It may be noted that the results in these tables are based on data supplied by participating economies to the ICP global and regional implementing agencies and produced in accordance with the ICP methodology endorsed by the ICP Technical Advisory Group. As such, these results are not produced by participating economies as part of their official statistics.

Table A1.1: Summary Results for Gross Domestic Product, 2021

Economy	Purchasing Power Parity ($ = 1.00)	Exchange Rate ($ = 1.00)	Expenditure ($ billion)		Shares (World = 100.00)		Expenditure Per Capita ($)		Expenditure Per Capita Indexes (US = 100)		Price Level Indexes		Reference Data	
			Real	Nominal	Real	Nominal	Real	Nominal	Real	Nominal	US = 100	World = 100	Expenditure (LCU billion)	Population (million)
Developing ADB Member Economies	**...**	**...**	**60,652.6**	**29,329.2**	**39.79**	**30.49**	**14,798**	**7,156**	**21**	**10**	**48**	**77**	**...**	**4,098.8**
Armenia	148.24	503.77	47.2	13.9	0.03	0.01	15,922	4,685	22	7	29	47	6,992	3.0
Azerbaijan	0.46	1.70	203.9	54.8	0.13	0.06	20,298	5,458	29	8	27	43	93	10.0
Bangladesh	28.30	85.10	1,325.6	440.8	0.87	0.46	7,786	2,589	11	4	33	53	37,510	170.3
Bhutan	19.61	73.94	10.4	2.8	0.01	0.00	13,803	3,661	19	5	27	42	205	0.8
Brunei Darussalam	0.53	1.34	35.3	14.0	0.02	0.01	80,203	31,786	113	45	40	63	19	0.4
Cambodia	1,426.96	4,098.72	77.4	27.0	0.05	0.03	4,667	1,625	7	2	35	55	110,506	16.6
China, People's Republic of	3.99	6.45	28,821.6	17,813.5	18.91	18.52	20,407	12,613	29	18	62	98	114,924	1,412.4
Fiji	0.91	2.07	9.8	4.3	0.01	0.00	10,963	4,818	15	7	44	70	9	0.9
Georgia	0.87	3.23	69.3	18.6	0.05	0.02	18,691	5,016	26	7	27	43	60	3.7
Hong Kong, China	5.87	7.77	488.4	368.9	0.32	0.38	65,877	49,760	93	70	76	120	2,868	7.4
India	20.73	73.92	10,963.1	3,074.3	7.19	3.20	8,019	2,249	11	3	28	44	227,243	1,367.2
Indonesia	4,808.43	14,308.14	3,530.6	1,186.5	2.32	1.23	12,948	4,351	18	6	34	53	16,976,751	272.7
Kazakhstan	129.06	426.03	650.5	197.1	0.43	0.20	34,231	10,370	48	15	30	48	83,952	19.0
Korea, Republic of	827.27	1,143.95	2,514.5	1,818.4	1.65	1.89	48,594	35,142	68	50	72	115	2,080,198	51.7
Kyrgyz Republic	19.92	84.64	39.3	9.2	0.03	0.01	5,736	1,350	8	2	24	37	783	6.9
Lao People's Democratic Republic	3,031.70	9,697.92	61.0	19.1	0.04	0.02	8,315	2,599	12	4	31	50	184,982	7.3
Malaysia	1.51	4.14	1,022.5	373.8	0.67	0.39	31,389	11,476	44	16	37	58	1,549	32.6
Maldives	8.21	15.38	9.8	5.3	0.01	0.01	17,309	9,243	24	13	53	85	81	0.6
Mongolia	870.18	2,849.29	50.1	15.3	0.03	0.02	15,247	4,657	21	7	31	48	43,555	3.3
Nepal	32.48	118.13	139.9	38.5	0.09	0.04	4,813	1,323	7	2	27	44	4,543	29.1
Pakistan	43.44	162.63	1,409.5	376.5	0.92	0.39	6,271	1,675	9	2	27	42	61,230	224.8
Philippines	19.38	49.25	1,001.8	394.1	0.66	0.41	9,091	3,576	13	5	39	62	19,411	110.2
Singapore	0.81	1.34	719.1	433.9	0.47	0.45	131,864	79,571	186	112	60	96	583	5.5
Sri Lanka	55.53	198.88	317.0	88.5	0.21	0.09	14,306	3,994	20	6	28	44	17,600	22.2
Taipei,China	14.40	28.02	1,504.8	773.1	0.99	0.80	64,120	32,941	90	46	51	81	21,663	23.5
Tajikistan	2.54	11.31	39.7	8.9	0.03	0.01	4,053	912	6	1	22	36	101	9.8
Thailand	11.15	31.98	1,452.1	506.2	0.95	0.53	20,838	7,264	29	10	35	55	16,189	69.7
Türkiye	2.73	8.89	2,662.2	816.4	1.75	0.85	31,638	9,702	45	14	31	49	7,256	84.1
Uzbekistan	2,591.11	10,609.98	285.0	69.6	0.19	0.07	8,162	1,993	11	3	24	39	738,425	34.9
Viet Nam	7,120.01	23,159.89	1,191.0	366.1	0.78	0.38	12,090	3,717	17	5	31	49	8,479,667	98.5
Developed ADB Member Economies	**...**	**...**	**7,366.7**	**6,912.8**	**4.83**	**7.19**	**47,132**	**44,227**	**66**	**62**	**94**	**149**	**...**	**156.3**
Australia	1.42	1.33	1,557.5	1,657.5	1.02	1.72	60,639	64,532	85	91	106	169	2,207	25.7
Japan	98.69	109.75	5,566.7	5,005.5	3.65	5.20	44,355	39,884	62	56	90	142	549,379	125.5
New Zealand	1.46	1.41	242.5	249.7	0.16	0.26	47,426	48,834	67	69	103	163	353	5.1
Asia and the Pacific (33)	**...**	**...**	**68,019.3**	**36,242.0**	**44.63**	**37.68**	**15,985**	**8,517**	**23**	**12**	**53**	**84**	**...**	**4,255.1**
Africa	**...**	**...**	**7,605.3**	**2,631.7**	**4.99**	**2.74**	**5,655**	**1,957**	**8**	**3**	**35**	**55**	**...**	**1,344.8**
Europe	**...**	**...**	**28,249.5**	**21,891.6**	**18.53**	**22.76**	**51,876**	**40,200**	**73**	**57**	**77**	**123**	**...**	**544.6**
United States	**1.00**	**1.00**	**23,594.0**	**23,594.0**	**15.48**	**24.53**	**70,988**	**70,988**	**100**	**100**	**100**	**158**	**23,594**	**332.4**
Rest of the World	**...**	**...**	**24,944.5**	**11,827.4**	**16.37**	**12.30**	**23,939**	**11,351**	**34**	**16**	**47**	**75**	**...**	**1,042.0**
World	**...**	**...**	**152,412.5**	**96,186.7**	**100.00**	**100.00**	**20,271**	**12,793**	**29**	**18**	**63**	**100**	**...**	**7,518.8**

... = not available/applicable, $ = United States dollars, ADB = Asian Development Bank, ICP = International Comparison Program, LCU = local currency unit, US = United States.

Source: ADB estimates using data from World Bank. DataBank: ICP 2021. https://databank.worldbank.org/source/icp-2021# (accessed 4 June 2024).

Table A1.2: Summary Results for Individual Consumption Expenditure by Households and Nonprofit Institutions Serving Households, 2021

Economy	Purchasing Power Parity ($ = 1.00)	Exchange Rate ($ = 1.00)	Expenditure ($ billion)		Shares (World = 100.00)		Expenditure Per Capita ($)		Expenditure Per Capita Indexes (US = 100)		Price Level Indexes		Reference Data	
			Real	Nominal	Real	Nominal	Real	Nominal	Real	Nominal	US = 100	World = 100	Expenditure (LCU billion)	Population (million)
Developing ADB Member Economies	**...**	**...**	**29,093.3**	**13,297.4**	**36.27**	**25.20**	**7,098**	**3,244**	**15**	**7**	**46**	**69**	**...**	**4,098.8**
Armenia	164.23	503.77	30.3	9.9	0.04	0.02	10,239	3,338	21	7	33	50	4,981	3.0
Azerbaijan	0.48	1.70	101.1	28.7	0.13	0.05	10,065	2,858	21	6	28	43	49	10.0
Bangladesh	29.21	85.10	885.1	303.8	1.10	0.58	5,198	1,785	11	4	34	52	25,857	170.3
Bhutan	21.36	73.94	5.0	1.4	0.01	0.00	6,605	1,908	14	4	29	44	107	0.8
Brunei Darussalam	0.61	1.34	7.7	3.5	0.01	0.01	17,504	7,899	36	16	45	69	5	0.4
Cambodia	1,577.41	4,098.72	46.1	17.8	0.06	0.03	2,781	1,070	6	2	38	59	72,790	16.6
China, People's Republic of	4.01	6.45	10,953.1	6,812.8	13.66	12.91	7,755	4,824	16	10	62	95	43,953	1,412.4
Fiji	0.94	2.07	7.7	3.5	0.01	0.01	8,646	3,945	18	8	46	69	7	0.9
Georgia	1.07	3.23	46.7	15.5	0.06	0.03	12,582	4,187	26	9	33	51	50	3.7
Hong Kong, China	6.39	7.77	291.7	239.7	0.36	0.45	39,345	32,332	82	67	82	125	1,863	7.4
India	19.47	73.92	7,127.6	1,877.3	8.89	3.56	5,213	1,373	11	3	26	40	138,767	1,367.2
Indonesia	5,353.56	14,308.14	1,764.1	660.0	2.20	1.25	6,469	2,421	13	5	37	57	9,443,965	272.7
Kazakhstan	142.36	426.03	304.5	101.8	0.38	0.19	16,026	5,355	33	11	33	51	43,353	19.0
Korea, Republic of	943.42	1,143.95	1,013.4	835.7	1.26	1.58	19,584	16,151	41	33	82	125	956,018	51.7
Kyrgyz Republic	24.32	84.64	27.5	7.9	0.03	0.01	4,019	1,155	8	2	29	44	670	6.9
Lao People's Democratic Republic	3,260.25	9,697.92	26.7	9.0	0.03	0.02	3,634	1,222	8	3	34	51	86,947	7.3
Malaysia	1.55	4.14	577.2	216.6	0.72	0.41	17,720	6,650	37	14	38	57	898	32.6
Maldives	10.25	15.38	3.7	2.5	0.00	0.00	6,544	4,362	14	9	67	101	38	0.6
Mongolia	957.84	2,849.29	24.1	8.1	0.03	0.02	7,342	2,468	15	5	34	51	23,086	3.3
Nepal	33.83	118.13	111.7	32.0	0.14	0.06	3,844	1,101	8	2	29	44	3,780	29.1
Pakistan	42.53	162.63	1,219.5	318.9	1.52	0.60	5,425	1,419	11	3	26	40	51,862	224.8
Philippines	20.75	49.25	704.2	296.6	0.88	0.56	6,390	2,691	13	6	42	64	14,609	110.2
Singapore	1.06	1.34	160.0	126.1	0.20	0.24	29,336	23,114	61	48	79	120	169	5.5
Sri Lanka	58.30	198.88	184.8	54.2	0.23	0.10	8,339	2,444	17	5	29	45	10,771	22.2
Taipei,China	15.70	28.02	618.1	346.4	0.77	0.66	26,340	14,759	55	31	56	85	9,706	23.5
Tajikistan	3.22	11.31	25.2	7.2	0.03	0.01	2,575	733	5	2	28	43	81	9.8
Thailand	11.71	31.98	728.9	266.9	0.91	0.51	10,459	3,831	22	8	37	56	8,537	69.7
Türkiye	3.02	8.89	1,325.9	451.0	1.65	0.85	15,757	5,360	33	11	34	52	4,009	84.1
Uzbekistan	2,906.58	10,609.98	151.9	41.6	0.19	0.08	4,350	1,192	9	2	27	42	441,498	34.9
Viet Nam	7,510.82	23,159.89	619.8	201.0	0.77	0.38	6,292	2,040	13	4	32	49	4,655,057	98.5
Developed ADB Member Economies	**...**	**...**	**3,543.6**	**3,638.3**	**4.42**	**6.90**	**22,672**	**23,277**	**47**	**48**	**103**	**156**	**...**	**156.3**
Australia	1.51	1.33	719.8	816.4	0.90	1.55	28,023	31,783	58	66	113	172	1,087	25.7
Japan	109.22	109.75	2,691.7	2,678.6	3.36	5.08	21,448	21,343	44	44	100	151	293,986	125.5
New Zealand	1.53	1.41	132.1	143.3	0.16	0.27	25,831	28,024	54	58	108	165	203	5.1
Asia and the Pacific (33)	**...**	**...**	**32,636.9**	**16,935.6**	**40.69**	**32.10**	**7,670**	**3,980**	**16**	**8**	**52**	**79**	**...**	**4,255.1**
Africa	**...**	**...**	**5,054.9**	**1,792.2**	**6.30**	**3.40**	**3,759**	**1,333**	**8**	**3**	**35**	**54**	**...**	**1,344.8**
Europe	**...**	**...**	**13,422.5**	**11,373.3**	**16.71**	**21.54**	**24,568**	**20,817**	**51**	**43**	**85**	**129**	**...**	**546.3**
United States	**1.00**	**1.00**	**16,043.0**	**16,043.0**	**20.00**	**30.41**	**48,269**	**48,269**	**100**	**100**	**100**	**152**	**16,043**	**332.4**
Rest of the World	**...**	**...**	**13,070.1**	**6,626.7**	**16.29**	**12.56**	**12,543**	**6,359**	**26**	**13**	**51**	**77**	**...**	**1,042.1**
World	**...**	**...**	**80,209.4**	**52,762.0**	**100.00**	**100.00**	**10,668**	**7,017**	**22**	**15**	**66**	**100**	**...**	**7,518.8**

... = not available/applicable, $ = United States dollars, ADB = Asian Development Bank, ICP = International Comparison Program, LCU = local currency unit, US = United States.

Source: ADB estimates using data from World Bank. DataBank: ICP 2021. https://databank.worldbank.org/source/icp-2021# (accessed 4 June 2024).

Table A1.3: Summary Results for Actual Individual Consumption by Households, 2021

Economy	Purchasing Power Parity ($ = 1.00)	Exchange Rate ($ = 1.00)	Expenditure ($ billion)		Shares (World = 100.00)		Expenditure Per Capita ($)		Expenditure Per Capita Indexes (US = 100)		Price Level Indexes		Reference Data	
			Real	Nominal	Real	Nominal	Real	Nominal	Real	Nominal	US = 100	World = 100	Expenditure (LCU billion)	Population (million)
Developing ADB Member Economies	**...**	**...**	**34,455.4**	**15,077.5**	**35.39**	**24.64**	**8,406**	**3,678**	**16**	**7**	**44**	**70**	**...**	**4,098.8**
Armenia	141.52	503.77	38.0	10.7	0.04	0.02	12,842	3,608	24	7	28	45	5,384	3.0
Azerbaijan	0.42	1.70	128.6	31.9	0.13	0.05	12,800	3,171	24	6	25	39	54	10.0
Bangladesh	26.83	85.10	971.6	306.4	1.00	0.50	5,707	1,799	11	3	32	50	26,071	170.3
Bhutan	18.61	73.94	6.7	1.7	0.01	0.00	8,852	2,227	17	4	25	40	125	0.8
Brunei Darussalam	0.55	1.34	10.4	4.2	0.01	0.01	23,492	9,597	45	18	41	65	6	0.4
Cambodia	1,431.84	4,098.72	54.5	19.0	0.06	0.03	3,284	1,147	6	2	35	56	78,008	16.6
China, People's Republic of	3.90	6.45	13,114.6	7,919.8	13.47	12.94	9,286	5,607	18	11	60	96	51,095	1,412.4
Fiji	0.88	2.07	9.1	3.9	0.01	0.01	10,212	4,347	19	8	43	68	8	0.9
Georgia	0.91	3.23	58.5	16.4	0.06	0.03	15,769	4,426	30	8	28	45	53	3.7
Hong Kong, China	6.07	7.77	330.5	258.2	0.34	0.42	44,577	34,831	85	66	78	124	2,007	7.4
India	18.78	73.92	7,854.5	1,996.0	8.07	3.26	5,745	1,460	11	3	25	40	147,541	1,367.2
Indonesia	4,852.44	14,308.14	2,083.7	706.7	2.14	1.16	7,642	2,592	15	5	34	54	10,111,243	272.7
Kazakhstan	124.65	426.03	389.0	113.8	0.40	0.19	20,469	5,989	39	11	29	47	48,482	19.0
Korea, Republic of	870.39	1,143.95	1,339.4	1,019.1	1.38	1.67	25,885	19,695	49	37	76	121	1,165,821	51.7
Kyrgyz Republic	20.36	84.64	36.1	8.7	0.04	0.01	5,270	1,268	10	2	24	38	735	6.9
Lao People's Democratic Republic	2,881.21	9,697.92	31.5	9.4	0.03	0.02	4,296	1,276	8	2	30	47	90,826	7.3
Malaysia	1.46	4.14	688.1	243.1	0.71	0.40	21,122	7,461	40	14	35	56	1,007	32.6
Maldives	8.98	15.38	5.1	3.0	0.01	0.00	8,907	5,200	17	10	58	93	45	0.6
Mongolia	824.57	2,849.29	31.0	9.0	0.03	0.01	9,455	2,736	18	5	29	46	25,594	3.3
Nepal	31.10	118.13	126.1	33.2	0.13	0.05	4,338	1,142	8	2	26	42	3,921	29.1
Pakistan	40.07	162.63	1,353.5	333.5	1.39	0.55	6,022	1,484	11	3	25	39	54,230	224.8
Philippines	19.23	49.25	813.4	317.6	0.84	0.52	7,381	2,882	14	5	39	62	15,642	110.2
Singapore	1.00	1.34	191.2	142.2	0.20	0.23	35,066	26,077	67	50	74	118	191	5.5
Sri Lanka	51.89	198.88	224.8	58.6	0.23	0.10	10,146	2,647	19	5	26	42	11,664	22.2
Taipei,China	14.57	28.02	775.9	403.3	0.80	0.66	33,061	17,185	63	33	52	83	11,302	23.5
Tajikistan	2.64	11.31	33.5	7.8	0.03	0.01	3,421	798	6	2	23	37	88	9.8
Thailand	10.80	31.98	935.8	316.0	0.96	0.52	13,429	4,534	26	9	34	54	10,105	69.7
Türkiye	2.47	8.89	1,861.4	518.3	1.91	0.85	22,121	6,160	42	12	28	44	4,607	84.1
Uzbekistan	2,418.63	10,609.98	208.0	47.4	0.21	0.08	5,956	1,358	11	3	23	36	502,991	34.9
Viet Nam	6,747.20	23,159.89	751.0	218.8	0.77	0.36	7,624	2,221	14	4	29	46	5,066,959	98.5
Developed ADB Member Economies	**...**	**...**	**4,848.2**	**4,572.8**	**4.98**	**7.47**	**31,018**	**29,256**	**59**	**56**	**94**	**150**	**...**	**156.3**
Australia	1.48	1.33	951.1	1,060.4	0.98	1.73	37,030	41,285	70	78	111	177	1,412	25.7
Japan	98.50	109.75	3,719.5	3,338.2	3.82	5.46	29,637	26,599	56	51	90	143	366,381	125.5
New Zealand	1.39	1.41	177.5	174.2	0.18	0.28	34,710	34,056	66	65	98	156	246	5.1
Asia and the Pacific (33)	**...**	**...**	**39,303.6**	**19,650.3**	**40.37**	**32.12**	**9,237**	**4,618**	**18**	**9**	**50**	**80**	**...**	**4,255.1**
Africa	**...**	**...**	**5,914.3**	**1,919.3**	**6.07**	**3.14**	**4,398**	**1,427**	**8**	**3**	**32**	**52**	**...**	**1,344.8**
Europe	**...**	**...**	**18,102.5**	**14,386.1**	**18.59**	**23.51**	**33,242**	**26,418**	**63**	**50**	**79**	**126**	**...**	**544.6**
United States	**1.00**	**1.00**	**17,500.4**	**17,500.4**	**17.98**	**28.60**	**52,654**	**52,654**	**100**	**100**	**100**	**159**	**17,500**	**332.4**
Rest of the World	**...**	**...**	**16,536.3**	**7,725.9**	**16.99**	**12.63**	**15,870**	**7,415**	**30**	**14**	**47**	**74**	**...**	**1,042.0**
World	**...**	**...**	**97,357.1**	**61,182.0**	**100.00**	**100.00**	**12,948**	**8,137**	**25**	**15**	**63**	**100**	**...**	**7,518.8**

... = not available/applicable, $ = United States dollars, ADB = Asian Development Bank, ICP = International Comparison Program, LCU = local currency unit, US = United States.

Source: ADB estimates using data from World Bank. DataBank: ICP 2021. https://databank.worldbank.org/source/icp-2021# (accessed 4 June 2024).

Table A1.4: Summary Results for Individual Consumption Expenditure by Government, 2021

Economy	Purchasing Power Parity ($ = 1.00)	Exchange Rate ($ = 1.00)	Expenditure ($ billion)		Shares (World = 100.00)		Expenditure Per Capita ($)		Expenditure Per Capita Indexes (US = 100)		Price Level Indexes		Reference Data	
			Real	Nominal	Real	Nominal	Real	Nominal	Real	Nominal	US = 100	World = 100	Expenditure (LCU billion)	Population (million)
Developing ADB Member Economies	**...**	**...**	**5,482.9**	**1,780.1**	**29.06**	**21.14**	**1,338**	**434**	**31**	**10**	**32**	**73**	**...**	**4,098.8**
Armenia	52.13	503.77	7.7	0.8	0.04	0.01	2,606	270	59	6	10	23	402	3.0
Azerbaijan	0.17	1.70	31.1	3.1	0.17	0.04	3,101	313	71	7	10	23	5	10.0
Bangladesh	15.42	85.10	13.9	2.5	0.07	0.03	81	15	2	0	18	41	214	170.3
Bhutan	7.34	73.94	2.4	0.2	0.01	0.00	3,216	319	73	7	10	22	18	0.8
Brunei Darussalam	0.28	1.34	3.7	0.7	0.02	0.01	8,288	1,698	189	39	20	46	1	0.4
Cambodia	692.40	4,098.72	7.5	1.3	0.04	0.02	454	77	10	2	17	38	5,219	16.6
China, People's Republic of	3.11	6.45	2,297.9	1,107.0	12.18	13.15	1,627	784	37	18	48	108	7,142	1,412.4
Fiji	0.56	2.07	1.3	0.4	0.01	0.00	1,479	402	34	9	27	61	1	0.9
Georgia	0.29	3.23	9.8	0.9	0.05	0.01	2,646	239	60	5	9	20	3	3.7
Hong Kong, China	4.54	7.77	31.7	18.5	0.17	0.22	4,280	2,499	98	57	58	131	144	7.4
India	17.64	73.92	497.5	118.7	2.64	1.41	364	87	8	2	24	53	8,774	1,367.2
Indonesia	2,282.19	14,308.14	292.4	46.6	1.55	0.55	1,072	171	24	4	16	36	667,278	272.7
Kazakhstan	51.24	426.03	100.1	12.0	0.53	0.14	5,269	634	120	14	12	27	5,130	19.0
Korea, Republic of	529.96	1,143.95	395.9	183.4	2.10	2.18	7,651	3,544	174	81	46	104	209,804	51.7
Kyrgyz Republic	5.97	84.64	11.0	0.8	0.06	0.01	1,605	113	37	3	7	16	66	6.9
Lao People's Democratic Republic	941.45	9,697.92	4.1	0.4	0.02	0.00	561	55	13	1	10	22	3,878	7.3
Malaysia	0.99	4.14	110.1	26.4	0.58	0.31	3,381	811	77	19	24	54	110	32.6
Maldives	3.75	15.38	2.0	0.5	0.01	0.01	3,434	837	78	19	24	55	7	0.6
Mongolia	260.51	2,849.29	9.6	0.9	0.05	0.01	2,933	268	67	6	9	20	2,508	3.3
Nepal	17.30	118.13	8.2	1.2	0.04	0.01	281	41	6	1	15	33	141	29.1
Pakistan	28.97	162.63	81.7	14.6	0.43	0.17	364	65	8	1	18	40	2,368	224.8
Philippines	11.92	49.25	86.7	21.0	0.46	0.25	787	190	18	4	24	54	1,034	110.2
Singapore	0.69	1.34	31.3	16.2	0.17	0.19	5,746	2,963	131	68	52	116	22	5.5
Sri Lanka	20.77	198.88	43.0	4.5	0.23	0.05	1,940	203	44	5	10	23	893	22.2
Taipei,China	8.58	28.02	186.0	56.9	0.99	0.68	7,926	2,427	181	55	31	69	1,596	23.5
Tajikistan	0.64	11.31	11.2	0.6	0.06	0.01	1,145	65	26	1	6	13	7	9.8
Thailand	6.04	31.98	259.4	49.0	1.38	0.58	3,722	704	85	16	19	42	1,568	69.7
Türkiye	0.83	8.89	720.4	67.3	3.82	0.80	8,561	800	195	18	9	21	598	84.1
Uzbekistan	708.70	10,609.98	86.8	5.8	0.46	0.07	2,485	166	57	4	7	15	61,492	34.9
Viet Nam	2,976.65	23,159.89	138.4	17.8	0.73	0.21	1,405	181	32	4	13	29	411,902	98.5
Developed ADB Member Economies	**...**	**...**	**1,667.6**	**934.5**	**8.84**	**11.10**	**10,669**	**5,979**	**243**	**136**	**56**	**126**	**...**	**156.3**
Australia	1.17	1.33	278.6	244.1	1.48	2.90	10,847	9,502	247	217	88	196	325	25.7
Japan	54.33	109.75	1,332.5	659.6	7.06	7.83	10,617	5,256	242	120	50	111	72,395	125.5
New Zealand	0.77	1.41	56.5	30.8	0.30	0.37	11,047	6,032	252	138	55	122	44	5.1
Asia and the Pacific (33)	**...**	**...**	**7,150.5**	**2,714.6**	**37.90**	**32.24**	**1,680**	**638**	**38**	**15**	**38**	**85**	**...**	**4,255.1**
Africa	**...**	**...**	**634.7**	**127.1**	**3.36**	**1.51**	**472**	**95**	**11**	**2**	**20**	**45**	**...**	**1,344.8**
Europe	**...**	**...**	**5,644.1**	**3,020.6**	**29.92**	**35.87**	**10,365**	**5,547**	**236**	**126**	**54**	**120**	**...**	**544.6**
United States	**1.00**	**1.00**	**1,457.4**	**1,457.4**	**7.73**	**17.31**	**4,385**	**4,385**	**100**	**100**	**100**	**224**	**1,457**	**332.4**
Rest of the World	**...**	**...**	**3,979.1**	**1,100.1**	**21.09**	**13.07**	**3,819**	**1,056**	**87**	**24**	**28**	**62**	**...**	**1,042.0**
World	**...**	**...**	**18,865.9**	**8,419.9**	**100.00**	**100.00**	**2,509**	**1,120**	**57**	**26**	**45**	**100**	**...**	**7,518.8**

... = not available/applicable, $ = United States dollars, ADB = Asian Development Bank, ICP = International Comparison Program, LCU = local currency unit, US = United States.

Source: ADB estimates using data from World Bank. DataBank: ICP 2021. https://databank.worldbank.org/source/icp-2021# (accessed 4 June 2024).

Table A1.5: Summary Results for Collective Consumption Expenditure by Government, 2021

Economy	Purchasing Power Parity ($ = 1.00)	Exchange Rate ($ = 1.00)	Expenditure ($ billion)		Shares (World = 100.00)		Expenditure Per Capita ($)		Expenditure Per Capita Indexes (US = 100)		Price Level Indexes		Reference Data	
			Real	Nominal	Real	Nominal	Real	Nominal	Real	Nominal	US = 100	World = 100	Expenditure (LCU billion)	Population (million)
Developing ADB Member Economies	...	...	**4,913.6**	**2,501.3**	**36.89**	**31.73**	**1,199**	**610**	**21**	**11**	**51**	**86**	...	**4,098.8**
Armenia	104.12	503.77	5.3	1.1	0.04	0.01	1,789	370	31	6	21	35	552	3.0
Azerbaijan	0.34	1.70	22.1	4.5	0.17	0.06	2,197	443	38	8	20	34	8	10.0
Bangladesh	25.16	85.10	77.7	23.0	0.58	0.29	457	135	8	2	30	50	1,956	170.3
Bhutan	10.64	73.94	2.7	0.4	0.02	0.00	3,548	511	62	9	14	24	29	0.8
Brunei Darussalam	0.32	1.34	10.0	2.4	0.08	0.03	22,685	5,444	395	95	24	41	3	0.4
Cambodia	1,303.28	4,098.72	2.1	0.7	0.02	0.01	127	40	2	1	32	54	2,753	16.6
China, People's Republic of	4.24	6.45	2,613.0	1,718.7	19.62	21.80	1,850	1,217	32	21	66	111	11,088	1,412.4
Fiji	0.80	2.07	1.7	0.7	0.01	0.01	1,900	736	33	13	39	65	1	0.9
Georgia	0.51	3.23	10.9	1.7	0.08	0.02	2,936	463	51	8	16	27	6	3.7
Hong Kong, China	5.72	7.77	38.4	28.2	0.29	0.36	5,181	3,809	90	66	74	124	220	7.4
India	25.99	73.92	619.8	217.9	4.65	2.76	453	159	8	3	35	59	16,108	1,367.2
Indonesia	3,688.29	14,308.14	244.7	63.1	1.84	0.80	897	231	16	4	26	44	902,552	272.7
Kazakhstan	71.48	426.03	60.6	10.2	0.46	0.13	3,189	535	56	9	17	28	4,332	19.0
Korea, Republic of	671.22	1,143.95	250.2	146.8	1.88	1.86	4,836	2,837	84	49	59	99	167,956	51.7
Kyrgyz Republic	11.54	84.64	5.6	0.8	0.04	0.01	817	111	14	2	14	23	65	6.9
Lao People's Democratic Republic	1,879.16	9,697.92	11.2	2.2	0.08	0.03	1,522	295	26	5	19	33	20,980	7.3
Malaysia	1.45	4.14	60.2	21.1	0.45	0.27	1,849	648	32	11	35	59	87	32.6
Maldives	5.91	15.38	1.3	0.5	0.01	0.01	2,314	889	40	15	38	65	8	0.6
Mongolia	505.91	2,849.29	7.9	1.4	0.06	0.02	2,401	426	42	7	18	30	3,987	3.3
Nepal	33.56	118.13	7.1	2.0	0.05	0.03	243	69	4	1	28	48	237	29.1
Pakistan	50.53	162.63	82.7	25.7	0.62	0.33	368	114	6	2	31	52	4,180	224.8
Philippines	17.34	49.25	114.8	40.4	0.86	0.51	1,042	367	18	6	35	59	1,990	110.2
Singapore	0.71	1.34	56.7	30.0	0.43	0.38	10,392	5,492	181	96	53	89	40	5.5
Sri Lanka	36.47	198.88	21.2	3.9	0.16	0.05	955	175	17	3	18	31	772	22.2
Taipei,China	12.20	28.02	110.6	48.1	0.83	0.61	4,713	2,052	82	36	44	74	1,349	23.5
Tajikistan	1.06	11.31	3.6	0.3	0.03	0.00	362	34	6	1	9	16	4	9.8
Thailand	9.09	31.98	155.2	44.1	1.17	0.56	2,228	633	39	11	28	48	1,412	69.7
Türkiye	1.69	8.89	201.5	38.4	1.51	0.49	2,394	456	42	8	19	32	341	84.1
Uzbekistan	1,696.60	10,609.98	35.9	5.7	0.27	0.07	1,029	165	18	3	16	27	60,981	34.9
Viet Nam	5,113.25	23,159.89	78.8	17.4	0.59	0.22	800	177	14	3	22	37	403,114	98.5
Developed ADB Member Economies	...	...	**671.4**	**556.4**	**5.04**	**7.06**	**4,296**	**3,560**	**75**	**62**	**83**	**140**	...	**156.3**
Australia	1.25	1.33	130.1	122.4	0.98	1.55	5,066	4,766	88	83	94	159	163	25.7
Japan	87.72	109.75	516.6	412.9	3.88	5.24	4,116	3,290	72	57	80	135	45,316	125.5
New Zealand	1.21	1.41	24.7	21.1	0.19	0.27	4,833	4,124	84	72	85	144	30	5.1
Asia and the Pacific (33)	...	...	**5,585.0**	**3,057.7**	**41.94**	**38.79**	**1,313**	**719**	**23**	**13**	**55**	**92**	...	**4,255.1**
Africa	...	...	**717.2**	**195.3**	**5.39**	**2.48**	**533**	**145**	**9**	**3**	**27**	**46**	...	**1,344.8**
Europe	...	...	**2,372.9**	**1,705.6**	**17.82**	**21.64**	**4,357**	**3,132**	**76**	**55**	**72**	**121**	...	**544.6**
United States	**1.00**	**1.00**	**1,908.8**	**1,908.8**	**14.33**	**24.21**	**5,743**	**5,743**	**100**	**100**	**100**	**169**	**1,909**	**332.4**
Rest of the World	...	...	**2,734.0**	**1,015.9**	**20.53**	**12.89**	**2,624**	**975**	**46**	**17**	**37**	**63**	...	**1,042.0**
World	...	...	**13,318.0**	**7,883.4**	**100.00**	**100.00**	**1,771**	**1,048**	**31**	**18**	**59**	**100**	...	**7,518.8**

... = not available/applicable, $ = United States dollars, ADB = Asian Development Bank, ICP = International Comparison Program, LCU = local currency unit, US = United States.

Source: ADB estimates using data from World Bank. DataBank: ICP 2021. https://databank.worldbank.org/source/icp-2021# (accessed 4 June 2024).

Table A1.6: Summary Results for General Government Final Consumption Expenditure, 2021

Economy	Purchasing Power Parity ($ = 1.00)	Exchange Rate ($ = 1.00)	Expenditure ($ billion)		Shares (World = 100.00)		Expenditure Per Capita ($)		Expenditure Per Capita Indexes (US = 100)		Price Level Indexes		Reference Data	
			Real	Nominal	Real	Nominal	Real	Nominal	Real	Nominal	US = 100	World = 100	Expenditure (LCU billion)	Population (million)
Developing ADB Member Economies	...	...	**10,190.9**	**4,281.5**	**32.88**	**26.26**	**2,486**	**1,045**	**25**	**10**	**42**	**80**	...	**4,098.8**
Armenia	74.99	503.77	12.7	1.9	0.04	0.01	4,296	640	42	6	15	28	954	3.0
Azerbaijan	0.25	1.70	52.3	7.6	0.17	0.05	5,203	757	51	7	15	28	13	10.0
Bangladesh	20.55	85.10	105.6	25.5	0.34	0.16	620	150	6	1	24	46	2,170	170.3
Bhutan	9.07	73.94	5.1	0.6	0.02	0.00	6,767	830	67	8	12	23	46	0.8
Brunei Darussalam	0.30	1.34	14.2	3.1	0.05	0.02	32,260	7,141	319	71	22	42	4	0.4
Cambodia	965.57	4,098.72	8.3	1.9	0.03	0.01	498	117	5	1	24	45	7,971	16.6
China, People's Republic of	3.70	6.45	4,930.6	2,825.7	15.91	17.33	3,491	2,001	34	20	57	109	18,230	1,412.4
Fiji	0.69	2.07	3.1	1.0	0.01	0.01	3,432	1,137	34	11	33	63	2	0.9
Georgia	0.39	3.23	21.4	2.6	0.07	0.02	5,758	702	57	7	12	23	8	3.7
Hong Kong, China	5.18	7.77	70.1	46.8	0.23	0.29	9,459	6,308	93	62	67	127	364	7.4
India	21.89	73.92	1,136.6	336.6	3.67	2.06	831	246	8	2	30	56	24,882	1,367.2
Indonesia	3,006.16	14,308.14	522.2	109.7	1.69	0.67	1,915	402	19	4	21	40	1,569,830	272.7
Kazakhstan	62.49	426.03	151.4	22.2	0.49	0.14	7,968	1,169	79	12	15	28	9,462	19.0
Korea, Republic of	607.96	1,143.95	621.4	330.2	2.01	2.03	12,008	6,382	119	63	53	101	377,760	51.7
Kyrgyz Republic	8.40	84.64	15.5	1.5	0.05	0.01	2,263	225	22	2	10	19	130	6.9
Lao People's Democratic Republic	1,469.03	9,697.92	16.9	2.6	0.05	0.02	2,306	349	23	3	15	29	24,859	7.3
Malaysia	1.23	4.14	159.8	47.5	0.52	0.29	4,906	1,459	48	14	30	57	197	32.6
Maldives	4.85	15.38	3.1	1.0	0.01	0.01	5,467	1,726	54	17	32	60	15	0.6
Mongolia	382.57	2,849.29	17.0	2.3	0.05	0.01	5,172	694	51	7	13	26	6,495	3.3
Nepal	25.30	118.13	14.9	3.2	0.05	0.02	514	110	5	1	21	41	378	29.1
Pakistan	39.89	162.63	164.1	40.3	0.53	0.25	730	179	7	2	25	47	6,548	224.8
Philippines	14.71	49.25	205.6	61.4	0.66	0.38	1,866	557	18	6	30	57	3,024	110.2
Singapore	0.69	1.34	89.8	46.1	0.29	0.28	16,469	8,455	163	83	51	98	62	5.5
Sri Lanka	28.48	198.88	58.4	8.4	0.19	0.05	2,638	378	26	4	14	27	1,665	22.2
Taipei,China	10.44	28.02	282.1	105.1	0.91	0.64	12,020	4,478	119	44	37	71	2,945	23.5
Tajikistan	0.85	11.31	13.0	1.0	0.04	0.01	1,327	99	13	1	7	14	11	9.8
Thailand	7.62	31.98	391.1	93.2	1.26	0.57	5,612	1,337	55	13	24	45	2,980	69.7
Türkiye	1.19	8.89	791.4	105.7	2.55	0.65	9,405	1,256	93	12	13	25	939	84.1
Uzbekistan	1,099.70	10,609.98	111.4	11.5	0.36	0.07	3,190	331	31	3	10	20	122,473	34.9
Viet Nam	4,040.95	23,159.89	201.7	35.2	0.65	0.22	2,047	357	20	4	17	33	815,016	98.5
Developed ADB Member Economies	...	...	**2,173.8**	**1,490.9**	**7.01**	**9.14**	**13,908**	**9,539**	**137**	**94**	**69**	**130**	...	**156.3**
Australia	1.26	1.33	385.9	366.5	1.25	2.25	15,023	14,268	148	141	95	181	488	25.7
Japan	68.75	109.75	1,712.1	1,072.5	5.52	6.58	13,642	8,546	135	84	63	119	117,711	125.5
New Zealand	0.97	1.41	75.8	51.9	0.24	0.32	14,821	10,156	146	100	69	130	73	5.1
Asia and the Pacific (33)	...	...	**12,364.7**	**5,772.4**	**39.90**	**35.41**	**2,906**	**1,357**	**29**	**13**	**47**	**89**	...	**4,255.1**
Africa	...	...	**1,361.6**	**322.4**	**4.39**	**1.98**	**1,013**	**240**	**10**	**2**	**24**	**45**	...	**1,344.8**
Europe	...	...	**7,422.3**	**4,726.3**	**23.95**	**28.99**	**13,630**	**8,679**	**135**	**86**	**64**	**121**	...	**544.6**
United States	**1.00**	**1.00**	**3,366.3**	**3,366.3**	**10.86**	**20.65**	**10,128**	**10,128**	**100**	**100**	**100**	**190**	**3,366**	**332.4**
Rest of the World	...	...	**6,474.9**	**2,116.0**	**20.89**	**12.98**	**6,214**	**2,031**	**61**	**20**	**33**	**62**	...	**1,042.0**
World	...	...	**30,989.7**	**16,303.3**	**100.00**	**100.00**	**4,122**	**2,168**	**41**	**21**	**53**	**100**	...	**7,518.8**

... = not available/applicable, $ = United States dollars, ADB = Asian Development Bank, ICP = International Comparison Program, LCU = local currency unit, US = United States.

Source: ADB estimates using data from World Bank. DataBank: ICP 2021. https://databank.worldbank.org/source/icp-2021# (accessed 4 June 2024).

Table A1.7: Summary Results for Gross Fixed Capital Formation, 2021

Economy	Purchasing Power Parity ($ = 1.00)	Exchange Rate ($ = 1.00)	Expenditure ($ billion)		Shares (World = 100.00)		Expenditure Per Capita ($)		Expenditure Per Capita Indexes (US = 100)		Price Level Indexes		Reference Data	
			Real	Nominal	Real	Nominal	Real	Nominal	Real	Nominal	US = 100	World = 100	Expenditure (LCU billion)	Population (million)
Developing ADB Member Economies	...	...	**18,874.8**	**10,651.5**	**49.72**	**42.25**	**4,605**	**2,599**	**30**	**17**	**56**	**85**	...	**4,098.8**
Armenia	184.16	503.77	8.0	2.9	0.02	0.01	2,707	989	18	7	37	55	1,477	3.0
Azerbaijan	0.62	1.70	24.4	8.8	0.06	0.04	2,433	881	16	6	36	55	15	10.0
Bangladesh	34.40	85.10	344.2	139.1	0.91	0.55	2,021	817	13	5	40	61	11,838	170.3
Bhutan	30.40	73.94	3.0	1.2	0.01	0.00	3,917	1,610	26	11	41	62	90	0.8
Brunei Darussalam	0.58	1.34	10.0	4.4	0.03	0.02	22,741	9,881	150	65	43	65	6	0.4
Cambodia	1,470.62	4,098.72	17.2	6.2	0.05	0.02	1,036	372	7	2	36	54	25,281	16.6
China, People's Republic of	4.25	6.45	11,381.4	7,498.8	29.98	29.75	8,058	5,309	53	35	66	99	48,378	1,412.4
Fiji	0.97	2.07	1.8	0.8	0.00	0.00	1,996	935	13	6	47	71	2	0.9
Georgia	1.06	3.23	11.8	3.9	0.03	0.02	3,185	1,049	21	7	33	50	13	3.7
Hong Kong, China	5.99	7.77	80.6	62.1	0.21	0.25	10,870	8,381	72	55	77	116	483	7.4
India	25.38	73.92	2,574.9	883.9	6.78	3.51	1,883	647	12	4	34	52	65,339	1,367.2
Indonesia	5,070.16	14,308.14	1,031.1	365.4	2.72	1.45	3,781	1,340	25	9	35	53	5,227,854	272.7
Kazakhstan	164.77	426.03	117.4	45.4	0.31	0.18	6,177	2,389	41	16	39	58	19,342	19.0
Korea, Republic of	780.21	1,143.95	843.8	575.5	2.22	2.28	16,307	11,122	108	73	68	103	658,353	51.7
Kyrgyz Republic	23.64	84.64	8.0	2.2	0.02	0.01	1,167	326	8	2	28	42	189	6.9
Lao People's Democratic Republic	3,934.54	9,697.92	21.4	8.7	0.06	0.03	2,914	1,182	19	8	41	61	84,137	7.3
Malaysia	1.66	4.14	180.1	72.0	0.47	0.29	5,529	2,211	37	15	40	60	298	32.6
Maldives	7.98	15.38	2.9	1.5	0.01	0.01	5,056	2,624	33	17	52	78	23	0.6
Mongolia	1,172.31	2,849.29	10.0	4.1	0.03	0.02	3,037	1,250	20	8	41	62	11,688	3.3
Nepal	44.07	118.13	30.5	11.4	0.08	0.05	1,050	392	7	3	37	56	1,345	29.1
Pakistan	60.05	162.63	137.3	50.7	0.36	0.20	611	226	4	1	37	56	8,247	224.8
Philippines	20.31	49.25	212.9	87.8	0.56	0.35	1,932	797	13	5	41	62	4,325	110.2
Singapore	0.82	1.34	158.6	96.7	0.42	0.38	29,077	17,737	192	117	61	92	130	5.5
Sri Lanka	74.74	198.88	61.9	23.3	0.16	0.09	2,795	1,051	18	7	38	57	4,629	22.2
Taipei,China	16.16	28.02	352.2	203.1	0.93	0.81	15,008	8,655	99	57	58	87	5,692	23.5
Tajikistan	3.12	11.31	10.4	2.9	0.03	0.01	1,058	292	7	2	28	42	32	9.8
Thailand	12.77	31.98	300.6	120.1	0.79	0.48	4,314	1,723	28	11	40	60	3,840	69.7
Türkiye	3.63	8.89	563.8	230.0	1.49	0.91	6,700	2,733	44	18	41	61	2,044	84.1
Uzbekistan	3,569.51	10,609.98	70.8	23.8	0.19	0.09	2,027	682	13	5	34	51	252,613	34.9
Viet Nam	8,748.39	23,159.89	303.8	114.8	0.80	0.46	3,084	1,165	20	8	38	57	2,658,069	98.5
Developed ADB Member Economies	...	...	**1,733.5**	**1,722.4**	**4.57**	**6.83**	**11,091**	**11,020**	**73**	**73**	**99**	**150**	...	**156.3**
Australia	1.44	1.33	351.0	380.7	0.92	1.51	13,664	14,820	90	98	108	163	507	25.7
Japan	105.36	109.75	1,334.5	1,281.1	3.52	5.08	10,633	10,208	70	67	96	145	140,608	125.5
New Zealand	1.79	1.41	48.0	60.6	0.13	0.24	9,385	11,860	62	78	126	190	86	5.1
Asia and the Pacific (33)	...	...	**20,608.3**	**12,374.0**	**54.29**	**49.08**	**4,843**	**2,908**	**32**	**19**	**60**	**90**	...	**4,255.1**
Africa	...	...	**1,112.5**	**548.1**	**2.93**	**2.17**	**827**	**408**	**5**	**3**	**49**	**74**	...	**1,344.8**
Europe	...	...	**6,470.4**	**4,714.8**	**17.04**	**18.70**	**11,882**	**8,658**	**78**	**57**	**73**	**110**	...	**544.6**
United States	**1.00**	**1.00**	**5,031.4**	**5,031.4**	**13.25**	**19.96**	**15,138**	**15,138**	**100**	**100**	**100**	**151**	**5,031**	**332.4**
Rest of the World	...	...	**4,739.3**	**2,541.6**	**12.48**	**10.08**	**4,548**	**2,439**	**30**	**16**	**54**	**81**	...	**1,042.0**
World	...	...	**37,961.8**	**25,209.8**	**100.00**	**100.00**	**5,049**	**3,353**	**33**	**22**	**66**	**100**	...	**7,518.8**

... = not available/applicable, $ = United States dollars, ADB = Asian Development Bank, ICP = International Comparison Program, LCU = local currency unit, US = United States.

Source: ADB estimates using data from World Bank. DataBank: ICP 2021. https://databank.worldbank.org/source/icp-2021# (accessed 4 June 2024).

APPENDIX 2

Product Lists as Instruments to Enhance Representativity and Comparability

Developing regional product lists for price surveys is a crucial step in the International Comparison Program (ICP). The items included in these lists must represent the purchases of goods and services in the participating economies and they must overlap sufficiently with the ICP's global core list so that regional purchasing power parities (PPPs) can be used to calculate global PPPs.

Comparability within the ICP is ensured by providing well-defined specifications for each product and including branded products with specific "make and model" details wherever feasible. This task is challenging in Asia and the Pacific due to the diversity of the region's economies. The regional items list for the ICP must represent consumption patterns and investments across geographically and culturally diverse economies of the region, including highly advanced and high-income economies such as Singapore and Hong Kong, China, and lower-middle-income economies such as Cambodia and Nepal.

While the Asian Development Bank (ADB), as the regional implementing agency for the ICP in Asia and the Pacific, prepares and updates product lists for all ICP price surveys in close collaboration with the participating economies, this appendix details specific measures taken for three lists: (i) household consumption, (ii) construction, and (iii) machinery and equipment.

Household Product List

Among all ICP surveys, the price survey for household products is the most resource-intensive. In the 2021 ICP cycle for the Asia and Pacific region, the household product list included 990 items and, in the 2024 ICP cycle, it has 1,050 items. The key challenge for the region, with its diverse economies, is to ensure good representation of subregional consumption and alignment with global core items.

The 2005 ICP household product list for Asia and the Pacific, the first with ADB as the regional implementing agency, was developed after strong collaboration with price experts from the participating economies and careful reviews of the consumer price index (CPI) item baskets in the participating economies. In subsequent cycles, the list has been updated by ADB after extensive consultations with the price experts of the participating economies, including face-to-face regional workshops. These updates ensure that the new and emerging items are incorporated, obsolete items are deleted, and product specifications improved for correct identification for price collection.

To ensure effective collaboration on the list for the 2024 ICP cycle, ADB developed an online interactive tool to expediently gather suggestions from participating economies on product specifications, new items, and deletion of obsolete products (Figure A2.1). This interactive platform evoked great interest and generated numerous suggestions, which were consolidated for further discussions in a regional workshop to finalize the draft product list for the 2024 ICP cycle.

Ensuring Representativity in the Household Product List

Regional workshops on the household product list are conducted with discussions organized by subregions of the Asia and Pacific region to ensure adequate representation of items of consumption in each subregion. For example, rice is important in almost all economies of the region,

Figure A2.1: Online Survey Tool for Updating the 2024 Household Product List

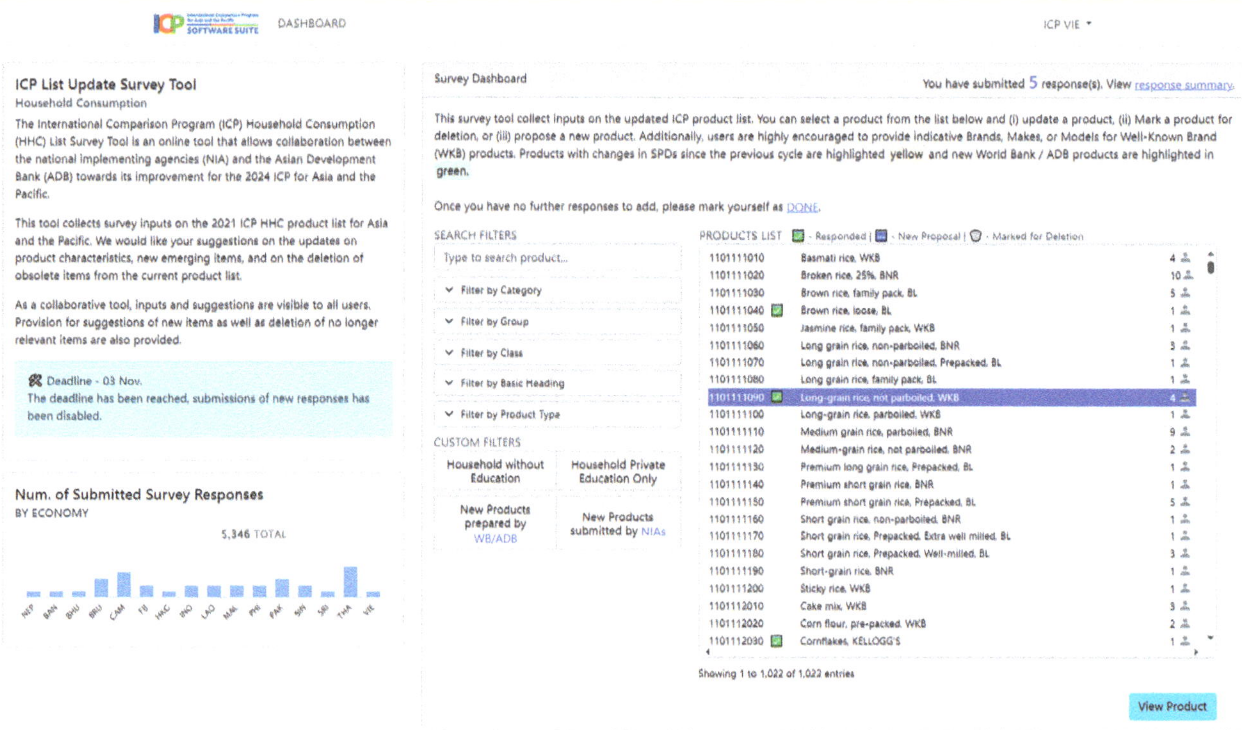

Source: Asian Development Bank screenshot.

but varieties such as basmati are more common in South Asia. Lentils are also more widely consumed in South Asian economies, which also have a different focus on clothing items such as sarees.

There are also subregional and economy-level differences in communication services, with high internet speeds and unlimited data plans commonly subscribed in high-income economies and data plans of lower speeds often typical in other economies. Similar challenges arise with fast-moving technology items and motor cars. In high-income economies, the latest technology releases and vehicle models are more quickly purchased while older versions and models remain popular in lower-middle-income economies.

Incorporating this diversity into the ICP household product list for the region requires collective effort, ensuring each economy can price representative items for household consumption. It means that each economy is able to price an adequate number of representative and important items for each basic heading of household consumption.

Ensuring Comparability in the Household Product List

Regional discussions on the household product list also focus on balancing localized product representation with the ICP's global core products list to facilitate effective global comparisons. In the 2024 ICP cycle, the allocation of items between the regional and global lists provides a balance across household consumption categories: almost 43% of the products are exclusive to Asia and the Pacific; another 43% overlap with the global core list; and about 14% are global core items included to strengthen region-to-global linking.

Table A2.1 shows the distribution of household product items by regional exclusivity, regional-global commonality, and global core linkage for the 2024 ICP cycle in Asia and the Pacific.

Table A2.1: Distribution of Items in the Household Product List for Asia and the Pacific, 2024

Consumption Categories	Number of Products			
	AP	AG	GL	Total
Food and nonalcoholic beverages	137	121	56	314
Alcoholic beverages, tobacco and narcotics	8	9	2	19
Clothing and footwear	56	27	19	102
Housing, water, electricity, gas and other fuels*	7	10	2	19
Furnishings, household equipment and routine household maintenance	82	34	20	136
Health**	18	139	2	159
Transport	50	33	16	99
Communication	10	19	6	35
Recreation and culture	33	32	12	77
Education	0	7	1	8
Restaurants and hotels	16	5	9	30
Miscellaneous goods and services and net purchases abroad	31	12	9	52
Household consumption	**448**	**448**	**154**	**1,050**

* A separate ICP Housing Rental Survey will be conducted to collect actual rental prices and Housing Volume indicators for dwelling services will also be compiled separately.

** 49 global pharmaceutical items (parent items) are excluded from the count since average prices of these items will be derived from the split pharmaceutical items.

AG = Asia and the Pacific and Global Product Overlap, AP = Asia and the Pacific Product, GL = Global Core List Product.

Source: Asian Development Bank compilation and analysis.

The consultations led by ADB to develop the region's household product list exemplify the level of cooperation among participating economies to ensure national and regional representativity and price comparability in the household survey.

Item Splitting in the Household Price Survey

The validation of household price data is crucial for ensuring comparability across economies. Prices are gathered by different price enumerators who visit market outlets periodically (usually every month or quarter) to ascertain the prevailing prices. The product description of each item guides the enumerators in collecting accurate prices for the prescribed item specifications.

During the early stages of price validations for the 2011 ICP cycle in Asia and the Pacific, large and unusual variations in the prices of specific items were observed. Different reasons were identified for such variations, including pricing of items with different specifications due to the items with the prescribed specifications not being available in local markets.

A possible reason for the pricing of different specifications—and a common issue during price validation—is "brand clustering". This is where different brands with similar specifications are treated as substitutes in multiple economies. For instance, home appliances such as steam and dry irons, air conditioners, refrigerators, phones, and similar durable goods are available in several models from different brands, and one single model and/or brand may not be the most popular across all economies. Brand clustering can conceal genuine price differences, leading to price dispersion within an economy and poor intereconomy comparability.

To address this issue, "product splitting" is necessary to improve data quality. This involves splitting the initially identified item into more than one item with brand attributes. To continue the example above, in the 2011 ICP cycle, the item "steam and dry iron" was split into three different items, i.e., "steam and dry iron (Panasonic)," "steam and dry iron (Philips)", and "steam and dry iron (other brands)" to cater to the requirements of different markets and ensure comparability. In subsequent ICP cycles, the split items were added as independent items.

Another important example of product splitting adopted in the Asia and Pacific region is for pharmaceutical items. Initially, these items were classified only as originator and generic medicines, based on the World Health Organization's List of Essential Medicines. However, due to high price variability across economies, further splitting was necessary.

In the 2011 ICP cycle in Asia and the Pacific, originator drugs were split by brand name while generic drugs were classified by source (either locally produced or imported). This practice has been continued in the subsequent ICP cycles. In the 2021 ICP cycle, the original 49 parent pharmaceutical items (which are also part of the ICP global core list) were expanded into 117 child items for data collection.

For example, under the parent item "acetaminophen/ paracetamol, 500 mg, tablet/capsule", the product list provides two child items for generic medicines with different sources and five child items for originator brands: Calpol (GlaxoSmithKline), Crocin (Solvay Pharma), Panadol (GlaxoSmithKline), Panodil (GlaxoSmithKline), and acetaminophen/paracetamol (other brand). Economies reported prices from the list of 117 child items, which were then used in calculating regional PPPs for the basic heading "pharmaceutical products". This practice, which ensures relevance to local market structures and consistency with global standards, has been maintained in the ICP cycles for Asia and the Pacific.

Construction Product List

The construction product list has also had issues around the standardization protocols used to achieve representativity and comparability.

In the 2005 ICP cycle, a standardization approach using a "basket of construction components" was applied, which aimed to price standard construction outputs. However, practical difficulties in implementation, including variation in specifications and a heavy data burden, limited this approach's effectiveness.

In response, from the 2011 ICP cycle onwards, the "input" approach has been adopted for the ICP. This is a much simpler approach, requiring collection of prices for a list of standard inputs—construction materials, labor (skilled and unskilled), and equipment rentals—used in residential, nonresidential, and civil engineering work. This list was developed by the ICP Global Office and includes 50 construction inputs and one regional item: 33 items for materials, 10 items for equipment rental, and 8 items for labor inputs. The list is uniformly adopted by all ICP regions.

While conducting a detailed review of the full 2024 ICP product list, ADB identified the need to regionalize the construction product list, in a similar way to the household product list, to suit the specifics of the Asia and Pacific region.

After assessing national construction input surveys from some of the region's economies, and following consultations with experts from the implementing agencies in a regional workshop, ADB added three new items for construction materials items and four new items for rental equipment (one labor input item was already included as a regional item in the 2017 ICP list). The addition of these seven new regional items in the 2024 ICP product list improved the overall representation for construction products.

The seven items added for Asia and the Pacific were shared with the ICP Global Office, which decided to include them in the global list of construction items for the 2024 ICP cycle. Thus, ADB input has again demonstrated how regional knowledge can contribute to improving global product lists.

Machinery and Equipment Product List

The machinery and equipment (MEQ) price survey is challenging due to the detailed technical specifications that should be met while collecting the item prices. Even minor differences in technical specifications can lead to significant price variation. Adding to this complexity, staff in statistics offices are generally not trained to carry out MEQ surveys, as they might be for household and consumer price surveys.

The MEQ product list, developed by the ICP Global Office, ensures worldwide comparability of MEQ items, which economies often import under commercial arrangements with multinational brands and/or via trade with other economies. The list facilitates the pricing of particular makes and models of MEQ to ensure comparability.

The MEQ product list for the 2024 ICP cycle has 214 items, of which 106 are "specified" items and 108 are "unspecified" items. Specified items are attributed to specific brands and models, while their unspecified counterpart items allow economies to price other brands that are more representative of the acquisitions made by domestic firms. Under the latter pricing option, the unspecified item must have specifications identical or equivalent to the corresponding specified item to guarantee price comparability across economies.

From a representativity perspective, the importance of unspecified items can be gauged by assessing the pricing practices of the 21 economies of Asia and the Pacific participating in the 2021 ICP cycle under ADB's regional stewardship. Of these 21 economies, 15 priced more than 50% unspecified MEQ items, with two small economies pricing at least 75% unspecified MEQ items. On average, 55% of the MEQ items priced by all economies in the region were unspecified items.

However, comparison of prices of unspecified MEQ items is complicated by the fact that wide price variations for these items have been observed across economies. Extensive validation at the regional level is required to confirm the comparability of items priced, but this requires detailed information on item specifications for every price quotation to assess if the correct specifications were priced.

Regionalizing the Machinery and Equipment Product List

To address the need for item comparability and improving regional representativity of the MEQ product list, ADB has started regionalizing the MEQ product list. This began with the 2021 ICP cycle, when indicative models were provided for 42 of the 91 unspecified items in the product list for the MEQ survey in Asia and the Pacific. The process was continued for the 2024 ICP cycle in the region. ADB experts researched MEQ items to identify indicative brands and models for unspecified MEQ items, and the experts in the implementing agencies of the participating economies were asked to suggest popular brands and models available in their markets. Indicative brands and models have now been added for 64 of the 108 unspecified MEQ items in the 2024 product list, easing the price collection and validation process for this survey. This pricing of indicative brands and models improves price comparability and strengthens regional representation in the MEQ product list.

In addition to including the indicative brands and models, ADB identified 35 additional items of MEQ while updating the 2024 ICP product list for the MEQ survey. These 35 new regionally available items (17 specified and 18 unspecified) were included in the regional MEQ product list after consultations with all participating economies. Some additions were necessary because a few of the region's larger economies are becoming exporters and are supplying MEQ items to other economies in the region. Other additions were made to reflect the needs of smaller and developing economies. These 35 new regional items have also been included in the ICP global list by the World Bank, enhancing the comparability and representativity of the global product list, reflecting regional contributions to improve global comparisons.

Item Splitting in the Machinery and Equipment Survey

Staff in statistics offices of participating economies often lack the technical expertise to assess detailed product characteristics, particularly for complex or high-value machinery items. While major specified items—typically imported and associated with recognized makes and models—can be priced more easily, unspecified items as discussed above present difficulties due to local variations in features, quality, and origin.

To address these constraints, ADB engages an international expert to conduct regional workshops focused on MEQ product identification, survey implementation, and price validation.

Economies are also encouraged to consult local technical experts and provide detailed product specifications for review by ADB. Emphasis is placed on identifying the essential characteristics that determine product comparability. The international expert engaged by ADB helps the ADB team in reviewing economy submissions to assess whether products priced with closely matching but nonidentical features could be accepted for inclusion in price comparisons. If the analysis of the product characteristics reveals the possibility of segmentation based on quality differences, then splits are introduced based on product quality.

As an illustration of this process, in the 2021 ICP cycle, a particular power tool (with the item identification "heavy duty cordless combi – unspecified") demonstrated high price variability across economies. A closer examination revealed that the prices submitted for this item could be grouped into two homogenous price groups. When detailed specifications were collected, it was found that some economies had priced the item with a battery voltage of 18 volts while others had priced the item with a battery voltage of 36 volts. This led to the decision to split the item into two using the quality information revealed by the analysis.

However, there are instances when the price of an item exhibits considerable variability and the economies are unable to provide sufficient information about the product characteristics of unspecified MEQ items, making it impossible to split the items according to differences in product characteristics. At the same time, it is not considered useful to discard the prices that have been collected with great effort and confirmed by economy representatives.

An Expert Group commissioned by ADB suggested using variability in the collected prices to identify items that could be split. Items were recommended to be split into two clusters if their price coefficient of variation exceeded 40 or if the standard deviation of country-product-dummy residuals of prices exceeded 0.40 (Table A2.2, Column 2). Using average prices in Hong Kong dollars, the average item prices submitted by the economies were grouped into two clusters, i.e., above and below the average price for all economies. This assumes each price cluster represents a distinct level of similar quality characteristics which is consistent within the cluster: the cluster above the average price reflecting a consistently higher quality and the cluster below the average price indicating a consistently lower quality.

In the 2021 ICP cycle, one item was split using product-specific information while price-based splitting, following the advice of the Expert Group, was applied to 23 unspecified items (Table A2.2, Column 4). These 24 splits increased the total number of items for comparison from 179 to 203 for regional PPP calculations.

Of the original 179 items in the MEQ product list for the 2021 ICP cycle, the number of items priced by each economy ranged from a low of 21 items to a high of 82 items. The price clustering based splitting approach, although less efficient than the product characteristics based approach, provides a reasonable basis for making use of the prices collected by the economies.

Table A2.2: Number of Items Priced and Splits by Basic Headings for Machinery and Equipment, 2021

Basic Heading	Original Items			Split Price Clusters	
	SD of CPD ≤ 0.4 or CV ≤ 40	SD of CPD > 0.4 or CV > 40	Total	Additional Items for Splitting Process	Total (Original and Split)
	(1)	(2)	(3)	(4)	(5) = (3) + (4)
Machinery and equipment	155	24	179	24	203
Fabricated metal products except MEQ	5	5	10	5	15
Electrical and optical equipment	61	7	68	7	75
General purpose machinery	22	4	26	4	30
Special purpose machinery	47	5	52	5	57
Road transport equipment	20	3	23	3	26

CPD= country-product-dummy, CV= coefficient of variation, MEQ = machinery and equipment, SD= standard deviation.

Notes: The table assesses data from the 2021 cycle of the International Comparison Program in Asia and the Pacific. It presents the outcomes of the price clustering procedure applied to 24 items across the five basic headings of MEQ survey, as shown in column (2). Items were assessed based on two criteria: a price CV greater than 40 or a SD of CPD residuals exceeding 0.4. Items exceeding either threshold were split into two groups (low and high).

Source: Asian Development Bank compilation and analysis.

Glossary

Term	Definition
Actual individual consumption by households (AICH)	AICH is the sum of individual consumption expenditures by households, expenditures by nonprofit institutions serving households, and individual consumption expenditure by government at purchasers' prices.
Basic heading	A basic heading is, in principle, a group of similar well-defined goods or services for which a sample of products can be selected, with the products being both representative of their type and of the purchases made in economies. In practice, a basic heading is defined as the smallest aggregate for which expenditure data are available.
Benchmark	A benchmark is a standard or point of reference against which an estimate can be compared, assessed, measured, or judged. In the International Comparison Program, the reference year is often referred to as the "benchmark year" or simply as the "benchmark." Purchasing power parities are calculated using price data from a full list of household and nonhousehold products and weights derived from the expenditures on gross domestic product for a specified reference year.
Big Mac index	The Big Mac index was developed and used by The Economist to illustrate the use of purchasing power parities. It is based on the price of a McDonald's Big Mac hamburger compared across economies.
Classification of individual consumption according to purpose	This classification is used to identify the objectives of both individual consumption expenditure and actual individual consumption.
Collective consumption expenditure by government	The final consumption expenditure provided by general government on collective services. The collective services are provided simultaneously to all members of the community or to all members of a particular section of the community, such as all households living in a particular region.
Comparability	Comparability is a requirement for economies to price products that are identical or, if not identical, equivalent. Pricing comparable products ensures that differences in prices between economies for a product reflect actual price differences and are not influenced by differences in quality. Two or more products are said to be comparable either if their physical and economic characteristics are identical or if they are sufficiently similar that consumers are indifferent to the variances between them.

Term	Definition
Comparison resistant	The term "comparison resistant" was first used to describe nonmarket services that are difficult to compare across economies because (i) they have no economically significant prices with which to value outputs; (ii) their units of output cannot be otherwise defined and measured, or the institutional arrangements for their provision and the conditions of payment differ from economy to economy; and (iii) their quality varies between economies, but the differences cannot be identified and quantified. Increasingly, the term is being used to describe capital goods and many market services whose complexity, variability, and economy specificity make it difficult for them to be priced comparably across economies.
Compensation of employees	Compensation of employees refers to total remuneration, in cash or in kind, payable by enterprises to employees in return for work done by the employees during a given accounting period.
Component	A component is a subset of goods or services, or both, which make up some defined aggregate.
Consumer price index (CPI)	The CPI is an index of price changes within an economy across time.
Country-product-dummy method	This is a multilateral method used to obtain transitive purchasing power parities (PPPs) at the basic heading level through regression analysis. This method is anchored on the "law of one price" which simply states that the observed price of a commodity in an economy is the product of the international average price of the commodity, general price level in the economy, and a random disturbance term. This method regresses log of price observed, on country and product dummy variables and hence the label. The method produces measures of reliability for the estimated PPPs.
Dwellings	Dwellings are buildings that are used entirely or primarily as residences, including any associated structures (such as garages) and all permanent fixtures customarily installed in residences. Movable structures, such as caravans, used as principal residences of households are included.
Expenditures	Expenditures are values of the amounts that buyers pay, or agree to pay, in exchange for goods or services that sellers provide to them or to other institutional units designated by the buyers.
Final consumption	Final consumption comprises all goods and services consumed by individual households or the community during a given period to satisfy their individual or collective needs or wants.
Fixity	Fixity is the principle that purchasing power parities between economies in a region (and therefore the volume relativities based on purchasing power parities) do not change when the results from that region are combined with those from another region (or regions).

Term	Definition
Gini–Eltetö–Köves–Szulc method (GEKS)	A method used to calculate PPPs for basic headings or to aggregate basic heading PPPs to obtain PPPs for each level of aggregation up to GDP. The GEKS method is a procedure that enables transformation of nontransitive binary purchasing power parities into transitive purchasing power parities, so that comparisons made between any pair of economies are mutually consistent. The GEKS method produces transitive purchasing power parities that are as close as possible to the nontransitive purchasing power parities originally calculated in the binary comparisons of two or more economies. In practice, the GEKS method is relevant only to the second part of this process (i.e., making the purchasing power parities transitive). Real expenditures obtained using GEKS-based purchasing power parities are not additive, so the sum of the real expenditures for the components of gross domestic product does not equal the real expenditure on gross domestic product.
Goods	Goods are physical objects for which a demand exists, over which ownership rights can be established, and whose ownership can be transferred from one institutional unit to another by engaging in transactions on the market. They are in demand because they may be used to satisfy the needs or wants of households or the community, or used to produce other goods or services
Government final consumption expenditure (GFCE)	GFCE is the final consumption expenditure by government, consisting of expenditure (including imputed expenditure) incurred by general government on both individual consumption goods and services and on collective consumption services.
Gross capital formation (GCF)	GCF is a measure of the total value of gross fixed capital formation, changes in inventories, and acquisitions less disposals of valuables for a given unit or sector.
Gross domestic product (GDP)—expenditure-based	When estimated from the expenditure side, GDP is a measure of the total value of the final consumption expenditures of households and general government and gross capital formation plus the balance of exports and imports.
Gross fixed capital formation (GFCF)	GFCF measures the total value of a producer's acquisitions, less disposals, of fixed assets during a given accounting period. It includes certain additions to the value of nonproduced assets (such as subsoil assets or major improvements in the quantity, quality, or productivity of land) realized by the productive activity of institutional units.

Term	Definition
Household products	Household products refer to the consumption of households for the following components: • Food and nonalcoholic beverages • Alcoholic beverages, tobacco, and narcotics • Clothing and footwear • Housing, water, electricity, gas, and other fuels • Furnishings, household equipment, and routine maintenance of the house • Health • Transport • Communication • Recreation and culture • Education • Restaurant and hotels • Miscellaneous goods and services (personal grooming, personal care, personal effects, financial services, and other services).
Individual consumption expenditure by household (ICEH)	ICEH is the total value of actual and imputed final consumption expenditures incurred by households for goods and services consumed by the households. In the context of the International Comparison Program in Asia and the Pacific, ICEH also includes the individual consumption expenditure by nonprofit institutions serving households.
Local currency unit (LCU)	An LCU is a monetary unit in which economic values are expressed in an economy.
Lorenz curve	Developed by Max Lorenz in 1905, the Lorenz curve is a graphical representation of the distribution of income or wealth. The horizontal axis of the graph represents the percentiles of population, while the vertical axis represents the cumulative income or wealth of those percentiles.
Multilateral comparison	A multilateral comparison is a simultaneous price or volume comparison of more than two economies that produces consistent relations among all pairs of economies, i.e., one that satisfies the transitivity requirement.
National annual average price	A national annual average price is a price that has been averaged over all localities of an economy to account for regional variations in prices, and over the days, weeks, months, or quarters of the reference year to allow for seasonal variations in prices as well as general inflation and changes in price structures.
Nominal expenditure	The term "nominal expenditure" is used when expenditure in local currency units is converted to a common currency using market exchange rates. Nominal expenditure may be presented either in terms of a common currency or as an index number relative to the region's total nominal expenditure.
Nonprofit institutions serving households (NPISHs)	NPISHs are entities not predominantly financed and/or controlled by government and that provide goods or services to households free or at prices that are not economically significant.
Per capita expenditure	Per capita expenditure is obtained by dividing total expenditure by the total population of a given economy or the reference geography.

Term	Definition
Price	The monetary value of one unit of a particular good or service.
Price level index (PLI)	Also referred to as "comparative price levels", the PLI is the ratio of a purchasing power parity to the corresponding exchange rate. It shows how the price levels of an economy compare with each other. It is expressed as an index on a base of 100. A PLI greater than 100 means that, when the national average prices are converted at exchange rates, the resulting prices tend to be higher on average than prices in the base economy. At the level of gross domestic product, PLIs provide a measure of the differences in the general price levels of economies.
Productivity adjustment	Productivity adjustment is an adjustment made to the wages and salaries of employees in different economies so that the remuneration reflects the same level of labor productivity.
Purchasing power parity	A purchasing power parity is a relative price that measures the number of units of economy B's currency that are needed in economy B to purchase the same quantity of an individual good or service as one unit of economy A's currency will purchase in economy A.
Real expenditure	Real expenditures are measures obtained by using purchasing power parities to convert final expenditures on product groups, major aggregates, and gross domestic product expressed in the local currency units of different economies into a common currency, by valuing them at a uniform price level. They are the spatial equivalent of a time series of gross domestic product for a single economy expressed at constant prices. Expenditures so converted reflect only volume differences, providing a measure of the relative magnitudes of the product groups or aggregates being compared across economies. At the level of gross domestic product, real expenditure is used to compare the sizes of economies. They may be presented either in terms of a particular currency or as an index number.
Reference purchasing power parity	The PPP used for basic headings for which it is difficult to collect price data to calculate the PPP. The PPP of a closely related basic heading or a group of basic headings for which prices are collected is used as a reference PPP. See also *Basic heading*.
Resident	An institutional unit is resident in an economy when it has a center of economic interest in the economic territory.
Services	Services are the result of a production activity that changes the conditions of the consuming units or facilitates the exchange of products or financial assets.
Structured product description	A structured product description is a standardized description that lists the characteristics relevant to a particular narrow cluster of products so that all specifications for a particular type of product are defined in the same way and specify the same parameters.
Total consumption	Total consumption is the total value of individual consumption expenditures by households, nonprofit institutions serving households, and government final consumption expenditure at purchasers' prices.

References

Alfani, F., D. V. Aaron, A. Atamanov, R. A. C. Aguilar, C. Diaz-Bonilla, N. P. Devpura, R. Dewina, et al. 2025. June 2025 Update to the Poverty and Inequality Platform. World Bank. http://documents.worldbank.org/curated/en/099510306052516849.

Asian Development Bank (ADB). 2007. *2005 International Comparison Program in Asia and the Pacific: Purchasing Power Parities and Real Expenditures.* https://www.adb.org/sites/default/files/publication/29145/ppp-real-expenditures.pdf.

———. 2008. *Research Study on Poverty-Specific Purchasing Power Parities for Selected Countries in Asia and the Pacific.* https://www.adb.org/sites/default/files/publication/29130/poverty-specific-ppp.pdf.

———. 2012a. *2009 Purchasing Power Parity Update for Selected Economies in Asia and the Pacific: A Research Study.* https://www.adb.org/sites/default/files/publication/30437/2009-ppp-update-research-study.pdf.

———. 2012b. *Supply and Use Tables for Selected Economies in Asia and the Pacific: A Research Study.* https://www.adb.org/sites/default/files/publication/30121/supply-and-use-tables-research-study.pdf.

———. 2017. *Compendium of Supply and Use Tables for Selected Economies in Asia and the Pacific.* https://www.adb.org/sites/default/files/publication/378246/compendium-supply-use-tables-selected-economies.pdf.

———. 2020. *2017 International Comparison Program for Asia and the Pacific: Purchasing Power Parities and Real Expenditures: Results and Methodology.* https://www.adb.org/sites/default/files/publication/639696/icp-2017-results-methodology.pdf.

———. 2021. *Constructing Purchasing Power Parities Using a Reduced Information Approach: A Research Study.* https://www.adb.org/sites/default/files/publication/674276/purchasing-power-parities-reduced-information-approach.pdf.

———. 2023. *Key Indicators for Asia and the Pacific 2023.* 54th edition. https://www.adb.org/publications/key-indicators-asia-and-pacific-2023.

———. 2024a. *2021 International Comparison Program for Asia and the Pacific: Purchasing Power Parities and Real Expenditures: A Summary Report.* https://www.adb.org/sites/default/files/publication/992941/2021-icp-asia-pacific-summary-report.pdf.

———. 2024b. *Steering ADB's Corporate Strategy to Success: Corporate Results Framework, 2025–2030: Policy Paper.* https://www.adb.org/sites/default/files/institutional-document/1003566/adb-results-framework-2025-2030-policy-paper.pdf.

Balk, B., A. N. Rambaldi, and D. S. P. Rao. 2022. Macroeconomic Measures for a Globalized World: Global Growth and Inflation. *Macroeconomic Dynamics*. Cambridge University Press. 26 (2). pp. 1–47 and pp. 314–360. https://doi.org/10.1017/S1365100520000152.

Deaton, A. 2004. Measuring Poverty. *Working Papers*. No. 170. Woodrow Wilson School of Public and International Affairs, Research Program in Development Studies. Princeton University.

Deaton, A. and O. Dupriez. 2011. Purchasing Power Parity Exchange Rates for the Global Poor. *American Economic Journal: Applied Economics*. 3 (2). pp. 137–66. https://thedocs.worldbank.org/en/doc/742501487995206666-0050022017/original/DeatonDupriezFinalPaper.pdf.

Dikhanov, Y., N. Hamadeh, W. Vigil-Oliver, T. B. Degefu, and I. Song. 2017. Poverty-Specific Purchasing Power Parities in Africa. *Policy Research Working Paper*. No. 8150. World Bank. https://documents1.worldbank.org/curated/en/271051500404610210/pdf/WPS8150.pdf.

Food and Agriculture Organization of the United Nations (FAO), International Fund for Agricultural Development, United Nations Children's Fund, World Food Programme, and World Health Organization. 2025. *The State of Food Security and Nutrition in the World 2025*. https://doi.org/10.4060/cd6008en.

Hajargasht, G., A. N. Rambaldi, and D. S. P. Rao. 2025. Convergence in the World Economy: Evidence from the Last Fifty Years. *CEPA Working Papers Series*. Number 022025. School of Economics: University of Queensland.

Heston, A. 2013. "Dwelling Services." In Measuring the Real Size of the World Economy, edited by World Bank. Washington, DC: World Bank.

International Comparison Program Inter-Agency Coordination Group. 2022. From local prices to the global economy: A unique global collaboration that underpins the International Comparison Program. *Statistical Journal of the International Association for Official Statistics*. 38 (3), 1067–1080.

Inklaar, R. C. 2019. *Productivity Adjustment in ICP*. Paper presented at the 4th Technical Advisory Group Meeting, International Comparison Program. 28–29 October.

International Monetary Fund (IMF). World Economic Outlook Database: April 2025. https://www.imf.org/en/Publications/WEO/weo-database/2025/april (accessed 31 July 2025).

Madison, A. 2006. China in the World Economy: 1300–2030. *International Journal of Business*. 11 (3).

Rao, D. S. P, A. N. Rambaldi, G. Hajargasht, D. Chotikapanich, and W. E. Griffiths. 2022. UQ International Comparisons Database: UQICD V3.0. https://uqicd.economics.uq.edu.au (accessed 20 May 2025).

Ravallion, M., G. Datt, and D. van de Walle. 1991. Quantifying Absolute Poverty in the Developing World. *Review of Income and Wealth*. 37. pp. 345–361.

The Economist. Big Mac Index. https://www.economist.com/big-mac-index (accessed 7 May 2025).

United Nations. 2025. *System of National Accounts 2025*. Pre-edit version. https://unstats.un.org/unsd/nationalaccount/docs/2025_SNA_Pre-edit.pdf.

United Nations Economic and Social Council (ECOSOC). 1968. National Accounts and Balances: International Comparison of Production, Income, and Expenditure Aggregates. Prepared for the 15th Session of the United Nations Statistical Commission. New York: United Nations. https://unstats.un.org/UNSDWebsite/statcom/session_15/documents/1968-364-Comparison-E.pdf.

———. 1999. Evaluation of the International Comparison Programme. New York: United Nations Economic and Social Council.

———. 2016. Statistical Commission: Report of the Forty-Seventh Session. 8–11 March 2016.

United Nations Statistical Commission (UNSC). 2001. *Report of the Friends of the Chair: An Assessment of the Statistical Criticisms made of the Human Development Report, 1999*. http://unstats.un.org/unsd/statcom/doc01/2001-18e.pdf.

World Bank. 2013. *Measuring the Real Size of the World Economy: The Framework, Methodology, and Results of the International Comparison Program—ICP*. https://thedocs.worldbank.org/en/doc/927971487091799574-0050022017/original/ICPBookeBookFINAL.pdf.

———. 2015. *Operational Guidelines and Procedures for Measuring the Real Size of the World Economy: 2011 International Comparison Program*. https://thedocs.worldbank.org/en/doc/777881487094209758-0050022017/original/OGeBook.pdf.

———. 2016. International Comparison Program: Classification of Final Expenditure on GDP. https://thedocs.worldbank.org/en/doc/708531575560035925-0050022019/original/ICPClassificationdescription20191205.pdf.

———. DataBank: ICP 2017. https://databank.worldbank.org/source/icp-2017 (accessed 4 June 2024).

———. 2020. *Purchasing Power Parities and the Size of World Economies: Results from the 2017 International Comparison Program*. https://openknowledge.worldbank.org/handle/10986/33623.

———. DataBank: ICP 2021. https://databank.worldbank.org/source/icp-2021# (accessed 4 June 2024).

———. 2021. *Purchasing Power Parities for Policy Making: A Visual Guide to Using Data from the International Comparison Program*. https://openknowledge.worldbank.org/entities/publication/dc4deba0-339b-5dca-af4c-4881445d1dce.

———. 2023. *Minutes of the International Comparison Program Technical Advisory Group Meeting. November 6-7, 2023*. Washington, DC: World Bank. https://thedocs.worldbank.org/en/doc/ff6b38a602fa57f4f0367fa6ccd06825-0050022023/original/Final-ICP-TAG-November-6-7-2023-Minutes.pdf

———. World Development Indicators. https://databank.worldbank.org/source/world-development-indicators (accessed 15 April 2025).

www.ingramcontent.com/pod-product-compliance
Lightning Source LLC
Chambersburg PA
CBHW041756220926
51847CB00014B/218
9789292776008